The House
in France

The House
in France

A MEMOIR

Gully Wells

B L O O M S B U R Y

LONDON · BERLIN · NEW YORK · SYDNEY

First published in Great Britain 2011

Copyright © 2011 by Gully Wells

The moral right of the author has been asserted

First published in the United States in 2011 by Alfred A. Knopf, a division of Random house,
Inc., New York, and in Canada by Random House of Canada Limited, Toronto

Grateful acknowledgement is made to Sayre Sheldon for permission to reprint 'Lines for Mrs. C.'
By V. R. ('Bunny') Lang. The photograph of Gully Wells at Oxford is courtesy of Cherwell

Bloomsbury Publishing Plc
36 Soho Square
London W1D 3QY

www.bloomsbury.com

Bloomsbury Publishing, London, Berlin, New York and Sydney
A CIP catalogue record for this book is available from the British Library

ISBN 978 1 4088 0809 9 (hardback)
ISBN 978 1 4088 1988 3 (trade paperback)

10 9 8 7 6 5 4 3 2 1

Printed in Great Britain by Clays Ltd, St Ives plc, Bungay, Suffolk

For Rebecca, Alexander, and Peter

The House
in France

Je Reviens

Every summer for almost twenty years I would gather up my children and take them to stay with their grandmother in her house in France. There they would do the things that children do—paddle in the inflatable pool set up beneath an ancient lime tree, throw bits of baguette at the bloated goldfish in the village fountain, demand to be taken to the beach, swing in the hammock, and if they were *really* bored, push handfuls of gravel through the holes in the hubcaps of her car. But once they reached the age of reason, it was the "Drawer of Death" that fascinated them the most. Visiting this macabre mausoleum was something they would never have dared to do on their own. It was far too frightening, and precious for that, so its curator had to be persuaded to take them upstairs to the living room, settle them down on the sofa, and then slowly slide the drawer out so they could examine its contents together. Who knows why my mother decided to start her collection, but each summer there were always new acquisitions in her witch's *Wunderkammer* to drive them mad with delight.

The cabinet itself was something she had bought in the Friday market in Le Beausset, where, in among the sweet-scented Cavaillon melons, purple pyramids of fresh figs, courgette blossoms, and viscous green local olive oil, were a few stalls of junk: inky black cast-iron pots too heavy to lift; linen napkins as big as pillowcases, embroidered with swirly, illegible initials; a brass lamp in the form of a gently pornographic naked nymph, with a tattered pink silk shade; and quite a few objects whose purpose, and use, even the seller was at a loss to explain.

On the shelves of the glass-fronted top of the cabinet were arranged some conventionally pretty pieces of china, which of course the children had absolutely no use for. It was the drawer beneath that they were after. And no wonder. Who could resist a bird's nest full of dead grasshoppers, or the pale-green-and-orange butterflies, shaped like miniature stealth bombers? The collection had begun innocently enough with a few furry bumblebees, a starfish no bigger than a thumbnail, and some translucent cicada skins; but then, over the years, altogether more intriguing creatures were added. A shriveled toad, a sinister black centipede, lizards, and scorpions all huddled together with the broken remains of a mouse's skeleton. And there, hiding behind a snail shell, was one of the dreaded hornets, which had built their nest in the old olive tree and were capable, or so my mother always claimed, of dispatching a baby with a few strategic strikes. The tiny silver snake that I had found flattened on a dirt track in Sicily, and mailed to my mother in a cigarette box, lay alongside the corpse of a New York–size water bug that had met its maker behind my fridge in Greenwich Village and made its last journey across the Atlantic in a Ziploc coffin. United in death, they sat in their dusty Provençal tomb all year, to emerge only briefly into the daylight at the beginning of the summer, in order to terrorize Rebecca and Alexander.

I FINALLY WENT BACK to the house six years after my mother died. I was too much of a coward to do it sooner. Living in New York made her death seem less real, and I could trick myself into thinking that if I just got on a plane and flew to Marseille, drove to Le Beausset, and headed up the hill, through the vineyards, past the old yellow schoolhouse on the left, I would see the cypress trees ahead, turn the corner, hear the click-clacking of the wooden beads, and she would emerge from the front door to greet me. She would be standing there in one of the faded cotton dresses that she only ever wore in France—not chic enough for New York or London, they lived in the house year round—and some old espadrilles. Her pale sapphire eyes would light up as soon as she saw me, and I could hear her voice inside my head telling me to come quick and taste the Brie—so runny its sides had to be shored up with little wooden sticks—she had bought in the market that morning. I kept this reassuring fantasy going for as long as I could, but gradually, as the pain began to fade, and after I had already survived (bruised but still relatively sane) the dismantling of her home in London, I knew the time had come.

What is it about a certain house that allows it to take on, as if by some strange process of architectural osmosis, the precise character of its owner? How can a complicated, intelligent human being and an inanimate structure, stuffed full of random rubbish, resemble each other so closely that they might as well be twins? It isn't something that happens quickly; in fact it usually takes decades, and it isn't universal—sometimes it never happens at all. In my mother's case the symbiosis was long established and deeply rooted. My problem with returning to the house was not just that it reminded me too much of her but that it also made me angry. How dare it be basking—stupidly, complacently, lazily—in the warm sunlight of Provence, when she no longer could? How could it possibly have had the ill grace to survive her? Surely it ought to have gone up in flames, like a dutiful Indian wife, on that dark dismal day at the crematorium in Golders Green?

But once I actually walked through the clackety beads and into the familiar, cool, terra-cotta-tiled kitchen, I realized that I had gotten it all completely wrong. Instead of sadness and fury I felt oddly relieved to have come home to a place that knew me so well. I forgave the house for being alive. Standing there, I gazed around the room and realized that nothing had changed: In fact it scarcely looked any different than it had when we first moved there in 1963. The beams, the same shape as the tree trunks they were made of (the long dead builders had scarcely bothered to hack at them; maybe it had been a rush job, or perhaps they were just too tired) were still hung with old baskets, straw hats, dried flowers, and the odd bunch of dusty bay leaves, rosemary, and fennel. The loaf of bread, baked in the form of a wheat sheaf, that I had found in a *boulangerie* in Sainte-Anne d'Évenos, was still there on the wall; and the marble-topped dining table, bought from a man with one arm at a *brocante* in Toulon, still ran down the middle of the room, surrounded by rickety, rush-seated wooden chairs, just like the one in van Gogh's painting of his bedroom in Arles. That first summer one of my stepfather's many ex-girlfriends, an elegant blond lady named Alvys, had come to stay on her way to Italy, and had sat there at the table, with her chic tortoiseshell glasses balanced on her perfect retroussé nose, sewing a pair of curtains for the kitchen window. I looked at the faded ocher-colored fabric and remembered the precise moment, only a few days after she'd left, when my mother told me she had been killed in a car crash, with her lover, on a mountain road above Ravello.

It must have been after nine o'clock before we (my husband, Peter; the children, Rebecca and Alexander; and my brother, Nick, plus his girl-friend, Stephanie—I had made quite sure that I was carefully cocooned for my *rentrée*) all sat down to dinner at the long marble table. The wine was a Domaine Tempier, *cuvée* La Migoua, made from grapes grown on the hills that surrounded our hamlet of the same name. The *pâté de cam-pagne*, studded with pistachios, the Brousse (a creamy fresh goat cheese), and the sweet red tomatoes all came from the market. The basil grew in a huge, cracked terra-cotta pot out on the terrace, buffeted almost hori-zontal by the mistral, which had started up that morning. The mistral is a mysterious wind, a joker that gets its kicks by barreling down the chimney of the Rhône Valley, in order to drive the inhabitants of the Midi completely mad.

The *pharmacien* in the village, a man with a tight, mean mouth, humor-less eyes, and a neatly pressed white coat, told me years ago that it had a special penchant for odd numbers, so that "he" always blew for three, five, or seven days. Or, presumably, for seventeen or thirty-three or any other odd number that took "his" fancy. In addition to his fondness for certain numbers, the mistral is also the most appalling snob, torment-ing only those who, like us, had the misfortune to live at the terminally unfashionable western end of the Mediterranean. "He" also used to be a godsend for anyone accused of a *crime passionel*, since defense lawyers regularly argued, with perfectly straight faces, that their clients had been obliged to murder their wives on account of mistral-related insanity.

The wine was finished, the *tarte aux pommes* and crème fraîche had disappeared, and slowly, we made our way upstairs. My daughter was sleeping in my old room, on the curlicued, white wrought-iron bed that used to be mine, with its saggy mattress and antique quilt festooned with blowsy pink roses. And I found myself in my mother's room. I could hear our neighbors next door on their terrace, squabbling as usual, the wife's voice becoming louder and more aggrieved with every glass of her well-deserved (imagine forty-five years of marriage to *him*) *vin d'orange*, and, in the distance, some dogs started howling at the mistral. I gave up, got out of bed, and crept into the living room. The enormous blackened fireplace stared back at me like the entrance to a cave, and there, on my mother's desk, was the paving stone, used as a paperweight, that had been uprooted from the rue Gay-Lussac in Paris during the *événements* of May '68, and had been given to her, as a radically chic memento of those thrilling days, by our neighbor Francette Drin. Above the sofa hung a poster of a *fraise des bois* plant. Its heart-shaped leaves and thin etiolated stems spread languidly across the paper; the tiny, jewel-like, red berries shone in the moonlight, and there in the corner was a cross-section of its delicate white flower. Just like the drawings I used to do in biology class in school. The words "Deyrolle et Fils" were printed at the bottom, with the address, "46, rue du Bac, Paris VII." My mother's favorite shop in the entire world. Its ostensible business was to supply the harried teachers of France with the tools to help them impart their knowledge of the natural world to their uncaring students. But to her they were decorators. Stuffed tarantulas, jagged lumps of purple quartz, the life cycle of the flea (one of their smaller posters), the many stages of cheese making, ditto winemaking, an iridescent Amazonian beetle the size of a small dog, snake skeletons in all sizes: There was nothing they didn't stock.

As I gazed around the room, my eyes inevitably fell upon the "Drawer of Death." Earlier in the evening, at the back of the old armoire in the kitchen, I had seen an earthenware jar, and when I looked inside I knew precisely what it contained. Very quietly I went downstairs, scooped a teaspoonful of the ashes into the palm of my hand, and returned to the living room. On the top shelf of the cabinet, beside a slightly chipped Limoges teacup, scattered with forget-me-nots and sky blue ribbons, I noticed a small cockleshell. Carefully emptying the ashes into the shell, I slid open the drawer, gently placed it in the bird's nest, closed the drawer, and tiptoed back to my mother's bed.

La Famille

My PARENTS HAD BEEN DIVORCED since before I could remember. It struck me as perfectly normal that I should live with my mother in London and then be sent off each vacation—like an airmail package—from Heathrow, with a label pinned to my lapel, to stay with my father wherever he happened to be. In fact it was a great deal better than normal because I had both of them entirely to myself. I was a double only child, a situation that suited me admirably.

I may have thought, in the supremely self-centered way of all children, that I had each of them all to myself, but of course I didn't. Both my father and mother were enormously attractive. My mother had a perfect model's body—fifties style, with a real bosom, tiny waist, and beautiful legs—combined, somewhat unfairly, with a stainless-steel brain. She was not conventionally pretty, her nose was too long to be cute, her jaw too strong, and her tongue way too sharp for some, but she did have that irresistible, ineffable x factor that meant she was never short of company. My father, on the other hand, was absurdly handsome, good-humored, and easygoing, with that sunny and ultimately deeply irritating—to her, at least—optimism that some lucky Americans seem to be born with. They were not well matched.

They had met at the American Embassy in Paris, where they both worked, and in a letter to her parents, my mother describes her impressions of the "Embassy Adonis," as she called her new friend:

> I have met a terrific man who is second secretary here and a big wheel in the Economic Section. Terribly rich, terribly handsome, and Yale

'39 and Yale Law and very blond (quite revolting that) and has the most beautiful car I've ever seen. A 1948 Oldsmobile . . . sleek and grey and convertible. And he took me out once and then big blank silence and so sad and heavy it was too, until today when he invited me to go for a quick tour of the château country in the big sleek grey car this weekend.

At the time my father was unofficially engaged to a nineteen-year-old girl back home in America who had the advantage of being (a) the daughter of Ambassador Harrison and (b) hugely rich. Sadly, my mother had been totally mistaken about the Wells family fortune, which turned out to be almost nonexistent. For a well-born WASP, oddly lacking a serious trust fund, who wanted to make his way in the Foreign Service, a rich, well-connected wife was probably as much of a necessity as impeccable manners and a perfectly tailored dinner jacket. But the ambassador's daughter decided that maybe she was just too young to get married, and the spoiled "little beast, in her recently-turned-20 fashion, has just announced that she wants to shop around a bit more." Which left the playing field wide open for my mother.

They went to stay in a haunted château in Normandy; they went skiing in an Austrian village with the wonderful name of Obergurgl; they went to diplomatic receptions at the Élysée Palace; they went to a very fancy dinner party on the quai Bourbon, overlooking the Seine, where, she wrote to her mother, "There was absolutely nothing to drink BUT champagne and wonderful lobster salad and things in molds and oriental houseboys dishing it out," where they met "the two younger Kennedy daughters, Eunice and Pat, who are in Paris for the holidays. And very nice little girls they are too, oddly enough." (My grandmother's snobbery was pretty universal, and the Boston Irish were the primary objects of her contempt. The Kennedy family may have been exempted, but somehow I doubt it.)

All in all my future parents were clearly having a ridiculously good time. Reading my mother's letters, I kept looking for evidence of that heart-stopping, feverish affliction that infects what is left of your mind and makes everything you cared about before he took over your life totally irrelevant. But instead I found this description of juggling the "Embassy Adonis" with another gentleman named Bill:

Al [my father] has just decided in true Neanderthal fashion, that
After All I am the girl for him. But I am playing a tricky game these
days . . . . I placate him and Bill and at the same time try not to alien-
ate any of the 2nd string . . . all the time getting myself all fouled up.
It's a difficult game to play and one at which I am not very good. With
Al you get a polo playing, stag hunting, good-at-cocktail-parties ris-
ing young diplomat who some day will be Minister to Tanganyika.
Not dumb, well informed, with lots of the right ideas . . . but short on
imagination and with about as many shadings in color as a piece of
white drawing paper. Now, with our Bill you have a nice, sweet, kind
and generous man who finds a great deal of difficulty in coping with
the nasty materialistic world. He knows wonderful people and funny
things and is so much brighter in many ways than Al. He is related to
the world's most fabulous collection of nuts . . . his great uncle is the
Marquis d'Ormonde . . . his cousin is Lady Phyllis Delamere, easily
the worst behaved of the whole Mountbatten tribe. Unfortunately he
doesn't seem to want to carve out an empire for himself. Just wanders
around ordering new gold monocles from Cartier, and waiting for
his grandmother to die. The choice is a really hard one; my big complaint is that I can't mix the two of them together and come up with
one Complete Man.

In the end the stag-hunting Adonis won. A large only slightly flawed
sapphire was dislodged from his father's tiepin back in Brewster, New
York, and taken to Cartier's to be transformed into a ring, and the wedding invitations were sent out.

Their friends in Paris couldn't understand what had possessed them
to get married. My mother, a self-described "wild savage" with a tendency to view life through her own darkly ironic prism, took any chance
she could to *épater la bourgeoisie* and anybody else who happened to be
within firing range. Fools were not tolerated, authority had to be ques-
tioned, "nice" people were dull, and the worst crime—up there with cruelty to animals—was to be a bore. She liked to stay up too late and smoke
too much, and her martini glass was invariably half empty, not because
she was a drinker but because that is how she saw the world. My father,
whose own family could not have been more bourgeois, saw no point in
shocking anybody, had no problem with "nice" people, and tended to
give those in power the benefit of the doubt. His mind was more practical
than intellectual, his inclination was to see the best in any situation, and

he had an enviable talent for extracting a huge amount of pleasure from every moment in the day—and therefore from life. He liked to go to bed early, eat too much chocolate ice cream, and his champagne glass always overflowed. I suspect they both fell in love with those qualities in the other that they themselves didn't possess. He adored her spirit, strength, and wit, and she loved his uncomplicated cheerfulness and the reassuring solidity of his large, conventional, and seemingly prosperous family. Why not get married? It must have seemed like an incredibly good idea at the time.

When I was about seventeen and old enough to understand such things, my mother told me that she knew the night before her wedding that it was never going to work. But how could she have backed out then? The guests, the presents, the flowers, the champagne, the *petits fours*, the cake. Not to mention the fact that she was being given away by my father's formidable patrician boss, Ambassador David Bruce, whom even she hesitated to embarrass. (Since the wedding took place just a month after the engagement, her parents had decided that there wasn't enough time, or probably money, for them to get from Boston to Paris.)

As it turned out, the friends and my mother were right, and my parents were divorced, quite happily, within four years. She left my father— surprised, quite possibly relieved, but not, I think, too distraught—in Burma, where he was first secretary at the American Embassy. And instead of going home to New York or Boston, she moved with me to London. Not an easy decision, but she was an adventuress. In Rangoon she had made friends with their neighbors, Sue and Basil Boothby, who were with the British Embassy, and they offered to lend her their house in London, which at least solved the problem of where we would live. It was one of those tall terraced houses built around 1830 with two rooms on each floor and lots of stairs in between. The kitchen was in the basement with a window that let in a bit of daylight, if there was any to spare— this still being the era of *Bleak House* pea-soup smog—and an Aga that needed to be fed on demand, like some monstrous, ravenous baby, with constant buckets of coal. After we had settled into the house she somehow persuaded the *New York Times* that she was the person they needed to report on fashion and "London life," and her salary, combined with her alimony, was just enough to live on. Slowly she built up quite a glittery social life, something she was always inordinately good at, while I set off for school each morning, in my gray flannel uniform (pleated skirt, blazer, and hat: straw in the summer, felt in the winter) and came home at teatime to play with my dolls and hamster.

After my mother and father divorced, there were always gentlemen—and lady—callers around. But in my cozy little solipsistic bubble this didn't faze me, which must have had as much to do with the tact and charm of the callers as it did with my unshakable confidence in my parents' love. I knew that I was the most important person in both their lives, and that none of the callers could ever change that. My great good luck was that I had no memory of them married or fighting (they both claimed they never had) or separating, and so was able to accept the situation without any of the angst and suffering that most children of divorced parents go through. Even though my mother tended to skip over the more sentimental aspects of motherhood, like smothering me in kisses and actually saying out loud how much she loved me, I never doubted for a single moment that she did. And it was only when I fell crazily in love for the first time, at nineteen, that I experienced again that all-consuming passion that I had felt for her as a child.

She was always interested in whatever I thought and was doing, and kept in close touch with my father, writing him long, chatty letters about me. ("Yesterday, when she was driving me completely crazy, I told her quite sternly to *behave*, to which she replied, looking aggrieved, 'But I *am* have.' What could I say?") He would then painstakingly stick them into leather-bound albums—one for each year of my life, with the date embossed in gold on the spine—along with my report cards ("Singing: distressing") and endless color photographs of our travels together. There I am at six, in an inky blue velvet dress, with a white lace collar, standing in front of an elaborate four-poster bed, at some gloomy *Schloss* we had stayed at in Austria. The enormous eiderdown rises up behind me like a bank of snow, and I look into the camera with an expression of secret satisfaction. My surroundings, my dress, and my traveling companion were all exactly as I wanted them to be. And there we are in the Piazza San Marco, dressed in matching lederhosen (what *could* he have been thinking?), surrounded by squabbling pigeons.

Later on the same trip we stayed at a hotel on a beach, where we somehow acquired a creature in a polka-dot bikini and gold hoop earrings, who talked way too much and showed no sign at all of leaving us alone, however much I scowled at her. The photograph in the album shows the three of us in a pedalo, her generous bosom bursting out of two pointy cones, her head thrown back in a paroxysm of laughter, with my father inexplicably smiling at her. I remember whispering to him that we should all pedal way out to sea, make her jump overboard for a refreshing dip, and then the two of us could race back to the shore. It seemed like a flawless plan, and it worked for a while, but as we sat down to dinner she reappeared, this time in a strapless dress with a huge pouffy skirt, her dark, curly hair held back by a twisted silk scarf. And, again quite inexplicably, my father stood up and pulled out her chair so she could join us. But when we left a few days later there was no sign of her, and we set off in our little white convertible with the red leather dashboard, bound for Portofino.

Now, fifty years later, I see that her totally understandable crime had been to focus all her charms on the object of her desire, and who can blame her? But the other, more permanent callers—both my mother's and my father's—were much cleverer and understood that if you want to win the heart of somebody attached to a small, overindulged daughter, you actually need to seduce *two* people. Since my father lived the life of a bachelor diplomat, first in Vienna and then in Bonn, at a time when there was actually a certain amount of spurious glamour attached to that profession, he had many ladies to entertain. But with me away in London, he didn't have to juggle them too much. For my mother things were a bit trickier. I must have been a little like the complacent, hoodwinked husband whose wife is having a series of affairs. I sailed along, oblivious of the fact that her dinner guests were anything more than friends of the family, and in the end I was aware of only two contenders, although she later told me there had of course, been a few more. And why not? Looking back, I realize that I picked up, by osmosis, from both my mother and father (and from my future stepparents, who were also gifted teachers of this subject) the useful and life-enhancing idea that love affairs, and therefore men, should be associated with excitement and happiness, and never with guilt and angst.

The first contender I became aware of was a man named Robert Neild, who lived in Cambridge, where he was an economist at Trinity College, which can't have taken up a great deal of his time, because he seemed to be mostly at our house in London. Robert had the most convoluted eyebrows I'd ever seen. They formed a wild ginger thatch above his crinkly blue eyes, and I unblinkingly accepted his arrival on the scene, rather as

if he'd been a nice new sofa that had just been delivered by Harrods and
taken up residence in our drawing room. I must have been about three or
four years old when the sofa arrived, and over the next year or so, became
very attached to it—so attached that I remember going to school and
announcing to nobody in particular that my mother was going to marry
Robert. And maybe she was. It seemed like a reasonable idea, and I was
an extremely reasonable child, or so she always told me. But then one day
the Harrods van turned up again on our doorstep and took the sofa away.
The curious thing is that I don't remember being in the least bit surprised
or upset, because no sooner had he gone back to the Trinity warehouse in
Cambridge than another, equally delightful gentleman caller appeared to
take his place. God knows there must have been a bit of Sturm und Drang
associated with this rearrangement of the furniture, but to everybody's
credit, it took place offstage and was so skillfully executed that it left no
impression on me at all.

The new Robert was called Freddie Ayer, and my mother met him at
a dance at St. Antony's College in Oxford in the summer of 1956. This is
how she described it in a letter to her old friend in Rangoon, Sue Boothby:

> I have fallen madly, madly, I tell you madly, in love for the first time in
> my whole misshapen ill-spent life—and with an impossibly hopeless
> man. It all fell on me . . . in the drafty fan-vaulted sewer of a basement
> at that goddamn dance in Oxford that Philip dragged me to. I knew I
> shouldn't have gone. But they all seemed so harmless, so egg headed,
> not to mention egg on the chin that my flaring nostril guard was down
> utterly. Then—I didn't look at him and didn't listen to his name—but
> what seemed to be a particularly egg headed, scruffy middle-aged
> professor asked me to dance. And being a well brought up girl I didn't
> say for him to fuck off. And then there I was—in about twenty seconds
> flat my head began to reel and I felt like being sick out the window and
> it hasn't stopped since. Stayed at that eightsome reel til 4 bloody thirty
> in the morning. Absolutely green with angst that this maniac wouldn't
> be on the 6pm train to London as we had exchanged blood illuminated
> promises to be. But he was. And since then, I meet this menace for five
> minutes at the Ritz bar and I lie to Robert to go see him at 10.30 or mid-
> night and we have what I believe are called in novels, Stolen Moments.
> I'm still sick regularly every other day or so, and it gets worse and
> worse—added to which, it is, of course, impossible. He's had a wife,

his children are grown up and he's had every woman in London and
keeps a tidy six-year old (?) mistress in the Maginot line background.
He's about 100 years old and is everything I've ever wanted. His name
is Ayer, or Eyre or Air or Ere, I don't really know how he spells it and
he's a philosopher. So far as I can gather from his books etc he's the big
deal in logical positivism etc. I am utterly miserable and quite unable to
do anything.

Well, she got most of it right. He actually spelled his name "Ayer," and
he *was* a big deal in logical positivism, and he *did* have two children, Val-
erie and Julian, and he *had* had love affairs with an awful lot of women—
and not just in London. The mistress turned out to be an Australian
painter named Jocelyn Rickards, who'd been around for six years or so,
but he also had a possessive ex-wife, Renée, who was his *real* Maginot
Line against ladies who might get any fancy ideas of moving in too close
on him. It seems to have been an arrangement that suited him extremely
well. He lived in a tiny flat in Shepherds Market in Mayfair, which Renée
had found and decorated for him in an Elsie de Wolfe meets Kierkegaard
minimalist style. According to his autobiography:

> Renée's taste in decoration had been formed in the 1930's, when there
> was a fashion for white walls, off-white furniture and a scarcity of orna-
> mentation. In fact the white walls suited my small rooms, and although
> I only had one picture, a portrait of myself by e. e. cummings, and lit-
> tle or no bric-a-brac, I had comfortable chairs and a sufficient stock of
> books with which to furnish both my sitting room and study. That oth-
> ers might view it differently was brought home to me one evening when
> I was entertaining some pupils to drinks. They all left at a fairly late
> hour, and as I was closing the door, I heard a voice reaching me from the
> stairs, "Poor old bugger, all alone *thinking* in those cold, cold rooms."

Which only goes to show how little we know about our teachers'
private lives. As it turned out, the "poor old bugger," *pace* his students'
description, was only forty-six when he and my mother met, and soon
after that, the Harrods van turned up again, and the moving men came
wheezing up the stairs and installed the new sofa in the drawing room in
Holland Park Avenue. To my six-year-old self, Freddie didn't seem terribly different from Robert, except that his eyebrows were under some kind

of control, and it looked as though he might be staying a bit longer than his predecessor. My mother may have fallen madly, dangerously, hopelessly in love for the first time in her "misshapen ill-spent life," but for Freddie the affair was just that—an affair. He was never a man of action, and for someone whose life was seemingly caught up in a series of passionate love affairs, he was curiously passive. His view of the beginning of their liaison could not have been more different from hers:

> Dee had been having an affair with a Cambridge economist but gave him up on my account. I was not yet sufficiently committed to her to renounce all other attachments, or even to profess to do so. Jocelyn, with whom I had arrived at a friendly *modus vivendi*, disapproved of my taking up with Dee, not out of jealousy but because she did not like her or think us suited to one another. Renée tended rather to approve of her as a counterweight to Jocelyn. I enjoyed her company, spent a fair amount of time in Holland Park Avenue and let events take their course.

Letting "events take their course" had never been my mother's style. If it had been, she would never have run away from her god-awful family and joined the Canadian army at seventeen (where she, unsurprisingly, rose to the rank of sergeant major), would never have bought that one-way ticket to Paris, would never have married my father, and would never have left him in Rangoon and moved to London. And then she would never have fallen for the "menace" at that dance in Oxford. But now that she had done all those things, she was determined to have him. It was not going to be easy.

Poor Freddie. All he wanted was for his well-ordered, carefully compartmentalized life to go on as it always had. During the day his beautiful mind was busy grappling with issues such as proving that the major domains of empirical knowledge could be reconstructed in terms of the data of direct experience and the single relation of remembered similarity between them, but once that was out of the way, it was time for a whiskey and soda, dinner at the Café Royal, either with a group of friends or one of the lucky ladies, followed by dancing at the Gargoyle Club. There were so many things to love about Freddie, but maybe the most seductive of all was his combination of intellectual brilliance (which extended way beyond the wilder shores of logical positivism) with a delight in all the pleasures life had to offer. His old friend e. e. cummings once wrote him a birthday poem, which captured this charming duality in his nature rather nicely:

> Considering the gravity of your language
> And the levity of your nature
> (or, at times, the levity of your language
> and the gravity of your nature)
> it is clear that keeping your balance
> comes easier than it does to teetering us.
> You walk on the tightropes as if they lay on the ground,
> And always, bird eyed, notice more than we notice you notice; and the
> observation follows always with the clarity
> of a wire slicing cheese.

And many years later, in the midseventies, Leon Wieseltier, who was then his pupil, described Freddie as "an eighteenth-century rationalist voluptuary—he could have been one of Diderot's friends. I remember asking him about Camus, 'I don't know his work well, but he and I were friends: we were making love to twin sisters in Paris after the war.'"

Clever my mother certainly was—Freddie told me that she was the most intelligent woman he had ever known—but his philosophical work was way beyond her and although in the first rush of love she did go out and buy all his books, she later confessed to a friend that she couldn't read them "without Dr. Johnson's dictionary close by and a finger tracing laboriously under every printed line." I'm not too sure that even then she could make much sense of them, and yet what did it matter? Freddie talked about his work with other philosophers, not with his friends, and being by nature promiscuous, intellectually and otherwise, his conversation skipped happily and entertainingly all over the place. As with his dancing, he enjoyed a partner who could follow his lightning lead, and as with his tennis, he needed an opponent who could slam the ball back just as hard as he served it. He had found both in my mother.

At the beginning she was careful not to rock his carefully balanced boat. Understanding the danger of putting any pressure on him, she presumably didn't allow him to see or hear just how hard her heart was beating. At the sizzling, red-hot start of their liaison, when Freddie had to go to Poland to give some lectures, she waited impatiently for his first letter, snatching it from the bewildered postman's hand before he had even had a chance to stuff it through the letter box. Although Freddie was a great letter writer—he had absolutely no patience with the telephone—there were a couple of problems. The first was his handwriting, which looked like an army of embryonic ants marching across the paper in strict parallel lines and was therefore totally indecipherable. But with a magnifying glass and practice, it was usually possible to figure out the vague contours of his message. And that was the second problem. The first two words of the letter my mother had grabbed from the postman were "Dear Dee." *Wrong:* Things did not improve as she read on. A brisk description of Professor Glowczewski's shortcomings as an interpreter of Wittgenstein was followed by Freddie's impressions of Warsaw—"chilly, but the vodka is plentiful"—his lack of appreciation of the charms of a lady philosopher, who was "large, and by no means attractive"—ending up with this measured critique of his hotel bedroom: "My bed, though hard, is not lumpy." The letter ended with two more illegible words, one of which she thought *might* be "Love," the other, presumably, being "Freddie."

It can't have been terribly difficult for her to conceal the extent of her passion from Freddie, because he was never the most perceptive man when it came to other people's feelings. How else could he possibly have thought that Jocelyn wasn't jealous? Did he actually believe that his current *maîtresse en titre* was just looking out for his best interests when she told him that he and this American adventuress were not "suited to one another"? So it is probably safe to say that my mother didn't need a degree from the Yale School of Drama to convince Freddie that all they were having was a delightful affair. She surrounded him with interesting people—not too hard since he seemed to know everybody in London—and she was able to throw in a few disreputable Americans just to liven up the mix. Then she made it her business to provide him with a cozy setup at her house. A place to write and regular meals with all his favorite food: Frank Cooper's Oxford Marmalade (coarse cut) on his toast at breakfast, Gentleman's Relish at teatime, and a rosy pink leg of lamb for dinner, with a good bottle of claret, and Stilton and "digestive biscuits" to follow. Forget dessert, vegetables, or salad: Freddie didn't do sweet or green. She was always a bit of a Jewish mother when it came to fattening people up, and I remember that years later, when one of my boyfriends said he was hungry, she had to remind me that men liked *two* things, and one of them was food.

Her formula must have worked, because slowly they became more of an established couple. I grew accustomed to seeing him sitting in his armchair with our fat old dachshund, Monster, on his lap when I came home from school, and accepted him as part of our family. He never replaced my real father, and why should he? My father lived in Germany, took me skiing in the winter, and to Italy in the summer in his snappy white Mercedes convertible with the red leather seats that smelled like new shoes. Freddie lived in London, took me to French restaurants, fed me my first snail, and didn't know how to drive. They could not have been less alike, and I loved them both. From as far back as I can remember I've had this insane idea—which can only have originated with my two fathers—that men were created to amuse me, comfort me, love me, tell me interesting things, and generally give me pleasure. I'll admit that over the years my faith has been tested just a little by one or two men, and mocked by many more women, but mostly—and luckily—this deeply unfashionable belief has turned out to be a self-fulfilling prophecy.

DIFFERENT AS THEY WERE, Freddie and my father did have one trait in common: They were not assertive, demanding, or difficult and would do just about anything to avoid confrontation. I have always assumed that this was one of the things that attracted my mother to both of them. Her primal need to be the one in charge prevented her, quite wisely, from being attracted to, or choosing, men too similar to herself. She was the sharpest, funniest, and most generous person on earth; she delighted in her talent to shock and amuse people, but the flip side to this captivating spirit was darker. She had grown up as a self-described "crafty, quick witted savage," and it was her toughness and absolute refusal to be defeated that had helped her get where she wanted to go. Sometimes it was simply boredom that brought on the compulsion to stir things up, and she once cheerfully admitted to me that her patent cure for tedium was to start an argument. Worked every time. And so what if it escalated into a fight, with a bit of shouting and collateral damage? Many years after they were married I would sometimes hear Freddie muttering under his breath, as he paced around his study, "That dreadful woman, that dreadful woman." But when they first met, she was just "quick witted." The "crafty savage" was for later.

My mother must have felt she was making a bit of headway when, in June 1957, Freddie invited her to see his son, Julian, play cricket at Eton. We took a train, and I remember pointing out to Freddie the "water buffalo" (as cows were called in Burma) dotted about in the fields as we sped by. We finally arrived at a big green lawn, with a tent set up on one side, full of ladies in silly hats and men clutching umbrellas, just in case it rained. I was given strawberries and cream; while the grown-ups sipped Pimm's and fed me the slices of cucumber and stalks of mint—infused with the strange taste of alcohol and Angostura bitters—floating in their dimpled beer mugs. In the distance tiny figures, dressed all in white, were scattered about on the grass. Occasionally one of them would summon up the energy to thwack the ball, and then walk laconically toward the stump to graze it with his bat, while the spectators would clap even more laconically and murmur, "Well played."

Needless to say, I found the game totally incomprehensible and extremely dull: All I wanted was to see Julian. I knew he was Freddie's son and sensed that for my mother, meeting him was important. Determined to be on my best behavior, I politely shook his hand when he was introduced to me and as soon as his back was turned, tugged at my mother's skirt and pointed out, quite truthfully, in the dangerous way that children can, "Mummy, Julian doesn't look a bit like Freddie. He doesn't look like him *at all*." She ignored me. So I said it again, and, still getting no response, I repeated it a little louder. Finally she bent down, put her face very close to mine, and said, "Shut up." I don't recall being offended, but I did shut up, and probably wandered off in search of some more strawberries.

It was only many years later that she told me why the tall, dark, and pointlessly good-looking Julian bore no resemblance whatsoever to his father. While married to Freddie, Renée had had an affair with Stuart Hampshire, another philosopher, and Julian was Stuart's son. But nobody had ever bothered to tell him. Or, at least, plenty of malicious gossips had hinted over the years that *they* knew, but his three parents apparently took a rather more casual view of the situation. For my mother bushes were not something you beat about. And so, when she finally met Renée, she got straight to the point and asked her when she was going to tell Julian about his origins. Renée replied, "It's not up to me. Freddie and Stuart are his parents." Yet more evidence that the English were completely out of their minds.

Julian's housemaster at Eton had even written to Renée urging her to come clean with her son: "I am certain that to learn the truth from anyone other than you and Freddie would be a mistake, perhaps even a danger, for him." But neither of them was brave enough to tell poor Julian the truth, and he discovered it only from a girlfriend when he was an undergraduate at Oxford. Isaiah Berlin remembered that Julian came to him in a state of extreme distress, wanting to change his name. I don't know what Isaiah's advice was, but he always had a prissy, puritanical attitude toward Freddie's romantic arrangements and disapproved of the louche nature of his marriage. When Stuart Hampshire had confessed to Freddie, in 1937, that he and Renée had fallen in love, Freddie seems to have taken the news quite calmly and, amazingly, even agreed to spend Christmas in Paris with them. Yet more evidence, for my mother, of his near-autism when it came to emotion.

Intellectually Freddie was a child of the Enlightenment and worshipped at the altar—designed in severe neoclassical style by Jacques-Louis David—of reason and tolerance. This was the foundation of his approach to philosophy and may have served him well in his politics, his assault on religion, and even in his sex life, but love and logic have never been happy bedmates. So, not too surprisingly, the festive ménage à trois in Paris ended in tears, and Freddie, feeling a bit sorry for himself, returned to London alone. But his mood didn't last long. He soon took up with a pretty young undergraduate at Somerville College in Oxford, who, in the incestuous nature of life, turned out to be a friend of Isaiah's. One of Freddie's closest friends, Philip Toynbee, wrote in his diary that Berlin, not for the first or last time, had tried to interpose himself between Freddie and a girlfriend: "Isaiah has been rushing from one to the other, urging them not to go to bed with one another. What an old fool he is."

Over martinis at their club, Freddie told Philip all about the debacle in Paris and his new girlfriend, and they "agreed that seduction was enormous fun" and that they "shared a genuinely adventurous attitude." That silly old fool Isaiah had no idea what he was missing.

Meanwhile life at Holland Park Avenue trundled peacefully along, or

at least that's how it felt to Freddie and me, but for my mother, who was engaged in the amorous equivalent of a Napoleonic military campaign, the situation was far from calm. Here's how she described her progress to Sue Boothby:

The Prof. and I are still having the battle of the brains and you can just guess who is winning. He is a nimble one he is, but I have never lived far away from the abattoir and learned early that there's more than one way to skin cats even cats on hot tin roofs like him. Sometimes I feel more encouraged than others . . . my latest hurdles have been fairly important ones: I've been taken to Eton twice (unprecedented that) to see the beautiful son. Once we took him to lunch at that chi-chi joint in Bray, and the other time we went to watch him play soccer against Westminster and then drove on to Oxford where Freddie had to give a talk. The son likes me (gleaned from the daughter who was there for lunch). Then, I've met the misty all-powerful wife and (absolutely unprecedented this Freddie claims) she isn't hostile. My sister has made friends with the daughter and has even been included in cosy family dinners in Hampstead with Renée and Lord Listowell [*sic*], the man she got after Stuart Hampshire.

But all this lateral infiltration will never poison the well so long as the mainspring is untouched you may claim—we don't ignore that for one moment let me tell you, but there's no good mauling that unless the host of protective friends and family on the side are fixed too. They're important to him, and I don't think that *one* blackball excludes or I'd have been out months ago, but I think some votes are 20 times more important than others. The Maori (Jocelyn Rickards) has been in Rome for a while now trying to trap an Italian, but he wriggled out and I hear she's heading this way. I don't think she's much to worry about except that she's out-and-out hostile and *is* an Influence. Even so, I see a couple of huge jumps left and then the homestretch is in sight. It is the most nerve wracking thing I've ever been in—and it seems to go on and on for years although I see by the calendar it's only 9 months.

Still and all, I think it's worth the struggle—my only fear is that I won't pull it off and will then find I've used up all my elasticity and sanity in the big effort and will just be a gibbering blob for the rest of my life. Which would be brief for, naturally, I would plaster damning notes all over London and then jump off Big Ben. It really does give pause for reflection though on the ultimate wisdom of not putting all the eggs in one basket. Though, if you don't, you can never hatch the number of chickens you want. I guess that most people just learn to settle for fewer chickens.

But just as soon as my mother felt she was within sight of victory, yet another dragon would rear its ugly head. The next one was called Lady Elizabeth von Hofmannsthal. And she was far from ugly. In fact she was one of the most beautiful women in London. The daughter of the Marquess of Anglesey, she was married to a wonderful man named Raimund, the son of the Viennese poet and librettist of *Der Rosenkavalier,* Hugo von Hofmannsthal. (At the very end of his life Freddie confessed to me that he had been in love only three times: with Renée, with Liz, and with his third wife, Vanessa.) It wasn't as though Liz was about to abandon her family (she and Freddie had known each other for twenty years, and when the affair had started or ended was all a bit hazy), but she was an Influence, and her vote counted. Again my mother confided to Sue:

Wish somebody would poison that f—ing Lady L.Von H. *She* is the biggest fly in anyone's ointment and I think fills F's head with stories of how ruthless and uncivilized I am and will make him miserable. She has just had a baby stuck in her tubes and I wish to god it had popped her off. But modern science has pulled her through and she is sitting around in feathered bed jackets getting in my way.

AND VERY FETCHING she must have looked swathed in chiffon and swansdown, sipping tea in her *lit à la polonaise* with its pale pink chintz curtains, held back by silken ribbons and tassels. Birch logs glowed in the fireplace, and above its marble mantelpiece hung a portrait of Liz's equally beautiful mother, who had the same creamy, magnolia skin, blue eyes, and almost-black hair as her daughter. The dressing table stood in front of the bay windows, festooned in a flouncy white petticoat, and on her bedside table, beside a flowering jasmine plant, was the all important telephone: the electronic conduit for pouring venom into Freddie's ear.

How, you may be wondering at this point, is it that I am so familiar with the decor of Lady Elizabeth's boudoir? Well, years later, when my mother and Liz had become friends, and I was old enough to go to grown-up dinner parties, I would be invited quite often to the Hofmannsthals, since

I was roughly the same age as their son Octavian. Looking back, it does seem a little incredible, but in some houses, in those dim and distant days, the ladies actually followed their hostess out of the dining room after the dessert, leaving the men alone so they could have their brandy and cigars unencumbered by feminine company. It didn't seem like such a bad idea to me, because at that point in the evening you were always longing to pee, and also needed to brush your hair and spackle on more makeup. And the bonus was that you got the chance to poke around in your hostess's bathroom, examine the contents of her medicine cabinet, see what interesting pills she might be taking, and douse yourself in her perfume. Having done all that, you'd then lounge about in her bedroom for a while—sometimes a bit too long—and, if you were lucky, exchange delicious little *petits fours* of gossip.

I don't want to give the impression that the Siege of Freddie occupied *all* my mother's time or formidable brain, because she actually loved her work and was just as determined to succeed in journalism as she was to become Mrs. A. J. Ayer. Having started out writing about fashion and London life for the *New York Times,* she quite soon moved on to reviewing movies, and then became the lead book reviewer for the *Sunday Express.* Her highly opinionated pieces began to create a stir and caught the attention of the *Express*'s proprietor, Lord Beaverbrook. The Beaver, as he was known, was Canadian, and incredibly right wing, and I think my mother enjoyed winding him up, and he, being the consummate newspaperman that he was, undoubtedly enjoyed the controversy that she attracted. In 1959 my mother wrote a scathing review of a book called *Beloved Infidel,* by Sheilah Graham. It may not have interested the Beaver particularly, but it was all too relevant to Freddie's byzantine private life.

The title was taken from a poem that Scott Fitzgerald had written about Sheilah, and the subject of the book was their love affair. They had met at a party to celebrate her engagement to the Marquess of Donegall, given by Robert Benchley in July 1937, at his Garden of Allah bungalow in Hollywood. Fitzgerald was writing scripts to pay for his daughter's education and his wife's catastrophic medical bills, drinking way too much, and trying to finish *The Last Tycoon.* Sheilah was a syndicated Hollywood gossip columnist. The marquess was unemployed, as marquesses generally are, and returned to his estate in Ireland, without his fiancée, the day after the party. In *Beloved Infidel* she describes, in touching detail, her life with

Fitzgerald, who was to die in her arms on December 21, 1940. Sheilah had grown up dirt poor in the slums of London, with no education, but had parlayed her dazzling looks, charm, and street smarts into a career, first as a chorus girl and later, when she moved to New York and Hollywood, as a journalist. But it was Fitzgerald who made up for all the schools she never went to, when he became the private tutor in her "college of one," and drew up the long list of books that she would read and they would discuss together. The book that Sheilah subsequently published almost twenty years later was good enough for Edmund Wilson to review in *The New Yorker*, calling it "the best portrait of Fitzgerald that has yet been put into print." But my mother thought otherwise, and dismissed it in the *Sunday Express*, concluding "And I suppose in a way you have to hand it to this ex–East End orphan, once named Lily Sheil. Just *what* to hand her, I'd be hard put to say. But I do know it's nothing I'd touch with a ten-foot pole. With gloves on."

Whatever the merits of *Beloved Infidel*, the main issue, from her point of view, was that Sheilah and Freddie had been lovers in New York during the war. It's not as if she posed any threat, but my mother just could not resist sticking the knife in and twisting it around, especially with an audience of five million readers. The situation was made even more complicated by the fact that Sheilah had given birth to Freddie's daughter, Wendy, in September 1942. There had been no question of marriage (he was still, conveniently, attached to Renée), so she had rather nimbly turned around and married the hapless Trevor Westbrook, after a "whirlwind romance," and had presumably convinced him that the baby born "prematurely," but curiously large, was his. (Interestingly, her next child, Robert, born in Hollywood, was rumored to be Robert Taylor's son. One sperm bank for brains and one for beauty.)

Sheilah kept in touch with Freddie over the years, and used to bring Wendy to London to see him, without ever telling her the truth about who her real father was. At one of these cozy lunches, in 1959, it emerged that Freddie had actually seen the review before it went to press but had done nothing to prevent its publication. As if poor Freddie, who loathed all confrontation, would *ever* have dreamed of doing any such thing. All he could come up with in his defense was to tell her that he had said to my mother, "Don't you think that's a bit strong?" As if my mother, who loved all confrontation, could *ever* have been persuaded to tone it down.

Sheilah stormed out of the restaurant, leaving Freddie and Wendy to poke around at the remains of their lamb chops in embarrassed silence.

While my mother was writing her reviews for the *Express*, Freddie, in addition to his philosophical work, was also becoming something of a public intellectual and television star after he started appearing regularly on a program called *The Brains Trust* in 1956. I think we actually bought our first television set in order to watch him. The format was deceptively simple: Line up four brainiacs, throw in a moderator, add questions from the viewers, and see what happens next. Of course it helped that both the guests and the questions were of an unusually high caliber. Freddie was a natural performer and soon became one of the regulars on the show. Others included scientists like Jacob Bronowski and Julian Huxley, writers like his brother Aldous and Cyril Connolly, plus the odd Jesuit like Father d'Arcy, peers like Lord Longford, and Dr. Strangelove himself, Henry Kissinger. Freddie, a well-known atheist, and Father d'Arcy were, curiously, old friends, but when presented with a question like, "Do you believe in the Devil?" they were every television producer's dream team. In his autobiography Freddie describes their encounter like this:

> "No," I said immediately, "and not in God either," giving my reasons as briefly as I could. Father d'Arcy replied with less than Jesuitical urbanity and a lively discussion followed. Later, we were asked whether we believed in original sin and Father d'Arcy said that he did. I was tempted but forebore to point out that this committed him to belief in the literal existence of Adam and Eve. Father d'Arcy with whom my personal relations were always good, admitted after the programme that he would have been embarrassed if I had fastened this doctrine on to him, and thanked me for not doing so.

So Freddie not only scored points off Father d'Arcy intellectually, forcing him to lose his Jesuitical cool, but also graciously let him off the hook. The debate apparently provoked Lord Longford into making a speech in the House of Lords to the effect that since "we live in a Christian country such atheists as Julian Huxley and myself should not be permitted to appear on television." Naturally nobody paid the slightest bit of attention to the Lord Longford, and Freddie went on to appear on the show forty-three times. He was always disarmingly honest about how much he enjoyed his growing fame, and confessed years later that "My success on the Brains Trust had given me an uncritical appetite for publicity." There were many other television appearances, including a memorable one on Valentine's Day with Eartha Kitt, which he later came to regret:

> We were asked a question about romantic love and I tried to talk learnedly about the troubadours. Out of mischievousness or boredom she made a show of flirting with me. Instead of bringing my speech to an end, or better still responding in kind, I floundered on and was made to look thoroughly foolish.

Freddie knew he was better off with a Jesuit than with Eve and that tempting apple.

LIFE WITH MY MOTHER and Freddie was never boring. They both shared the same sense of humor and the fundamental idea that although life was clearly a serious business, there was no reason why it should not also be *fun*. Clever and funny. Funny and clever. That was what they were, and that was what I assumed everybody must be. Like all children, I accepted my own family and circumstances as being utterly normal. And it was only as I got older that I came to realize that not everybody commuted between Europe and America, got divorced, had multiple lovers, the odd illegitimate child, and, most surprising of all, that the world was actually full of people who were neither clever nor funny. The last revelation was the real shocker and much the hardest to adjust to.

I remember one trick they concocted together that involved, in Freddie's words, "our appealing but incontinent dachshund, Monster," who was inordinately fond of him. The idea was that the next time Freddie appeared on *The Brains Trust* he should contrive to say the dog's name really loudly, and we three should sit at home in front of the TV set and see what happened next. So there we were on the sofa, with a special box of Maltesers—his favorite chocolates—for Monster, when Freddie appeared on the screen, gabbling away about metaphysics, possibly with poor old Father d'Arcy again, and suddenly said, "I see no empirical reason to believe in the existence of God, any more than I do in the Loch Ness MONSTER." The experiment was a huge success. Monster lunged at the TV, barking wildly, the Maltesers scattered all over the floor, and we both fell about laughing.

When it came to my birthday they were both ridiculously indulgent. Not necessarily with extravagant presents, but with humoring my wishes, however ludicrous. The year I turned eight I was caught up in my ballerina fantasy. I went to classes every Wednesday in a dank church hall in Notting Hill Gate, where my lack of any musical sense was overlooked by my kindly teacher, a tiny, sparrowlike woman who spoke with an impenetrable "foreign" accent of no clear provenance. But since I didn't much care about the actual dancing, my complete absence of rhythm didn't matter. It was the clothes I was interested in. My deepest desire was to look like the tarty, twirling figure on top of the mirrored jewelry box that I had been given for Christmas.

Together my mother and I concocted what we thought was the perfect birthday tutu. The bodice was pink satin, the spaghetti straps were embroidered with rosebuds, and the skirt was cantilevered out from my nonexistent waist with multiple layers of tulle. White tights, ballet shoes encrusted with silver sparkles, like a Woolworth's Christmas tree ornament, and a tasteful not-too-large rhinestone tiara, completed the ensemble. Decked out like that, my mother knew there was only one place in the whole of London we could possibly have gone. King Edward VII and Lily Langtry had gorged on tournedos Rossini and peach Melba there; Oscar Wilde had entertained the fatally attractive Lord Alfred Douglas with quail's eggs and Veuve Clicquot there; and on top of all that, it was Freddie's favorite restaurant. Mirrors, gilt, crystal chandeliers, pink, pleated silk lampshades, red velvet banquettes, silver candelabras: the Café Royal had it all. I was led to our table—toes carefully pointed out, ballerina style—seated between my mother and Freddie, and given a menu only slightly taller than myself. I ordered *sole meunière*, my mother had oysters, which made her sneeze, as she always did when she felt too much money was being spent on food, and Freddie probably had turbot, as he usually did. For dessert there was a special cake that had been ordered ahead of time, with eight candles perched precariously on top of a pillow of whipped cream. As far as I was concerned the evening was a total triumph. And I like to think they may have had quite a good time too.

In fact my memories of them together at this point in their lives were entirely happy, but I was, of course, unaware of the continuing Siege of Freddie. By 1959 she was making serious progress and wrote to her friend Sue:

> Freddie seems to be worked up to a pitch of enthusiasm not likely to be possible again. He doesn't shake and tremble and mutter No no no No no noooo all night anymore and he on his own steam actually went to Somerset House and got a copy of his grandpa's will which has a trust fund thing out of which I hope to con the money for the house. He also even got a copy of his divorce papers and *that* I never even suggested as a thing to do. He is now off to New York to see Valerie [his daughter with Renée] get married tomorrow to a frightful sounding swotter from Rochester. He is bound to appreciate my fine sensitivity and European ways even more when he gets back, and that is why I want to find the house to pop him in quickly and slam the door.

Nothing like a trip to Rochester in the winter to concentrate the mind. But my mother still felt she needed to bring on her one last bit of heavy artillery, and for that she turned to a somewhat surprising ally. My father was living in Bonn at this point, working as a kind of senior aide-de-camp to Ambassador Bruce, entertaining his ladies, and taking me on our regular road trips around Europe. That year we were due to visit Sue and Basil Boothby in Brussels, where they had been posted by the Foreign Office after Rangoon, for the 1958 World's Fair:

> I think your cup runnething over as it does you are likely to have that old Al and Gully with you around the 22nd or so. And they are not only going to see the fair, they are going to the fucking flower fields of Holland and some midget village or something near Amsterdam.

After we toured the "fucking flower fields" and the "midget village" (quite fun, as I recall) I was put on a plane back to London, and my father returned to Germany, where he found a letter from his ex-wife waiting for him. Would he do her a huge favor, please? Could he write her a letter, saying that he was *outraged* and *disgusted* by the thought of his precious daughter living in such a sinful ménage, and what was my mother proposing to do about it? He roared with laughter, spent a happy evening composing a suitably indignant letter, and sent it off in the diplomatic pouch posthaste to London. Sadly the document hasn't survived, and my father

only told me about it, still laughing, after my mother's death. But it may
have been the piece of paper that broke Freddie's back, because in 1959 he
wrote, rather mournfully, to e. e. cummings's wife, Marion, in New York:

> I agree that I should probably not make a good husband. We don't in
> fact plan to get married, at least not straightaway, but for various rea-
> sons, including the attitude of Gully's father, it may be difficult for us
> not to. And anyhow, the point is not so much being married as living
> with one person. My being away at Oxford during the term may or may
> not make it easier. We are both full of forebodings, but it seems feeble
> to back out now, having gone so far.

Having confided his doubts to Marion, he then turned to his old mistress, Jocelyn, the "Maori," who was now living with the playwright John
Osborne, and invited himself to lunch. In his autobiography Osborne
describes what happened next:

> I found Jocelyn, her face streaked with tears, more upset than I had ever
> seen her. It confirmed my view that Ayer was possibly the most self-
> ish, superficial and obtuse man I have ever met, spitting out his com-
> monplace opinions to an audience mystified by the tricks of manipulated
> sleight-of-mind. He had announced that he was contemplating marriage
> to an American, but was undecided whether the match fulfilled his stan-
> dards of wisdom and self-esteem. He offered his ex-mistress a two-card
> choice: he was prepared to marry the American unless Jocelyn should
> feel impelled to offer herself as an alternative. Anyone less kindly would
> have kicked this pear-shaped Don Giovanni down the stairs and his
> cruel presumption with him. She could find nothing to say except, "But
> Freddie, it's too late."

And so, dear reader, the pear-shaped Don Giovanni married the
American adventuress.

My mother found a house, just off Fitzroy Square, into which she
popped Freddie and then quickly bolted the door. It was a smaller version of Holland Park Avenue: a typical London town house with endless
stairs and two rooms on each floor. My bedroom was right at the top, and
I chose a flamboyant, and probably ill-advised, wallpaper of cauliflower
size turquoise roses, a green carpet, and *broderie anglaise* curtains for

the windows. For all her bossiness, my mother was happy to leave me to make my own decisions, however ridiculous they might be, when it came to clothes, decor, and just about everything else. Freedom was something she believed in: If I wanted meringues for dinner, and leftover spareribs for breakfast, why not have them? With her, there were never any of those pointless decrees and nitpicking that other children I knew had to endure from their more conventional parents. She lived by the ethos that rules were there to be ignored, icons were for smashing (unless you had smuggled them out of Russia, as she did on a trip to Moscow), and that if you really wanted to do something, you should just go ahead and *do* it. Quite naturally I later rebelled against her, and became the prissiest, most conservative girl in all of swinging London.

The sixties blew into town and caught us both by surprise. My mother had always been a rebel and was thrilled that society had finally come around to her way of thinking. She had incredible legs, so what could be more flattering than a short leather skirt designed by her friend Mary Quant? She had dead-straight auburn hair, so who better to cut it than Vidal Sassoon? She was an anarchist, so why not let your young son run around naked and go to bed whenever he damn well pleased? She loved to shock, so what's wrong with smoking a joint or two in front of your kids? And while I was perfectly happy to go shopping for miniskirts and have my hair cut at Sassoon, I was a cautious, careful child who craved order and routine. The cautious child became a cautious teenager who behaved like a disapproving—but secretly admiring—maiden aunt, clucking her tongue at the wild antics of her naughty mother. Even if I *had* wished to misbehave, which I didn't, whom would I have done it with? As an A student at an all-girls school with a mild—but for me, totally debilitating—case of acne, I didn't have a long list of suitors eager to tempt me off the straight and narrow. In fact I had none. But in my early teenage years this didn't bother me at all, and I was quite happy devouring books and hanging about with my parents and their friends, wondering if I would ever have as much fun as they did when I finally grew up.

THE DAY OF THE WEDDING my mother and I got up before dawn and headed off to Covent Garden to buy flowers for the party that night.

We returned in a taxi filled to the roof with roses, delphiniums, mimosa, and enormous branches of apple blossoms, which we arranged before getting dressed for the ceremony at St. Pancras Town Hall. The lunch afterward was in the sun-filled, mirror-spangled dining room at the Ritz, overlooking St. James's Park. Three other couples had been invited to join us: Sue and Basil Boothby, Margie and Goronwy Rees, and Sonia and Michael Pitt-Rivers. I don't recall very much about the lunch except that I was seated beside Michael, with whom I fell instantly in love. The fact that he was old, married, and, I was later told, gay, did absolutely nothing to diminish my ardor. He was a dazzlingly handsome farmer with a large estate in Wiltshire that had been left to him by his father, a truly terrifying man who had been one of Oswald Mosley's more rabid acolytes. The rolling, carefully manicured green hills were sprinkled with bizarre and incongruous follies, brought back by his grandfather, an eminent Edwardian anthropologist, from his travels around the world. A tree house from Sumatra loomed over a bank of rhododendron bushes; an Iraqi meetinghouse, constructed entirely of rushes, stood beside the lake, and, on an island in the middle, a bark hut from Papua New Guinea was flanked by two weeping willows. It was the perfect backdrop for elaborate parties of an exotic nature, which usually involved Michael's dressing up as an Indian prince with lots of jewels and brocade, his flawless features enhanced by dusky Othello-toned makeup and meticulously applied kohl eyeliner. Sometimes elephants and tigers were brought into play.

A couple of years before the wedding, Michael had been arrested, along with his friend, Lord Montagu, after they had spent the weekend at Montagu's stately home entertaining some dashing young guardsmen they had picked up in Green Park. Homosexuality was a criminal offense in those days (Freddie was one of the leaders of the campaign to have the law repealed, which finally happened in 1967), and Michael was sent to jail. Ironically his jailer turned out to be a man called Tubb, who had served under him in the army during the war. So each morning, when he came into the cell with the prisoner's bowl of gruel, Michael would leap up and say, in his best British commander's voice, "Morning, Tubb," and poor Tubb, before he could stop himself, would snap to attention and reply, "Morning, sir"—which, Michael always said, was the only fun part about being in jail.

As soon as he was released he got married. Why, nobody could ever figure out. The lady he chose was George Orwell's mercurial widow, Sonia, and the marriage, predictably enough, was not a great success. They soon divorced, and Michael went on to live happily ever after with a cherubic, golden-haired young painter named William, who shared his passion for dressing up and riding around on elephants.

AFTER THE LUNCH at the Ritz there was a huge party at our new house. Probably shell-shocked, Freddie wrote in his autobiography, "I remember nothing of the party which followed our wedding." And he wasn't much more revealing about their honeymoon: "We went to Venice, which I found enchanting, despite the prevalence of German tourists. Then we stopped in Split, where we visited Diocletian's palace and from there went by sea to Dubrovnik where we settled into a moderately luxurious hotel outside the town."

But things started to look up a bit when they joined their close friend, Hugh Gaitskell, the leader of the Labour Party, in the palatial villa he had rented from the Yugoslav ambassador to London. No doubt Tito had been told all about the ambassador's distinguished guest, and various Communist-themed treats were laid on, like a trip down the Dalmatian coast on the president of Croatia's yacht, accompanied by the head of the Yugoslavian trade unions. A fun-packed week followed, until the day Freddie took it into his head to go swimming:

> Although the sea was rough and I am not a good swimmer, I succumbed to the temptation of joining the others in a bathe. There was no difficulty in plunging into the water and for a short time I quite enjoyed being buffeted by the waves. The difficulty was in getting out again. You had somehow to ride the crest of a wave and let it deposit you on the hotel terrace.

Riding the waves was never Freddie's forte, and eventually he was in real trouble and had to be rescued, ending up with his lungs full of seawater. A fever followed, and "No sooner was he aware of my condition than Hugh ordered me to bed." Since they were due to leave later that day, my mother seems to have been rather more concerned with catching the Orient Express than with Freddie's fever, and she persuaded her new husband that he was perfectly well enough to travel. Obediently he got up and started putting his clothes on. But then, "Hugh came into the room while I was dressing and in almost no time at all he had me back in bed."

It was a battle of the wills between the leader of the Labour Party and the Canadian sergeant major, with Freddie in the middle, pulling his underpants up and down. Amazingly the politician won. "I was very much impressed by this glimpse of Hugh Gaitskell in action. Dee is an exceptionally strong-minded woman but her will was no match for his." In the end good old Tito came through with an airplane and a promise that the Orient Express would be held up, if necessary, and they arrived back in London, tired but happy, ready to embark on married life together.

Le Dîner

A s s o o n a s m y m o t h e r m a r r i e d f r e d d i e, I started nagging her to have a baby. In fact, I had started nagging her years before, when she had been living with Robert. I yearned for a living, breathing creature that I could play with and dress up and add to my already enormous collection of dolls. But babies were not her thing, and she never pretended they were. And I think she was probably only half kidding when she wrote this letter to her mother about me as a newborn:

> She's still surviving but I can scarcely say the same about me—drives me nuts with the yacking and complete lack of logic and/or reason and/or gratitude that I've always associated with babies. . . . Must go now and throw the monster into its bath. I can't tell who hates it more—her or me. She gets orange juice now to keep her krapping which is a necessary function she forgets about from time to time and lies there screaming trying to remember what it was she forgot to do.

When I was born in Paris, she had an old Swiss crone waiting for her at the house (presumably the letter described one of those days when the crone had had the temerity to take some time off) when she brought me home from the hospital. In Burma I had an ayah, who taught me the Burmese names for all my clothes, so that, on the rare occasions when my mother dressed me, I would demand my *lungi* or my *ganji*s, and grow increasingly impatient when she couldn't produce them. And in London I had Cele, an Italian au pair, whom I adored, except when she told me about the time she had chopped a chicken's head off on her family's farm in Puglia.

In my mother's family there had been no kindly crones or gentle ayahs or pretty Italian au pairs. In fact, there had been nothing remotely kind, gentle, or pretty about her childhood. Her own mother, she always told me, was a monster. Depressed, violent, highly intelligent, capable of "mesmerizing charm," vicious, and nuts: She should probably never have had children at all. But of course she married a nice, mild-mannered man whom she could terrorize, and had four. My grandfather had started out working for the *Providence Journal*, in Rhode Island, but then moved to New Bedford, an old whaling town in Massachusetts, where he became a PR executive in the Bell Telephone Company. There wasn't a huge amount of money, but far, far worse than that were the toxic fumes belched out by his fire-breathing wife, which infected the entire family.

When my mother was two and a half she ran away from home. Her six-year-old brother was actually the mastermind behind the great escape, and just big enough to push her in the baby carriage, since he judged they wouldn't get very far if she had to walk. They rattled along a bumpy road and, according to my uncle, had several hours of sunlit peace, lolling about on a grassy hilltop, before they were yanked back, amid much shouting, to their gloomy house. But then again lots of kids play at running away from home, so that story never carried quite the same grisly heft as her next, far more horrific memory.

A few years after the abortive breakout, she brought a friend home from school, and they went in search of the litter of kittens her cat had given birth to a few days before. Where could they possibly be? My mother never forgot the smile on my grandmother's face when she told her that she had put the kittens, very gently, in the drum of an old washing machine in the basement, with some chloroform soaked rags, and closed the top. Really they hadn't suffered at all, it was a beautiful, peaceful death and it was all for the best. The Angel of Death had swooped down to save them from "this terrible world." This was not the first or last time that the Angel had indulged in her penchant for guiding cats along the road to a much, much better place. Years later, V. R. Lang, a wild and brilliant playwright, actress, and poet, whom my mother had met when they were both misbehaving in the Canadian army, wrote a poem about the murderous Mrs. Chapman. The first two verses go like this:

LINES FOR MRS. C.

About to annihilate, in a long succession of cat murders, two old stray cats
with ether, in her washing machine, with the cover on.

O you cats, go home to God,
She finds them and locks
Kitties, where the saints have trod,
them in the kitchen.
You go, you two, you too
Like thin flames upwards into
That which, electric and ethereal,
Is going to be your first square deal.

Kitties, go! Unspring those tails!
They are not convinced.
Cease wild scrabbling of those claws!
No longer roll those maddened eyes!
    —Trust me kitties!
I who love cats know their problems.
Tonight you will sleep in the arms of Jesus.

Whether all happy families are alike, *pace* Tolstoy, is debatable, but my
mother's unhappy family was positively Dostoyevskian in its misery. Of
course each person copes with trauma in a different way, and my mother's
method was to confront it head-on, fight back, and then get the hell out
as fast as she could. None of her three siblings were quite as outspoken
in their hostility toward their mother, but interestingly, when she died,
aged ninety-eight, not one of them came to her funeral. It is possible
that my grandmother took out more of her anger and bitterness on her
eldest daughter than on the others, but whatever the origin of her cruelty,
the result was that my mother regarded her as "the most untrustworthy,
destructive person I have ever known." A childhood like that leaves scars
that never heal, and as I got older I learned to look at my mother's character and behavior through the prism of this primal reign of horror.

Her attitude toward babies was also, I believe, directly related to her
upbringing. When she was eight, she told me, her mother became pregnant with her fourth child, and on the night she went into labor, amid
plenty of screaming and hysteria, her husband was not around, so she

rushed off to the hospital by herself. My mother was left, terrified and alone, for the next ten days, in charge of her three-year-old sister. Where my grandfather and uncle were in this scenario is a little unclear—maybe they just fled to work and school each morning, leaving her at home— but for my mother this was yet another traumatic memory to add to her growing collection. She grew up during the Depression, and there was not enough money for a nanny, and even if there had been, why waste it when you had a perfectly strong and capable eight-year-old girl at home?

Based on her own in-depth, hands-on, and far-too-extensive experience, babies were irrational creatures who spent most of their time screaming, refusing to sleep, and throwing their food at you. She thought it was just about understandable to have one, but any more was sheer madness. So when her younger sister grew up, got married, and became quite happily pregnant for the second time, she marched her off to the doctor, where they made an appointment for an abortion. And it was only after my mother had safely disappeared to the house in France for the summer that her sister had the unbelievable chutzpah to blow off the date she had never had any intention of keeping.

But when my mother finally married Freddie, her view of babies softened somewhat, and I began to feel that my years of nagging might just pay off. Later that year she wrote to Sue:

> I've been feeling so blah that I've been doing nothing but lurch from one chair to another. In a burst of positively Galileo-like dedication to science we finally called in our comic doctor. He thinks I'm pregnant, and though nothing would please me more than to be able to agree with him, I don't. It doesn't feel right. I can smoke etc and I know me; I wouldn't be able to if I really were. But it's too awful because it has got Fred's hopes all up (and mine too, in a way) and he is bounding around like Nijinsky, he's that pleased with himself, but I fear it will all end badly. In about 3 days when they discover I have lung cancer, exploded ovaries and ulcers.

As it turned out she wasn't pregnant, but neither did she have any other dire condition, and Freddie and I both went on hoping that next time our dreams would come true. His for a "real" son and mine for a new "doll." But in the meantime she switched her attention from her ovaries to Provence.

∾

IN THE SPRING OF 1962, for some reason or another—it may have been the dregs from her divorce settlement with my father—my mother found herself with more money than she knew what to do with. Or, at least slightly more than she actually needed to live on, so she decided it might be a good idea to buy a house in the south of France. As I recall, it was less than ten thousand dollars, which even in those days wasn't a huge amount, but it was just enough, she reckoned, for a very small hut at the wrong end of the Côte d'Azur. But where to begin?

One of Freddie's oldest friends was a man called Bill Deakin, who, as warden of St. Antony's College, Oxford, had been the host of that fateful party where my mother had fallen for "the menace." He also happened to have a house in a village called Le Castellet, not too far from Toulon. Bill was a sweet and gentle man, whom Freddie had met when they were both undergraduates at Oxford, and who went on to become head of his section at Special Executive Operations (SOE), in Rockefeller Center in New York, during the war. But they overlapped for only a few months because shortly after Freddie arrived, Bill was called back to London and then parachuted into Yugoslavia as leader of the first British mission to make contact with good old Tito, who, many years later, was to prove so helpful to Freddie and my mother on their honeymoon. Bill was married to Pussy, a delightfully bossy Romanian lady with the most beautiful skin I have ever seen which was still miraculously smooth and plump and polished when I last saw her a few months before she died in her eighties.

"Darling," she told me in a whisper, as she lay in bed, "you must clean your face with olive oil; do not allow water to touch it. Ever. And once a week you must cover it with a thick layer of honey and lie for at least one hour, with your head hanging lower than your body, so the blood can rush into your skin and feed it."

Looking back—and in the mirror—I realize I should have followed her advice.

MY MOTHER, FREDDIE, and I flew from London to Marseille, where they rented a car, which she drove, while he sat beside her attempting to read the map. As we sped along the coast road, just east of the *vieux port*, Freddie announced triumphantly, "I've got it. I've found Le Castellet." We whooped with delight, but as he issued directions, he kept turning the map around, to make it easier to read, until it was finally, and much more conveniently, upside down. When my mother finally realized what he had done—Freddie was, naturally, oblivious of his mistake—she exploded:

"Jesus H. Christ, Freddie, have you ever wondered why it was Bill who was parachuted into Yugoslavia, while they left you in Rockefeller Fucking Center, where all you did was take Sheilah Fucking Graham to the Stork Club every night? And you know what *that* stork ended up dropping on your plate, don't you?"

She was, of course, laughing as she said it, and it *was* funny, and even funnier that night at dinner when her account of Freddie's incompetence was followed by his mildly indignant reply: "Actually, I was in charge of the maps when we liberated Saint-Tropez, and we managed quite well then." Which only made her mutter "Jesus H. Christ" all over again.

FROM THE DISTANCE Le Castellet looked like one of those toy villages, perched on a hilltop, glimpsed in the background of an Italian Renaissance portrait. The surrounding plain was covered in a neat patchwork of parallel rows of vines, dotted with ocher-colored farmhouses, olive groves, and the occasional row of neatly tapered inky green cypress trees. Still enclosed by most of its original medieval walls, the village curled itself around the top of the hill like a giant stone snail. The houses clustered about the church—its tower was crowned by an elaborate wrought-iron cage containing a huge bronze bell—and the château next door, with its large *place* out front, where the Marquis de Quelquechose was gracious enough to allow the locals, usually just a few rickety old men, to play *boules* in his dust.

The medieval walls had a medieval gateway, about three centimeters wider than our car, which meant that Freddie the map reader became Freddie the traffic cop, as he stood there waving his arms about, trying to guide my mother through the narrow stone passageway. Never having learned to drive, with no visual sense of any kind, and completely unable to gauge distance, he was possibly even worse at his new job than his old one. Luckily for him we got through without scraping the sides of the car and so narrowly avoided, not just the walls, the ire of Hertz, but, far more important, a new barrage of swearing.

The Deakins—although it was actually bossy Pussy who had masterminded the real estate deals—had been clever enough to buy several connected, tumbledown houses in the 1950s, when such things were still quite affordable. The first house they had bought was the old village schoolhouse, whose back door led to the ramparts, and to the ruins of another house, its roof long since gone. The remaining stone walls enclosed a series of garden "rooms," which in turn led to a terrace with a staggering view of the entire valley, stretching all the way to the Mediterranean about ten miles away.

The night we arrived they had gathered together an assortment of people—mostly a mix of English and American—all of whom had bought houses nearby. The old hands were clearly there to give the neophytes much needed advice, warnings, and encouragement. I remember it was freezing cold and the schoolhouse's heating system, which probably dated back to the previous century, consisted of a couple of stoves fueled by some mysterious French substance called *mazout*, which produced a strong and distinctive smell but surprisingly little heat. The mistral howled through the village, and I could hear a rogue shutter banging against a wall upstairs. Fortunately there was also a huge fireplace, which we huddled around while Bill poured stiff drinks and Pussy crashed about in the kitchen tending to her legendary *boeuf en daube*.

"Darling, you must *always* marinate the meat for three days in the *best* bottle of wine you have, with some juniper berries, cloves, thyme, a bay leaf, and four strips of dried orange peel. Bill was furious when I once used a Château Margaux '53, which he said Churchill had given him, but the English are fools who know nothing of food. They even have something called 'cooking wine.' I have no idea what this could possibly be, and hope never to find out. So, next you gently brown the *lardons*, carrots, garlic, and onions in very-high-quality olive oil— preferably from the Domaine Souviou outside Le Beausset—and then add the meat, ripe plum tomatoes, and the strained marinade. The cooking pot *must* be covered with a soup plate containing half a cup of red wine, which you have to refill as it evaporates, and then you cook it for six or seven hours in the oven, with just a whisper of heat."

I may have been dumb enough to ignore her patent olive oil and honey

beauty formula, but I have followed—and passed on—her *daube* recipe
with evangelical fanaticism for more than forty years.

It is strange, after all this time, to look back and realize that the people
around the table, whom I was to know so well and for so many years,
were all strangers to me that night. As an only child I was used to spending most of my time with adults, and I actually enjoyed their company. I
didn't necessarily want to join in their conversation, but I loved watching them, listening to their chatter, like an anthropologist observing
the behavior of an odd but endearing tribe of nomads, whose song lines
meandered between England, France, and America. To avoid embarrassing them my usual cover was to act as a waitress, which meant I got to
roam around while doing my fieldwork, and also earned valuable brownie
points with my mother or the harried hostess. I remember standing, on
duty, in the kitchen with Pussy as she opened the oven door and brought
out the enormous earthenware pot with the soup plate of wine nestled in
the indentation on its lid. At that precise moment the scent of the wood
smoke mingled with the rich, almost gamey, wine-infused aroma of the
daube and the faintly dieselish *ma{out* smell, to produce my own private
Provençal "madeleine." And don't think I haven't tried to re-create it ever
since. I know how to make a wood fire, and I can cook a *daube,* but it is
the eau de *ma{out* that always eludes me. Unknown in New York, it may
not even exist any longer in France, besides which I have never again seen
a stove like the ones in the schoolhouse.

"À table, à table!" Pussy shouted, as I carried the plates into the dining room, piled high with *daube* and fresh noodles, bought that morning in the market in Toulon from the Italian woman down by the port,
who made them in her own kitchen and hung them out to dry on her
washing line. Bill did his best to bring some Oxford logic to the seating
plan, and may have gotten as far as placing my mother beside him, but in
the end everybody sat down, slightly drunk and very hungry, wherever
they wanted. Several bottles of the local Domaine Tempier had already
been opened, the fire snapped and spat out sparks like firecrackers and,
when everyone had finally been served, I settled in to observe the habits
of these strange new creatures.

Directly across from me was a woman named Sylvia who looked like
a Gypsy, or quite possibly an American Indian. Deeply tanned, she had
a nose like a hawk, espresso-colored eyes, and smoked a small, pungent

black cheroot, in between occasional bites of food. Big silver hoops dangled from her slightly pendulous earlobes, both her arms were stacked with silver and turquoise bracelets (could they have been a present from her tribal elders in New Mexico?), and I strongly suspected she wasn't wearing a bra. Apparently she had just bought a house in a place called Ollioules, which had come complete with a man called Monsieur Zancanaro, who was in charge of the vines, the olive trees, and the vegetable garden, and whose wife was incredibly useful around the house. Sylvia was every bit as bossy as my mother and Pussy, and grabbed Freddie's arm, her tribal bracelets clanking, and made him *promise* that he would not even *consider* buying anything that didn't include a Zancanaro-like couple as part of the deal. Freddie was looking a bit wild eyed at this point, and would probably have promised her anything—even his yet-to-be-conceived son, just to shut her up, get her hand off his arm and her cheroot out of his face.

Fortunately for Freddie she soon turned to the gentleman on her other side and almost immediately got into an argument with him about the Ott family. The Domaine Ott was, and still is, the largest and fanciest wine producer for miles around, and it seemed that Sylvia's neighbor was in the habit of selling them quite a lot of his grapes, and even occasionally had dinner with old Monsieur Ott. This, for some inexplicable reason, drove her nuts. She lit another cheroot and waved it about wildly until, in desperation, he swiveled around and focused his attention on the lady to his right—who turned out to be me.

"Hello, my name is Roger, and what, may I ask, is yours?"

When I said, "Gully," he reeled back as though I'd smacked him in the face and replied in his slow, upper-class English drawl: "Good God, what an *extraordinary* name. Surely you weren't *christened* that?"

So I rattled off the high-speed explanation for my distressing nickname: "Born in Paris—christened Alexandra—took a ship to Burma when I was one—on the way we went through the Suez Canal and met a magician in Port Said who said he was a 'Gully-Gully' man—he put his hand up my mother's skirt and produced some fluffy yellow chicks—after that whenever I cried my mother called me 'Gully-Gully,' which shut me up."

Roger considered this bizarre sequence of events for a long time in silence, his eyes fixing me with a slightly manic stare, and finally said:

"I am assuming that when you refer to the Gully-Gully men, you actually mean the Fuzzy-Wuzzy men. In Alexandria one used to chuck coins into the sea, which was incredibly deep, but the Fuzzy-Wuzzies would dive right in and stay under water for ages and ages. One always thought they might quite possibly drown—who knows, maybe some did—but then they'd bob up to the surface, happy as sand boys, clutching their prizes. I don't believe they ever did a stroke of work, but then again, they didn't need to because they made an absolute fortune from all those coins."

He drifted off into a gauzy reverie at the memory of this idyllic scene, and I realized that our conversation was over.

I looked around the table and wondered which of the luckless ladies was married to this Edwardian Neanderthal. Couldn't be the Gypsy, couldn't be the French academic's wife, couldn't be Pussy's sister-in-law, so that left the American with the albino complexion, the tightly curled blond hair, and the even more tightly coiled nerves. My mother always gravitated toward fellow Americans, and especially toward American women who, like herself, were married to Englishmen. Sleeping with the enemy engendered a special, cozy kind of camaraderie that allowed them to reflect, with secret satisfaction, on how far they had traveled from New Bedford/Baltimore/Chicago, while complaining endlessly, but not unhappily, about their husbands' peculiar backgrounds and habits.

Imagine sending your sons to boarding school at six: No wonder they were clueless about women. Imagine beating young boys at school: No wonder they became lifetime clients of Mamzelle de Sade later on. Imagine blowing your nose on phlegm-encrusted handkerchiefs instead of Kleenex: No wonder they had colds all the time. Imagine putting up with freezing bathrooms and bedrooms: No wonder they were filthy but not nearly filthy enough in bed. And they didn't even allow themselves to get started on English dentists and teeth. There was never any shortage of fresh outrages to be amazed at.

Lorna St. Aubyn, my mother's new American friend, was indeed married to Roger, and they had recently bought a house in Le Plan du Castellet, a tiny village in the valley below. Roger had been a doctor in England, but once they married he had stopped practicing, and now that they had moved to France, he was able to devote all his time to playing the piano and making Lorna's life as unpleasant as possible. It seemed that he was unusually gifted at both tasks. Lorna's mother had been an American heiress—ball bearings, mouthwash, coal mines, furniture wax—who knew where the money came from?—who had, in predictable Jamesian fashion, first married an Englishman, and after that some obscure French aristocrat. Lorna inherited her fortune, her eighteenth-century French furniture, her Tiepolos and Guardis, her doll-size shoes, handmade in Rome, and her aversion to American husbands. Roger's family, it was always understood, "had come over with the Conqueror" in 1066 and ended up in Cornwall, where they had lived, unadventurously and impecuniously, ever since. How these star-crossed lovers found each other I was never told, but by the time we met them that night, they had two small children, a terrifying English nanny, and a marriage handmade in hell.

When dinner was over Pussy, Lorna, and the Gypsy huddled together with my mother to fill her in on builders, plumbers, and a *menuisier* named Marius who, while full of irresistible Provençal charm, was a drunken thief and must be *avoided at all costs*. Bill and Freddie retreated, whiskeys in hand, to lurch down Rockefeller Center's tangled memory lanes, and I found myself sitting with a man who, in the thirty years I knew him, never once uttered a single serious word. He told me he was called Azamat. Sounded to me suspiciously like Mazout, but then again, when you are named after a lecherous Egyptian magician, there's not much point in being surprised at what other people choose to call their children. Azamat reminded me of an unbelievably attractive jester at a medieval court. He was quite small, with ghost-white skin, curly brown hair, and, unlike most men I had met, he actually *enjoyed* the company of children—maybe because he never seemed wholly grown up himself. I loved his enthusiasm for sudden, insane expeditions to places like the "OK Corral," a seedy amusement park on the way to Marseille, full of mangy horses and syphilitic old "cowboys," that no other adult would dream of going to. Unable to sit still and unwilling to concentrate on anything dull—work was never his thing—his not-inconsiderable talent and ineffable charm lay in simply making life more enjoyable—something that is not as easy as he always made it look.

Azamat was married to Sylvia, the Gypsy, and they had two children whose names—Selima and Kadir—were as strange and magical as his own. The reason, my mother later told me, that they all sounded

like characters from one of Scheherazade's more fanciful tales was that
Azamat was a direct descendant of Genghis Khan. Seriously. His family name was Guirey, and like the St. Aubyns, they too had "come over
with the Conqueror" except that *their* conqueror had killed a few more
people and they had ended up in the Crimea instead of Cornwall. When
Russia swallowed up the Crimea in the eighteenth century, the Guirey
khans became Russian princes and moved north to St. Petersburg, where
their lives calmed down considerably and revolved entirely around the
czar and his court. But all that changed quite abruptly in 1917, when there
was what a boyfriend of mine once called "a bit of a rumble and a rethink"
in Russia, and the Guireys fled, Azamat's branch of the family ending up
in America. His father had been a brilliant horseman, commanding one of
the czar's more glamorous cavalry regiments, so when he arrived in New
York he quite naturally started a riding school in Central Park.

Curiously—or maybe not—Sylvia's father had also been a White
Russian prince, called Serge Obolensky, who had also lived in St. Petersburg, where he had, quite enterprisingly, married Princess Catherine, the
daughter of Czar Alexander II. After the "rumble and the rethink," they
too became New Yorkers, and in the American fashion soon divorced,
Serge going on to marry Sylvia's mother, Alice Astor, in 1924. Alice
sounded like lots of fun. She was something of a free spirit; quite unlike
her charmless stuffy father, John Jacob IV (known as "Jack Ass" behind
his back), who had gone down on the *Titanic*, or her deeply unappealing brother, Vincent (whose last wife was the legendary Brooke). Alice
was fascinated by Egyptian magic and bonded with Aldous Huxley over
their shared interest, and she also claimed to have been one of the first
people to enter King Tutankhamen's tomb. Mean-spirited gossips back
home always said that Alice had confused the tomb with the Cairo branch
of Van Cleef and Arpels and had emerged from it with a dazzling gold
necklace in her bag. But then again nobody ever claimed to have seen the
trophy, so who knows?

In 1913 she played the lead in *The Nosed Princess*, which the *New York
Times* described as "a fairy comedy"; Cecil Beaton painted her portrait
dressed in a silk kimono; and along the way she acquired four husbands.
While married to Serge, it seems that Alice had an affair with Raimund
von Hofmannsthal, who was Sylvia's real father. (Alice and Raimund
eventually married, then divorced, and his next wife was the beautiful

Liz, Freddie's great love and my mother's bête noire. Prince Obolensky went on to become the vice chairman of the Hilton Hotel Corporation.) So even if Sylvia wasn't a DNA-certified Russian princess by birth, she became one when she married Azamat, always assuming you care about such things, which I'm not so sure she ever did.

Some of this my mother and Freddie told me the next morning at breakfast; the rest I pieced together over the years, and to this day the people sitting around the table that night are chattering away inside my head. Forty-six years later they are all dead, but I can still smell the cigarette smoke, hear Sylvia's bracelets clanking, taste Pussy's *daube*, feel Roger's scorn—and Lorna's fear—see Freddie's smile, giggle at Azamat's jokes, and hear my mother muttering "Jesus H. Christ" under her breath.

La Migoua

PUSSY SAID THERE WAS ONLY ONE estate agent in Le Beausset you could trust, and his name was Loulou Richelmi. The rest were all criminals who should have been put in jail years ago. It was our first morning at the Deakins', and my mother was preparing her battle plan. Bill was hiding behind a two-day-old copy of *The Times*, which Freddie had thoughtfully brought him from London, except that he'd already done the crossword *in ink* on the plane—his thoughtfulness toward an old friend, stuck in the wilds of Provence, certainly didn't extend to depriving himself of *that* daily pleasure.

"Bill, I am right, no?" Pussy wasn't going to allow her husband to escape so easily. "They are all thieves except for Loulou, aren't they?" Still shielded by *The Times*, Bill winked at me, smiling, and replied, "Thieves and criminals. And probably collaborators as well." Memories of the war were still fresh in 1962, and *espèce de collaborateur* was the insult of last resort.

Le Castellet was far too picturesque to have anything so useful as a bank, pharmacy, or any real shops, since its shrewd inhabitants had long ago figured out that it was much more profitable to sell postcards, cigarettes, crêpes, and grubby little bags of stale lavender to the tourists, who stumbled up the hill to gawk at the *village médiéval*. It had a tiny *boulangerie*, a fruit-and-vegetable stand, and an old lady with a makeshift post office in her front parlor—open only on Tuesday and Friday mornings—but any serious business or shopping had to be done in Le Beausset.

The medieval gateway had not expanded during the night, so Freddie was back on traffic cop duty as we squeezed through and headed down into the valley. Our road followed the gentle contours of the hill, its borders a pointillist jumble of scarlet poppies, Queen Anne's lace, and tiny yellow and blue flowers, and beyond, rows of blurry green vines—their new spring leaves just starting to unfurl—stretched across the plain. The mistral's fury had blasted every last scrap of cloud out of the sky, leaving behind an ocean of deep, assertive Matisse blue, and the spring sun was just beginning to breathe some warmth into the early morning air. A few men in work clothes trudged through the vineyards, and in the distance I saw another village, the mirror image of Le Castellet, clinging precariously to the top of an even-steeper hill. "That must be La Cadière," said Freddie, who, unfazed by yesterday's fiasco, had unfolded the map again, blocking my mother's view through the windshield—"Jesus, what are you doing now? I can't see a goddamn thing!"—and flapped his hand out the window in the vague direction of the village. The people in the car behind naturally assumed we were turning right, and when we didn't, roared past us screaming abuse at the half-witted "foreigners" from Marseille.

Pussy had set up an appointment with Loulou and scribbled his address on a bit of paper, but after parking the car, we still had enough time for Freddie to go in search of *Le Monde*, for me to buy a chocolate éclair, and for my mother to inhale her usual breakfast of coffee and cigarettes. As in all Provençal villages, life in Le Beausset revolved around the *place* at its center. In a roughly triangular space, shaded by plane trees, the *mairie* occupied one end, and an ancient stone fountain, overgrown with moss, its basin full of rotting leaves and the odd goldfish, stood at the other, while shops and cafés lined the two longer sides. In the summer, tables, chairs, and umbrellas were set up in the middle, but in April it was still too cold to sit outside, so we went in search of a café. The one we chose was called the Café Jean Jaurès, which didn't mean a great deal to my mother or to me, but when Freddie joined us, with his newspaper neatly folded under his arm, he was beaming.

"You clever girls," he complimented us. "Jean Jaurès has always been a particular hero of mine. As I'm sure you both know"—we didn't— "Jaurès was a great socialist president, and a defender of Dreyfus, who tried to prevent the outbreak of the First World War. Of course he failed, and for his pains was assassinated in 1914 by a man named, appropriately enough, Villain. And even worse, Villain was acquitted of the murder, in a frenzy of nationalism after the war. A total disgrace."

Freddie looked momentarily indignant at this travesty of justice but calmed down as soon as his *café crème* and croissant arrived. Since I was only eleven, and my mother had skipped huge chunks of school, copied what little work she did from other kids, and had fled to the Canadian army as soon as she could, we were both in need of some remedial tutoring in nineteenth-century French history. And who better than Freddie Ayer to have as your own private in-house teacher? As I got older he helped me even more, suggesting books in his library I might want to read, and patiently talking me through the "rumble and the rethink" of the Russian Revolution or Voltaire's contribution to the Enlightenment— and his penchant for pretty ladies—whenever I had some terrifying exam looming. He led me to Gibbon's *Decline and Fall of the Roman Empire* (I think I managed one volume), Lytton Strachey's *Elizabeth and Essex* (passion, power, death—what's not to like?), P. G. Wodehouse (not so much), Evelyn Waugh (wonderful, except for the crazy Catholicism), and he launched me on my lifelong love affair with history, which took me to Oxford and has lasted ever since. But that morning we had no time to dwell on the sad fate of Jean Jaurès, because we were already late for our meeting with the only uncrooked real estate broker in the entire village of Le Beausset.

Loulou Richelmi's office was hidden away down a side street, its doorway, windows, and facade almost obscured by an out-of-control wisteria vine, whose boa constrictor trunk seemed to be strangling the life out of the rickety building. A few malnourished cats loitered about in the patio out front. The door, painted the same dusty lavender blue as a Gauloise pack, was ajar so we walked in, and were greeted by a small man with pitch-black hair, who leapt up like a jack-in-the-box from behind his desk, "Ah, les amis de Madame Deakin!" After handshakes and more coffee, they settled down to business, which consisted of my mother's explaining, quite cheerfully, "Nous n'avons pas beaucoup d'argent," and then naming the actual number of francs in her new French bank account while Loulou rummaged about in the index file inside his head, until he came up with "deux possibilités." The first was in La Cadière and had been a chapel, which was appealing if only as a Freddie tease (imagine the famous atheist living in a church . . .), but there was the problem of the windows.

Loulou had to admit that they were perhaps placed a little too high on the walls, making it impossible to see out and allowing very little light to penetrate the gloomy interior. He seriously doubted that planning permission could ever be obtained to enlarge them. The second possibility was an old farmhouse without water or electricity, on the road to Le Beausset-Vieux, and after a quick call, Loulou announced that the man who had the key would meet us there in half an hour.

We drove out of the village on a road lined with pollarded trees—their branches had been attacked with such Gallic savagery that they resembled maimed veterans of the trenches—and then headed up the hill toward Notre-Dame du Beausset-Vieux. Like Le Castellet and La Cadière, Le Beausset had started out as a tiny settlement clinging to the top of a treacherous hill. The endless invasions, starting with the Phoenicians around 600 BC, followed by the Celts and then the Romans, who made these hilltops the only semisafe places to live. The Romans imposed their own laws and military discipline and, as long as the *Pax Romana* held, they were able to keep things under some kind of control, but with the fall of the empire and the barbarian invasions, all hell truly broke loose, and the settlements became fortified villages surrounded by massive stone walls. After the barbarians came the Moors from Spain, followed by a period of generalized chaos, violence, and banditry, lasting until the beginning of the sixteenth century, when everything calmed down enough for the "new" Le Beausset to be built in the valley below.

Five centuries later all that was left of the original village was an ancient chapel, the remains of the ramparts, and a narrow, vaulted room whose walls were covered with a patchwork of lurid ex-votos. Painted in the style of a Grand-mère Moses who favored scenes of thrilling mayhem rather than dreary New England farms, they depicted a series of disasters: shipwrecks, near-amputations, horrendous train crashes, and fires. And in each case the miraculous intervention of Our Lady of Le Beausset-Vieux had saved the day—and the lives of the victims. Some of the paintings were surprisingly recent, and every year, on the night of September 7, the Virgin's birthday was celebrated with a procession, followed by Midnight Mass in the chapel.

The road up the mountain was so narrow that there was no way for two cars to pass each other without a standoff. These often lasted for quite a while and inevitably ended in a humiliating capitulation by the defeated driver who was forced to back up. Sometimes they involved shouting, sometimes the drivers—if they were men—got out of their cars, egged on by backseat viragos, and threatened each other before one claimed victory, slammed his foot on the accelerator, and roared past his castrated opponent, scowling. Luckily the road was quite empty that morning. Loulou kept reassuring us that we were almost there, and as we approached the crest of the hill, he suddenly swerved off to the left, ground the stick shift down into first, and we started the slow climb up a rocky boulder-strewn, path.

"Et voilà, on est arrivé!" Loulou jumped out of the car, opened the door for my mother, and pointed at a scraggly collection of houses and sheds. It wasn't immediately clear which one was "ours." But just then the front door of the last house in the row opened, and a tubby man with gray hair and an uncertain smile walked toward us: the man with the key. First we took a tour of the "grounds," which encompassed several jungly terraces on the other side of the road, too overgrown to actually set foot on, as well as a dusty open space out front, shielded from the mistral by a thick stand of cypress trees, just big enough for a couple of cars to park in. There was no sign of a garden. But there was a large lime tree, almost as tall as the house, just outside the front door, which shaded not only the terrace beneath it but all the rooms with windows on that side, too, keeping them nice and cool and dark even at the height of summer. My mother, perversely, always regarded this as a huge advantage. Never big on daylight or the outdoors, she preferred a cozy cave with thick curtains, decorated in a subtle medley-*de-merde*. How about a dense chocolate mousse for the walls, the detail picked out in a lighter brown, and a mustard carpet for the floor? This was the actual color scheme of her London bedroom, and oddly enough it did have a certain back-to-the-womb allure.

Loulou, the consummate salesman, kept up his patter, pointing out the useful proximity of our neighbors—they surrounded us—who would keep an eye on the house when we were not here. "Regardez le beau paysage," he said, sweeping his arm toward the woods and vineyards, and, leading us around the corner, he revealed a kind of vertical shed glued onto the back of "our" house, surrounded by rubble. "Une autre maison," he said, beaming like some generous greengrocer throwing a free, only slightly bruised extra plum into the bag. The shed was more spacious than it looked, with three levels, connected by wooden ladders, each with one "room." He suggested we could make a rock garden from the rubble, and the shed would be the perfect place to put "Grand-mère," when she came to stay. My mother looked appalled. But now, he said, it was time for us to take a look inside *la grande maison*, and we all followed the man with the key back round the corner.

He opened the door and we stumbled into a large, pitch-dark space. The ground felt disturbingly uneven, but the key man was also the flashlight man, and he guided us toward an archway and down a couple of steps into an even-danker room, with no windows, no door, no light, and no air. This, Loulou told us, was *la cave* and would have been used for storing olive oil, sacks of grain, vegetables, and barrels of wine. My mother always claimed it was haunted, and it is true that people who slept there —we put in a window and French doors—often woke up exhausted after being burned at the stake or battling ax murderers all night long. The *cave* was also Freddie's study, so when his guests emerged at breakfast, stunned by the events of the night, he would always say, quite innocently, "Well, I can't say I've ever felt anything untoward in there," and my mother would then point out that he was an Aspergian atheist with the sensitivity of a snail. Ergo: "You wouldn't, would you?" He would smile and reply good-humoredly, "I won't deny the first part of your proposition, since I've always been proud to be an atheist, but I am not sure I am willing to concede my resemblance to a snail, sensitive or otherwise."

We returned to the original dark room, where the animals would have lived, hence the lack of windows, and groped our way up a staircase that led to the altogether more cheerful second floor. "Voilà le salon!" Loulou pointed to a room with a massive fireplace and a terra-cotta-tiled floor, and then showed us a big cupboard—eventually the bathroom—and a square, sunny room that overlooked the vertical shed. One more twisty staircase and we were on the top floor, a wide-open space with two tiny windows and a rough cement floor. Loulou said nothing would be easier than to divide it up into three, even four, bedrooms.

Curiously, for a peasant's farmhouse stuck in the middle of the country, several miles from the nearest village, it felt more like a tenement in the backstreets of Marseille. I suppose this had something to do with the house being quite tall and narrow, and the fact that, once inside, you could hear absolutely *everything*. The interior walls must have been made of papier-mâché, which meant that every single conversation, argument, weeping fit, sigh, fart, whisper, or cough was audible throughout the house. And then, as Loulou had correctly pointed out, there was the cozy proximity of the neighbors. Immediately next door was a defunct olive oil mill, and beyond that a house owned by Monsieur Barry, who drove up regularly on his tractor in order to rumble around inside it, doing what, nobody knew, since he never actually stayed there. Beside that was another structure, where he kept his farming tools, and beyond it the Kingdom of the Tricons began. Marcel Tricon was a traveling sales-man specializing in fancy foods—instant flan mixes, jars of Italian olives stuffed with pimentos, tinned pâtés—so he was mostly on the road, leav-ing his wife, Jeannine, and their three children, in the large house that anchored the other end of the hamlet of La Migoua. The Tricons elevated the entire tone of the neighborhood. Marcel knew how to fix anything and was constantly improving his property—building a fountain, turn-ing one of his outbuildings into a guest suite, varnishing a gnarled vine root and transforming it into a lamp—which only highlighted the *Tobacco Road* aspect of our house. But Marcel understood that Monsieur Ayer was an intellectual and could not be expected to occupy himself with such things, and God knows a woman wouldn't know how to, so I think he and Jeannine forgave us our lamentable lack of skills with the hammer and paintbrush. And in any case we were English and had therefore been deprived of the beneficent influence of *la civilisation française*, so what else could you expect?

Around the back of La Migoua, along with the vertical shed, were a few other crumbling buildings, all part of the Tricons' kingdom, as well as a tiny cottage owned by a rather stylish couple from Alsace, who migrated south every summer, hungry for the warmth and sexiness so lacking in their grim Germanic corner of France. Loulou suggested we might want to look inside "our" other house, the one where Grand-mère would be staying, and he led the way, scrambling up the rubble to the entrance on the second level. Freddie was not a climber, so he and the man with the key stayed behind, smoking their cigarettes and speculating on just when the mistral might make up "his" mind to bugger off and leave us in peace. Loulou was just showing us how a *très jolie* bedroom and an adjoining bath could be conjured up out of the shambles on the top floor, when we suddenly heard a violent scuffling outside, and Freddie crying out, "Oh God!" Could the man with the key have attacked him? Didn't seem like the best strategy for selling a house. My mother rushed to the window and saw the man writhing on the ground, obviously having some kind of major fit, while Freddie stood there, his hands shaking, trying to light another cigarette, and repeating, "Oh God, oh God, oh God!" Loulou took charge, pinned the poor victim down by sitting on his bouncy stomach, and frantically tried to shove a stick between his snapping-turtle jaws. I remember being fascinated by the flailing limbs, the swiveling eyeballs, the froth spewing out of his mouth (did he perhaps have rabies?), and by the wild hysteria and excitement swirling around the whole episode. Everybody agreed that it was *un grand mal* and that eventually it would pass and, with any luck, his tongue would still be intact. What happened next I don't recall, but I do know that by the end of the day, my mother and Freddie had agreed to buy their dream house.

AFTER WE RETURNED to London Freddie and I forgot all about La Migoua. I suppose we just assumed that somehow or other the house would be ready for us to move into the following summer. The "somehow or other" was my mother's job. In a letter to her friend Sue, she described our visit to the Deakins:

> We did really go mad in the south of France. Put a down payment yet on a shed (two sheds actually) that is hitched onto an olive oil press, which is on top of a rock and the only road up is very Dracula-like.
> It will, I fear, be a long time before House and Garden seeks *us* out to photograph. In the meantime great wranglings are going on with the local mayor—who Gully calls quite rightly a slimy eel—about the water supply. It seems they don't have much. On the other hand we don't have *any*. I do hope the old French tradition of fair play isn't today too dormant to be roused, else we will go on having none. Come to think of it, in the desert-like circumstances that surround Notre Rêve, the mayor shouldn't be called a slimy eel at all, but maybe a sidewinder or a horned toad.

The rest of the letter is about her efforts to make her younger sister, Beegoonie (the one who had the audacity to wriggle out of her much-needed abortion many years later), decamp from New York to London. My mother had decided that she needed to abandon her (totally unsuitable) boyfriend and (hopeless) job and to move into the Boothbys' house in Holland Park Avenue, just as she herself had done six years before. The question was when she would arrive, and how much rent she should pay: "I have big sisterly vibrations that she's having a hard time prying herself out of that exceedingly unattractive man's bed. Anyway, let's wait until she actually gets here and I will rip her purse from her hands and see really how much money she has."

Needless to say Beegoonie did as she was told and moved to London, where she established herself as one of Harry Evans's bright young journalists at the *Sunday Times*, married a delightful man, had two charming sons, and lived happily ever after in a beautiful house on Primrose Hill. Yet more proof—as if any were needed—of the infallibility of her older sister's judgment.

That spring and summer my mother was a very busy lady. In addition to organizing Beegoonie's life, she had her own to consider. The house in France was a wreck and needed to be made habitable by the next summer. Not such an easy thing to accomplish long-distance from London. But Lorna St. Aubyn, who was living there full-time, fixing up her own house, helped out by acting as my mother's surrogate, bullying the electricians, plumbers, carpenters, and painters into sticking to some kind of plausible schedule. So that took care of Provence, leaving her to juggle her work, her social life, Freddie, me, and her not entirely cooperative— or youthful—ovaries.

She had moved on from reviewing books and movies at the (reactionary) *Sunday Express*, and now had a regular column in the (progressive) *Daily Herald*, which suited her much better. She could write about anything she wanted and her political views, instead of driving the editor to apoplexy, marched in red-flag-waving sync with the socialist outlook of the paper. *The Herald* supported the Labour Party, which was led by their friend Hugh Gaitskell (who had so memorably defeated my mother in the Battle of Freddie's Underpants, on their honeymoon in Yugoslavia). And the Labour Party was closely allied to the Trade Union movement, whose most powerful member was the mighty Miners Union, which held a huge and boisterous rally every year at a seaside resort in the north of England. It invariably rained. In 1962 they decided to invite my mother to come and judge their beauty contest. In a letter to Sue she wrote:

Next week, I go (and am taking Gull and Fred) to the Lancashire Miner's Gala to pick Miss Coal Mine. We go one night to Wigan, for a pre-Gala dinner, then on to St Helen's, where Hugh [Gaitskell] makes the speech, I pick the bewty queen and then Lady Robens crowns her. I look forward to it enormously as have just seen a documentary film of the 1961 Gala in Durham. They rip the town to bits, and the after-dark sounds are entirely of breaking glass in the pubs and indignant shrieks from the ladies being mauled in the alleyways.

I suppose if Tom Wolfe had been around in London in the sixties, he would have dumped my mother and Freddie—and most of their friends—in with Mr. and Mrs. Leonard Bernstein, and tarred them all with the same Radical Chic/Bollinger/Socialist/Limousine/Liberal brush. And he would have been entirely right. They could not have been more serious about their support of progressive causes, and worked diligently (in Freddie's case) and vociferously (in my mother's) for things like the abolition of capital punishment, homosexual-law reform, and abortion rights. But they saw no reason why any of that should stop them from enjoying a restful weekend in the country, staying with friends who lived in large eighteenth-century houses, and were a bit hazy about how to find the road to Wigan Pier. Sometimes their hosts were old friends, like my secret passion, Michael Pitt-Rivers, the gay gentleman farmer in Wiltshire, who was married to Sonia Orwell, whose previous husband had written the book on Wigan Pier, and sometimes they were new friends, like the Duke of Bedford. The Bedfords had come into their lives through Bertrand Russell, whose ninetieth birthday party Freddie had organized. Here's how he described it in his autobiography:

It was held at the Café Royal and about seventy people came, personal friends, scientists, philosophers and their wives rather than Russell's political associates. [Freddie felt that Russell had been hijacked by the nuclear disarmament movement, and disapproved of its leaders. They were way too radical, and not nearly sophisticated enough, for his taste.] Speeches were made by Julian Huxley, E M Forster and myself to which Russell replied. . . . When I had asked Russell whether there was anyone he would like to add to the guest list, he said he would like to invite the head of his family, the Duke of Bedford. Owing to some longstanding family feud, he had never met him or set foot in Woburn Abbey.

The dinner was a huge success, and afterward the Bedfords "took Dee and myself to a nightclub where the Duke, a man of about my own age, proved remarkably adept at dancing the Twist." Soon after, Bertrand Russell was invited to Woburn Abbey for the weekend, and "when the time came for the visit, Ian [the duke] took fright and invited me with Dee to help keep Russell entertained."

I was also included, and remember being suitably wowed by the intoxicating combination of grandeur (the dining room was wallpapered in Canalettos, commissioned by the fourth duke on his grand tour in 1731) and intellect (Bertrand Russell sitting with Freddie on the sofa discussing Hume). Not so the duke's daughter-in-law the Marchioness of Tavistock who looked like a cross-dressing Pekingese—eyes too wide apart, nonexistent nose, body veering toward the masculine—and announced, just before Russell was due to arrive, that she thought she'd go wash her hair and was never seen again.

After lunch the elegant Twisting duke took the ancient diminutive philosopher on a tour of the house their ancestors had built. I watched them walk slowly down a long corridor lined with family portraits, Russell leaning on the duke's arm, stopping every now and then in front of one of the paintings to have a conspiratorial gossip about the misbehavior of a particularly wayward relative. Russell's small, birdlike face was full of animation, and you could hear the excitement in his high-pitched voice as he chattered away about these long-dead people whom he had known so well, as if they had only just left to go upstairs and change for dinner.

Freddie had given me a minitutorial on the Great Man in the car on the way to Woburn. And what had struck me was how similar they were: intellectually brilliant, skeptical, curious, resolutely rational, radical in their politics, and deeply appreciative of feminine charm. But what I loved hearing about most were Russell's long, atavistic tentacles that stretched so far back into the past.

Freddie told me that Russell had been orphaned as a young child and had gone to live with his grandfather, Lord John Russell, who had twice been prime minister, was one of the principal proponents of the great Reform Act of 1832, and had been born in the *eighteenth century*. That was the bit that really mesmerized me. Imagine: I was about to touch a man who had been brought up by somebody who had been alive in London *at the same time* as Robespierre had been busy with his guillotine in Paris. *And* the man I was about to meet had sat on Queen Victoria's well-upholstered lap, *and* his godfather (except he didn't believe in God) was John Stuart Mill, for God's sake. It was all too much, and I couldn't stop these ghosts from jiggling and nattering about inside my head as I was introduced to Russell and touched his feather-light hand, shaking it as gently as I would a newborn baby's.

JUST AFTER WE GOT BACK from France, I noticed that my mother had added a new element to her usual breakfast of cigarettes and Nescafé. There, on the tray with the Frank Cooper's Oxford Marmalade (coarse cut), the tin of Band-Aids, the sugar bowl, the ashtray, and the Gentleman's Relish, was a large glass jar containing a mélange of different-colored pills, mixed in with some translucent amber capsules. It turned out she had read a magazine article about the difficulty of conceiving in your late thirties, whose author, a handsome, gray-haired gynecologist from Queen Charlotte's Hospital, had recommended a cocktail of vitamins and a daily megadose of fish oil as a surefire solution to the problem. Since she had spent her childbearing years wrestling with recalcitrant diaphragms and having abortions, this was a new challenge for her—but one she was more than willing to take on. Every morning she would gulp down a handful of pills, and maybe it worked, because by the early fall she was indeed pregnant.

Freddie and I were thrilled, and even she seemed secretly pleased. Nothing much changed in her life; she still rushed about, wrote her column, and went to just as many dinners and parties as ever, where she drank and smoked just as much as ever. She told me that her doctor in Paris, when she was pregnant with me, had insisted it was *imperative* she drink *at least* one glass of the best possible red wine every day, and she proposed to follow his advice twelve years later in London. Not that her doctor, a charming and garrulous Irishman named Gerry Slattery, who loved making house calls, mostly on account of the whiskey (preferably single malt, though he would graciously accept any substitute) and the conversation (the iniquities of the Tory Party; the necessity of Edna O'Brien's winning a literary prize), would have disagreed with his French confrère's prescription for a healthy mother and baby. There must have been a few adjustments to her wardrobe, but only one dress sticks in my

memory. It was floor-length, high-waisted, emerald green velvet and festooned in mink—salvaged from an old jacket—at the neck and sleeves.
My mother had designed it herself, and when she wore it I was always
reminded of the wife in that Jan van Eyck painting of the solemn couple,
standing in front of the marital bed, with the chic convex mirror on the
wall behind them. Except that she tended *not* to put a dish towel, draped
over two horns, on her head like the lady in the picture.

The day my mother went into labor Freddie was lecturing in Copen-
hagen, which was just as well, because I suspect there could have been
a repetition of the "Oh God!" scene, when the man with the key had
started foaming at the mouth. But her friend Margie Rees, who knew all
about such things, having delivered five children of her own—while her
husband had probably been down at the King of Denmark pub having
a restorative cocktail or four—was on hand to take her to the hospital.
Freddie arrived back a couple of days later, and that evening we went
together to see her, and to admire his son, and my baby brother, Nicholas.
Peering through the window I remember thinking how different he was
from all the other pink and porky English babies in the hospital nursery. There they were, lined up like roly-poly puddings, swaddled in their
creamy suet blankets, the rolls of fat on their chubby little arms tied up
with invisible string; and there he was, skinny, dark haired, and alert,
staring back at us with his deep midnight blue eyes. For Freddie it was
love at first sight, and from that day on, as he wrote in the last line of his
autobiography, "My love for this child has been the dominating factor in
my life." Nick's secular godmothers were Dora Gaitskell and Nicole de
Bedford (as the duchess signed her name), and Bertrand Russell agreed to
be his godfather. Freddie loved the idea that his son would have a direct
link back to Jeremy Bentham, since Russell's own secular godfather had
been John Stuart Mill, and Mill's had been Bentham. The two ladies
coughed up regular Christmas and birthday presents, but I think all Nick
ever got out of the great man was this thrilling three degrees of separation
from his father's philosophical hero.

As soon as my mother got back from the hospital she began to look for
a nanny. Robin, a young nurse who had recently left the Middlesex Hospital, was delivered to our doorstep by an agency called Universal Aunts.
I think she was the first and only candidate for the job whom my mother
interviewed, and amazingly she agreed to move in and take over the care

of Nicholas the very next day. And not a moment too soon. There were no more rants and rages from her new charge, and calm and order prevailed as her reassuring, sane influence permeated the entire household. Not that she was a caricature English nanny; she was much too young and smart for that, and my mother despised that whole shtick anyway. Why bother to have a baby at all if you were just going to hand it over to some dragon in a uniform for the first seven years of its life and then ship it off to boarding school for the next ten? When, she wondered in a magazine piece, "would it dawn on the British that Nanny, Noddy, Frinton and a pony add up to a thin life for a small child. That prep school at seven, followed by Eton, means that a child is being brought up by strangers, is only a sometime visitor in his own home, and love is a holiday treat like going to a Christmas pantomime." Children should be seen *and* heard. Except when you didn't want them around, and then Robin was there to take over.

THE NEWS FROM LA MIGOUA was encouraging. By late spring Lorna reported back that the house was all but finished. Of course it had no furniture, and my mother, convinced that everything in France was wildly overpriced, decided to fill up a van in London, with beds and lamps and sheets and chairs and lightbulbs and detergent and Kotex and mattresses and tables and shampoo and saucepans, and drive it down there herself. Her birth coach, Margie Rees, signed on as codriver, and off they went. Robin was left in charge of Nicholas and me, and Freddie and Goronwy had lunch and dinner at the Garrick Club, since both their cooks had selfishly gone AWOL to sun themselves on the Riviera. (Neither Freddie nor Goronwy ever learned to drive or cook, or to do anything at all in or outside the house, and so were totally dependent on their live-in cooks/ handywomen/nannies/gardeners/cleaning ladies/hostesses/ chauffeurs. Mistress was the only role that my mother and Margie were not required to play.)

Finally, at the end of July, after my school got out, the day arrived. The car, a dumpy English approximation of an American station wagon, with pointless bits of wood glued onto its exterior, and two doors at the back that opened up like a kitchen cupboard, was outside, and we had a boat to catch in Dover that afternoon. Our suitcases, cardboard boxes, plastic bags, Nicholas's crib, packets of potato chips, economy-size rolls of toilet paper, and a case of Coke, were all piled up on the sidewalk. Clearly the suitcases belonged on the rusty roof rack, where it was Freddie's job to tie them down with a tangle of Medusa-like "snakes," equipped with metal hooks, one at each end of their long, stripey, elasticated bodies. After that the bags, boxes, and crib were stuffed in through the cupboard doors, while Robin and I clambered over the front seats (the "station wagon" had only two doors) and settled ourselves in the back. My mother then passed us everything else: first the baby, then all the other rubbish, which had to be wedged into whatever pockets of uninhabited space were left. I quickly learned to offload the cans and glass bottles onto Robin, so they could clank around her ankles, and keep the diapers and six-packs of toilet paper—which made a perfect pillow—for myself. Once the sidewalk had been cleared, Freddie got into the passenger seat, patted his pockets to make sure he had his glasses and passport, and my mother slipped behind the wheel, lit a cigarette, and said in her best cowboy voice, "Time to get outta Dodge and head south."

La Plage

THERE WAS NOTHING REMOTELY CHIC or comfortable about our journey to the south of France. Crammed into our soi-disant station wagon, we barreled through the endless, grisly suburbs of south London, hit a few miles of open road and the odd green field, and then found ourselves on the outskirts of Dover, where we followed the signs— a cheerful-looking tugboat bobbing around on wiggly lines—for the Channel ferry. A couple of hours of lurching about on deck, trying not to be sick, and we were in Calais, and from there we drove, already exhausted, to Paris. But not the Paris you may be imagining. We were headed for a dark—it was then about ten at night—and rather sinister railway siding, where we left the car with a man in blue overalls who loaded it onto the clanking train.

Festooned with plastic bags—our supplies for the night—we traipsed down the train's hot, crowded corridors in search of our compartment. Except that it wasn't ours at all. My mother had booked only four of the six *couchettes*, so two fat ladies were already firmly installed on the lower bunks, one with a Lone Ranger mask over her eyes, presumably trying to sleep, and the other eating a greasy sandwich while reading *France Dimanche*. We all said "Bonsoir" very politely, and I climbed up the ladder and lay down, my nose a couple of inches from the ceiling, and wondered ungratefully why I wasn't an orphan traveling alone in a wagon-lit with real sheets and a pillow, to stay with my elderly, homosexual guardian in his sugar-almond-pink villa overlooking Cap d'Antibes.

Something happened in the night, and when I woke up early the next morning, the world outside the train's window had been totally transformed. The landscape was illuminated, like one of van Gogh's paintings from the madhouse in Saint-Rémy, by the sharp, uncompromising clarity of the sun of the Midi. And it wasn't just the light that was so different from the opaque, misty look of England. The entire scene had been painted in a whole new palette of colors. The sky shone a fierce, brilliant blue; the roofs of the stone houses were faded terra-cotta; and the crumpled cubist mountains rose up in the distance in delicate shades of gray and violet. As the train shuddered to a halt, we gathered together our plastic bags, said *Au revoir* to the two fat ladies, and emerged into the heat and dust of a railway platform just outside Avignon. Nicholas started to wail, and Robin poked a placatory bottle into his mouth. Freddie and my mother lit cigarettes, and I took a deep breath, marveling that even the air of the south was perfumed with some mysterious new scent I couldn't begin to recognize. Sweet and almost sickly, it came from the sticky pink blossoms of the oleander bushes growing outside the stationmaster's neat little house alongside the tracks. Mixed with rosemary, wild mint, and thyme, it was the smell of Provence.

Wedged back into our cozy "station wagon," with Freddie, the map reader, in charge of guiding us on our way, we headed due south. But it wasn't long before we found an excuse to stop. How could we just zoom by and miss Aix-en-Provence? My mother saw the road sign up ahead and, surprisingly, became quite misty about her honeymoon there with my father.

"We stayed in a tiny hotel right on the Cours Mirabeau, which only happens to be the most beautiful street in all of France. And we had breakfast every morning on the terrace of Les Deux Garçons, which is just what we're going to do right now. Don't you want to see where your Mum and Dad had such a good time before you were born?" And before you left him four years later.

Of course I did. Not wishing to be outdone, Freddie then announced that he too had spent a night in Aix, during the war, with a French lady, whose name momentarily escaped him, and that he had never forgotten it. The town, that is. Genuinely curious about why Aix had left such an impression on him, since he never usually noticed his surroundings at all, she asked him, "And what picture comes into your head, when I say Aix to you?" Freddie closed his eyes, put the tips of his fingers together and

sat there thinking. And thinking. And thinking. And finally the magical
image came floating up from his subconscious,
"I see Mirabeau." (Mirabeau had been born in Aix.)
"And?"
"I see Mirabeau telling the king's representative in the National As-
sembly on June 23, 1789, 'Tell those who sent you that we are here by the
will of the people and will leave only by the force of bayonets.' Splendid
words, splendid man."
Which was only slightly better than his reply when my mother had
asked him the same question about Paris, when he had said, "I see a road
sign that says Paris."

LES DEUX GARÇONS first opened its doors for business in 1792, and its
various owners had seen no reason to change the shabby elegance of its
green-and-gold interiors since then. And why should they? The dappled
sunlight of the Cours Mirabeau was reflected in its ancient speckled mirrors, a lazy ceiling fan swooshed above our heads, while waiters darted
across the tiled floor, trays piled high with patisseries and coffee for the
ladies who had just come from the market. Their baskets were stuffed
full of tiny tomatoes the size of large pearls, feathery *girolles* mushrooms,
fragrant bunches of basil, and pink-and-white peaches with the complexion of a Boucher milkmaid. The ladies' *maquillage* had been perfectly
applied, and their fine-grained-leather handbags, silk foulards, and discreet but expensive jewelry betrayed the French bourgeoise's obsession with quality. Clearly they had been up early—it wasn't even nine
o'clock—patroling the market stalls on the outlook for delicacies to set
before their demanding families that night. Although I had not yet heard
of my future heroine M. F. K. Fisher, she happened to be living in Aix
with her two young daughters in the early sixties, and she had fallen
under the spell of the Cours. And they too would stop by Les Deux Garçons every day to have "breakfast on the terrace, and talk with whoever
stopped beside us, and usually stay longer than we'd meant to, in a kind
of daze of well-being and satisfaction about the rhythm and beauty of the
town, the people, the fountain music." Who knows, they might even have
been there with us on the terrace that morning.

After we had finished our coffee, my mother reckoned we had just enough time for a little promenade along what she now upgraded to "the most beautiful street in the whole world." A double row of plane trees shaded both sidewalks, filtering the early morning light and meeting in the middle to create the monumental vaulted nave of a leafy green cathedral. As a piece of town planning, the Cours is wonderfully free of any practical purpose. The concept of a wide urban boulevard had come from Italy at the beginning of the seventeenth century, and the Cours Mirabeau was constructed soon after, as a place where the Aixois aristocracy could parade around in their carriages, as the Italians did on their daily *passaggio*. This was not a road that actually led anywhere, other than up and down the complicated, slippery snakes and ladders of the social scene.

Elegant *hôtels particuliers* built of the local honey-colored stone, with gray shutters, line the street, and twirly wrought-iron balconies supported by gigantic Atlantes whose lapidary beards are as tightly curled as the hair under their muscular arms. It was Leonardo who said, "Let the street be as wide as the height of the houses" (why don't all architects just *listen* to him?), and in Aix they knew that perfect proportion, like Garbo's bone structure, is the secret of lasting beauty. The Cours is 440 meters long and generally 44 wide, while the houses are never more than four stories high, and it is this geometry that makes the result of the equation eternally pleasing to the eye. Not only did the architects do their math right, but they also believed that nature had to be included in the construct—and understood that there is something intrinsically satisfying about the combination of stone, water, and trees.

Water is what brought the Romans to Aix. On their conquering march through what was to become their Provincia, they discovered warm sulfuric water gurgling up from a series of underground springs, and built their first settlement around them, calling it Aquae Sextiae in honor of the consul Caius Sextius Calvinus. And two thousand years later the water is still bubbling away in the four fountains that punctuate the length of the Cours. My favorite is the Neuf Canons (just across from Les Deux Garçons), whose granite basin was constructed in Louis XV's time, with especially low sides for the thirsty sheep that were driven each year through the town on their spring migration to the hills. Sadly the sheep have all gone, but there are still plenty of dogs in Aix, who now use it as their local bar, stopping for a reviving slurp or two as they pass by.

∾

THE MAN WITH THE KEY, whose tongue Loulou had so skillfully preserved, would not have recognized the house. The haunted "cave" now had French windows and a tiled floor, and the ground-floor animals' quarters had been transformed into an enormous kitchen, with a real live fridge and a gas-propelled stove, and a large window that opened onto the shady terrace where the lime tree grew. On the second floor the one and only bathroom had been shoehorned into a cupboard at the top of the stairs, and although it did have a sparkling new bath and basin, and a loo that flushed straight into a sparkling new septic tank, it had no door. Actually there *was* a door, but instead of being attached with hinges, it leaned precariously against the doorframe, with huge, embarrassing, breezy gaps on either side. Having assured my mother that the door would be installed before we arrived, Monsieur Choremi revised his schedule and promised it would be done before we left. And, being a man of his word, he did indeed pull up in his battered Citroën, six weeks later, on the morning we were setting off for the station in Avignon, just as Freddie was once again wrestling with the Medusa snakes and the rusty roof rack.

Is there any point at all in having a beach nearby unless you go there every single day for as long as you possibly can? I thought not. And, although everybody else was moderately enthusiastic, none of them quite shared my fanatical and monomaniacal devotion to Bikini Beach. Without question it had everything you could possibly want: glamour, social life, pedalos, pizza, Orangina, trashy magazines, sugar-roasted nuts, ice cream, and that eternal—and irresistible—combination of sun, sand, and sex. As soon as breakfast was over, I started hopping about, offering to help my mother with the picnic, or Robin with the baby, and tempting Freddie with *The Times*. Rattling the Leaning Door of La Migoua, as he lolled in his soupy bath, I would remind him that if we didn't leave soon, there wouldn't be a single copy left in the whole of Les Lecques, and he would have to make do with *Le Monde*, which didn't even have a crossword. Finally, like an irritating sheepdog, I got them all rounded up, into the car, and we were on our way to the beach.

On our jaunts from Austria to Italy, in his white convertible that smelled of new shoes and had room only for the two of us, my father and

I had always played our own private version of "I Spy." As we turned a corner, a sliver of blue would suddenly appear in the distance, and I would shriek, "There it is!" and he would say, "You win" (I always did), and there before us was the mesmerizing Mediterranean. The "station wagon" was permeated by the smell of Ambre Solaire and tuna fish sandwiches, but that didn't stop me from playing the game silently, all by myself, and still feeling the same jolt of excitement when I caught that first glimpse of blue as we came over the crest of the hill.

There was absolutely no doubt in my mind that Bikini Beach was the most stylish patch of sand in the whole of Les Lecques. Which, of course, was not saying a great deal. I still had fantasies about my guardian in his pink villa, high above the *real* Côte d'Azur, but I was a sensible child, and understood that I was stuck with my terminally unfashionable family and so would have to make the best of it. I tried hard to smarten them up, but there was only so much a girl could do. Freddie's beach outfit consisted of a pair of beige linen shorts, which were not short at all, since they flapped around his knees and approached his armpits on top. Far worse were his underpants: Blue and even more voluminous, they extended a good few inches above his "waist," and below the hem of the shorts, giving them a nice, contrasting blue-border effect. With this he wore a short-sleeved khaki shirt and some faded espadrilles. My mother usually favored a more colorful look, like a loose, flower-patterned dress, topped off with a brightly spotted bandanna, to hold back her hair, so she could see to drive, for crissakes. Robin was let off the hook because she wasn't family, and Nick was a baby, so he didn't count.

The Queen of Bikini Beach, its very own Diana Vreeland, its social arbiter and strict enforcer of its byzantine code of conduct, was Monsieur Maurice. Of indeterminate age, hunchbacked, with mahogany skin, distended, licorice-colored nipples, and his hair dyed orangutan orange, he wore a yellow thong and patrolled the beach, rake in hand, keeping us all in order. His beaklike nose was covered in a matching yellow plastic guard, attached to his sunglasses in a Groucho Marx arrangement, like something from a joke shop. He was a savage snob, and his favorite reading material was *Point de Vue,* a magazine entirely taken up with the meaningless doings of deposed royals, with a particular focus on the rivalry between the two claimants to the tragically still-vacant throne of France. Monsieur Maurice worshipped the Gypsy (Sylvia), whom he always addressed as "Madame la Princesse."

The exclusivity of the beach was maintained partly by two fences, which kept the hoi polloi mostly at bay—although by law they had to be allowed to walk along the seashore—and partly by Monsieur Maurice's discriminating gate policy. Jaunty triangular blue flags marked the entrance on the boardwalk, and some rickety wooden steps led down to the sand, where a row of cabanas stood up against the cement wall. Sometimes a forlorn-looking family would appear at the top of the steps—their unappealing children clutching plastic buckets, the mother too fat, the father too thin—hoping to rent a couple of deck chairs and an umbrella for the afternoon, and would be told, before they had even opened their mouths, "C'est impossible. On est complet." How else could one possibly be expected to maintain "le standing" of Bikini Beach?

Mattresses covered in blue-and-white-striped canvas, deck chairs, small tables, and parasols were all arranged in parallel lines facing the ocean. As at the theater, the front row was the most desirable location, and was, understandably, reserved for Monsieur Maurice's favorites, while the rest of us were grateful to be allowed to camp out farther back, in front of the cabanas. But at least we were closer to Madame Carrère, whose plywood hut offered up all kinds of treats. A glossy map of multicolored ice creams was tacked to the outside, and behind the counter, a chalkboard advertised two kinds of sandwiches, pâté and ham; *fougasse*, a kind of primitive Provençal pizza, minus the tomatoes; and *salade niçoise*. The filthy, sagging shelves were stacked high with slices of stale fruitcake, studded with sticky cherries and wrapped in cellophane, bubble gum, chocolate, and every conceivable kind of candy. Our favorite drink was something a French marketing whiz had decided to call "Pschitt," which we thought was screamingly funny. The joke, of course, was entirely lost on Madame Carrère, who just handed over the bottle and wearily added its exorbitant cost to our parents' already inflated accounts.

"I got the last copy of *The Times*, as well as the *Telegraph* and the *Express*," Freddie arrived, flush with the triumph of his shopping expedition. Whenever we traveled, finding English papers occupied a good part of every outing, but in that summer of 1963 my mother and Freddie's appetite for news from home seemed to have escalated. As soon as

Freddie plopped himself down in his deck chair, he announced: "That tart Keeler has started to talk, and Stephen Ward has killed himself."

My mother snatched the paper from his hand and disappeared behind it, while he calmly opened another one, and nothing more was heard from either of them for at least an hour. I *knew* something was going on; I just couldn't figure out what it was. And nobody would tell me. It had all started before we left London, when I heard them talking about somebody called Profumo. He looked a bit startled—as well he might—in the photos I'd seen of him on the front pages, and he seemed to have lost most of his hair, and was in some kind of awful trouble with the prime minister, Harold Macmillan. The whole thing was incredibly complicated, and involved not just "that tart Keeler" but also her friend Mandy, and their doctor, Stephen Ward, who had been kind enough to invite them both to come and live with him in his pretty mews house. A Russian spy and a homicidal West Indian with a gun had walk-on parts, as well as some man called Astor, who Freddie said was a shit, and had been at Eton with him. How on earth the shit from Eton could be connected to the West Indian, or how the nice doctor (whom a friend of my mother's had gone to see with her bad back) had met the Russian spy, or why on earth the prime minister should care about *any* of these people, I could not begin to understand. And, just to add to the bouillabaisse of confusion swirling around inside my head, Freddie had some more news to share with us: "And that other tart, Margaret Argyll, is up in court too. It seems that the 'headless man' is Duncan Sandys, which, on top of Profumo, will drive Macmillan completely mad."

"We can but hope. And let's also hope that those two Tory sex maniacs lose him the next election" was my mother's only response from behind her paper.

Were the two "tarts" connected in some way? Did Margaret perhaps live with Mandy and Christine in the doctor's mews house? Clearly Mr. Profumo and Mr. Sandys both worked for the prime minister, and both were deranged by sex, which Mr. Macmillan was quite understandably furious about. But that still left the question of where Mr. Sandys's head had gone. Exasperated by my whining, my mother finally put her paper down and turned to me. "Okay, so here's the story: The Duchess of Argyll is in court because she's divorcing the duke. And they have a photograph of her kneeling in front of some naked guy she worshipped, called Duncan Sandys, who's so tall you can't see his head at the top of the picture."

"Is that *it?*"

"Yeah, that's it."

I decided to go swimming.

THE BAY AT LES LECQUES looked like something a child might draw. A perfect semicircle, with a pretty little toy town at one end and a rocky promontory at the other, a sandy beach in between, palm trees, and tiny white boats bobbing around in a Crayola-blue sea. The water may have looked blue, but that didn't guarantee anything. How dirty it was we didn't know or care, but it was true that you couldn't see through it very well, and we did quite often find strange things floating about, mainly plastic bags and once, rather excitingly, a real live turd. None of which, in my mind at least, detracted from the irredeemable glamour of Bikini Beach.

But as an amateur anthropologist I wasn't there just to have a good time; I had my fieldwork to do. Observing the differences between my British and French subjects was that summer's special project. Representing England—and who better?—I had Nanny St. Aubyn, whom Lorna had dropped off that morning, with her two small charges, Teddy and Minky. What the old dragon's real name was we never discovered, and anyway it didn't matter, because all *real* nannies automatically acquired the last name of their employers. Sartorially Nanny had made no conces sions to her day at the beach. Dressed in her usual starched uniform, thick white stockings, and lace-up shoes, she spent most of her time stopping the children from indulging in anything that could remotely be construed as having fun. They had to keep their tops on, sit in the shade, were not allowed to eat anything from Madame Carrère's hut, could go into the sea only up to their knees, and had to take a two-hour rest after lunch. She made a halfhearted attempt to strike up a conversation with Nanny Ayer before quickly realizing that she was dealing with an impostor. Not only did we call her Robin, but she addressed her employers as "Dee" and "Freddie," she was wearing a bikini, and it soon became all too clear that she did not know a single one of the nannies in Kensington Gardens whom Nanny St. Aubyn hung out with.

This was the sixties, and Bikini Beach had gone topless. Some were bananas, others torpedoes; skinny women had poached or—if they were unlucky—fried eggs; and one girl's were so perfectly rounded that they looked like the two halves of a juicy grapefruit. But it was the huge saggy ones, and their owners' amazing lack of embarrassment in displaying them, that fascinated me the most. They lolled about on their mattresses, their bosoms slopping over the ill-defined edges of their bodies, like over-the-hill houris in some downmarket seraglio, while their husbands calmly smoked, drank their beer, and read the sports pages of *Le Figaro*. Sometimes, though, the animal urges of the French male were just too strong to be contained. And then he would heave himself on top of the lady beside him, the matted thatch on his chest pressed seductively against her oily bananas, and start fiddling with the tangle of gold chains around her neck. This I recognized as a clear prelude to some much more serious fiddling later on. In London the couples smooching on the grass in Regent's Park were always a bitter disappointment, because whenever I got close to them—on the pretext of retrieving my skillfully tossed ball—they glared at me, and anyway they had far too many clothes on. But here they might as well have been naked and didn't seem to notice or care who was watching them. The French had to be the sexiest people on earth.

Sylvia, the Gypsy, lay on her striped mattress in the front row, her toes almost touching the water, smoking a cheroot, and drinking a tumbler of rosé. Occasionally she would scoop out an ice cube and let it dribble down the back of her neck before popping it into her mouth. She had discarded her top and lay on her stomach, dressed in nothing more than a triangular scrap of black fabric, her turquoise-and-silver tribal bracelets, and a shimmering slick of bergamot-and-almond oil, mixed specially for her by the man in the drugstore in Ollioulles. Monsieur Maurice hovered above her holding a collection of ice-cream wrappers and cigarette butts retrieved from the sand, longing for an excuse to strike up a conversation with Madame la Princesse.

"Oh là là, qu'il fait chaud!" was his safe opening gambit, but then, unfortunately, he noticed what she was reading. "Ah, Cocteau," he sighed, and paused soulfully, forcing Sylvia to put her book aside and listen to an emotional account of a fleeting visit to Tangiers, many years before— the mysteries of the Kasbah, the music of the nightingales, the scent of the roses, the potency of the kef, the heat of the sirocco, the beauty of the boys—when he had passed an entire evening in the great man's company. Sylvia pretended to pay attention, but, suddenly announcing that the heat was quite intolerable, she stood up and waded into the water, leaving him there, rake in hand, still lost in the dreamlike maze of the medina.

The Gypsy was much taken with all things artistic and liked to surround herself with poets, painters, and writers. Where this left Prince Azamat, other than playing backgammon at White's, I was never quite sure. She classified Freddie as an intellectual, so at least he was spared the discussions about Rothko or Pollock, but, on the other hand, he was expected to come up with something scintillating when she fancied a chat about a new edition of Apollinaire's poems or existentialism or, indeed, Cocteau. He dreaded these Sylvia seminars. But the Gypsy was not just a hungry consumer of art and ideas; she was also an artist herself, who showed her work in real art galleries in London, where real people paid real money to acquire them. My mother loved Sylvia and was a loyal friend, so I would be dragged to her openings, where we would marvel at how a simple string dishrag could, in the right hands, be transformed with a few, judicious dabs of paint, into something or other—what, we were never quite sure. My mother and I may not have known much about modern art, but we knew what we liked; and we liked Sylvia's dishrags because Sylvia had painted them.

At her last private view, arriving early to show support, and flailing around for something to say, my mother had, in desperation, singled out one of the larger pieces for special praise: "This is amazing . . , I've never seen anything like it . . , how *do* you create these?" Sylvia was genuinely pleased by her friend's enthusiasm and, worried that the dishrag in question would be snapped up once the hordes arrived, she kindly asked the gallery to put a red sticker on it immediately. A couple of weeks later a package, wrapped in brown paper, was delivered to our house, along with an invoice containing a surprising number of zeroes.

NANNY ST. AUBYN had never been so hot in all her life. She was fanning herself with one of Freddie's discarded newspapers, had soaked all their towels in water, and then draped them over the children's heads and shoulders.

"I can't think where Mrs. St. Aubyn could possibly be. She said she would be here to collect us on the dot of three, and now it is almost five o'clock." It was indeed hard to imagine what Lorna might be up to. Being tortured by Roger seemed the most likely possibility, but then again she might just be having a much-needed cocktail. Who knew? But Nanny was right: It was unbearably hot and Lorna was late.

While Teddy and Minky sat under their parasol, wrapped up like Egyptian mummies, forbidden to move, a couple of boys, no more than five or six years old, were running wild across the sand, fighting, screeching, and gorging themselves on candy and bottles of Pschitt from Madame Carrère's hut. Nanny St. Aubyn did not approve, and I could hear her muttering under her halitotic breath, something about "Regular little savages, these Frenchies." At that moment Sylvia emerged from the sea, and started walking toward us. In this heat, why bother with a towel? Standing beside Nanny, dripping and glistening, her bracelets clanking, her bananas tanned the same deep espresso as the rest of her sinewy body, she looked a bit like a regular savage herself.

For the Mademoiselle Lévi-Strauss of Bikini Beach, it was the perfect juxtaposition, and made all more delicious by the expression of disgust on Nanny's face, and by the arrival of Monsieur Maurice, who added the missing louche element to the tableau. Instead of his customary rake he was carrying a bulky blue file under his arm. He nodded to Nanny, addressing her as "Madame," bowed deeply to Sylvia, and, crouching down beside Freddie's deck chair, he asked Monsieur le Professeur if he would do him the honor of reading his novel. He had actually started writing it in Tangiers, more than twenty years ago, "Quand j'étais là avec Monsieur Cocteau, vous voyez," he explained, lowering his voice discreetly. Never one to miss an opportunity of bringing the conversation around to himself, Freddie then embarked on a story about some glittering dinner at the British Embassy in Paris, just after the war, when Lady Diana Cooper had introduced him to Cocteau as "our most brilliant philosopher."

"Elle était très diplomatique." Freddie laughed, pretending to dismiss his hostess's remark with this disingenuous joke, and then, remembering the manuscript, added that, speaking as one writer to another, "Je serais ravi de lire votre livre." Monsieur Maurice was so affected by the Professeur's response that he took off his sunglasses with the attached yellow plastic nose guard, and I saw his sunken, crocodile eyes light up and his tight little mouth crack into a misshapen smile as he handed over his precious life's oeuvre. Freddie dumped the file into the beach bag, on top of his wet bathing suit and a half-eaten tuna fish sandwich. (Later that evening I heard him muttering in his study, "I can't possibly go on reading this, it's filth. Pure pornography. *Homosexual* pornography. What on earth am I going to say to him? Oh God, Oh God!")

On the way back to the car, I turned around and saw Nanny standing there, red faced, feet firmly planted on the sand, her uniform now slightly stained, with only a damp hanky on her head to shield her from the fierce tropical sun. It looked as if she was trying to say something to the two dusky, bare-breasted natives—a man and a woman—on either side of her, but however slowly she spoke, they just waved their hands about, jabbered away in their own language, and paid no attention to her at all.

Le Marché

WHEN SHE WASN'T SHOUTING, my mother was more fun than anyone on earth. And, in those early years at La Migoua, before things started to fall apart with Freddie, she hardly shouted at all. Of course there were always the machine-gun blasts of swearing, but nobody minds being called a "cuntburger," as long as it's done with grace and good humor. Besides, we were all used to it. It never crossed my mind that newcomers like Robin and, after her, Amanda and then Beatrice, who lived with us to help out on those long hot summers in France, might be surprised, shocked, or even frightened by my mother's behavior. Robin did admit that she thought we were "a bit eccentric," and I once found Amanda crying in her room, but they soon adapted to—or were corrupted by—the odd but endearing ways of the Ayer-Wells ménage. At any rate, during the first few summers, all my mother's whirling-dervish energy was focused on fixing up the house, going to markets, cooking huge dinners, giving parties, and actually having an extraordinarily good time.

Usually we did our shopping in Le Beausset, where in those days there was only one small general store, called the Casino, on the main *place*. In addition the village had a couple of indifferent bakeries, a butcher, a greengrocer, and an itinerant fish truck that appeared on Thursdays and parked outside the post office. If we felt in need of something a bit more recherché, we would venture as far as Bandol, on the coast, where every Saturday there was a serious outdoor market set up around the fountain in the old part of the town. However, there was no going to the market without first dropping by the infamous Bandol dump. A smoldering Vesuvius populated by sad, soot-darkened specters who spent their days clambering about on the burning mountain, rearranging the garbage with rusty rakes: It was a scene straight from Dante's *Inferno* and mesmerizing in its pathos and horror. But since the job of "sanitation worker" didn't exist in rural France, we had no choice but to load up the back of the car with our stinking trash cans, drive twenty miles in the sultry heat, and then heave the contents onto the foothills of the mountain. Imagine having to *work* on the Bandol dump! The plight of these poor people should have driven me to join the junior branch of the local Parti Communiste, but instead I was inspired to dream up a simple, but satisfying, game that, I am ashamed to admit, I have been playing ever since: "Which Would You Rather?" Have your little finger amputated, drink somebody else's pee, go to bed with Prince Charles or . . . work on the Bandol dump? I even got Freddie to play it with me until he rebelled—"Darling, you really are too disgusting." And then, just for him, I came up with a subtle variation on the same theme: "Who Would You Rather?" Cleopatra or Marilyn Monroe. That tart Keeler or the Duchess of Argyll. Or, just to torture him, the Queen Mother or Madame Carrère. This game was much more to Freddie's taste.

AS MARKETS GO, the one in Bandol was impressive, but it was nothing stacked up against the mother of all markets in Toulon. It occupied the entire length of the Cours Lafayette, which—like its fancier cousin in Aix—is a broad boulevard shaded by enormous plane trees with peeling camouflage-bark that stretches on a gentle slope from a hill at the center of the city all the way down to the harbor. Lined on each side with wooden stands overflowing with fruit—raspberries in baskets lined with fuzzy vine leaves; figs about to burst their purple skins; heavy, fat little watermelons—and vegetables—skinny *haricots verts*, shiny aubergines, fragrant bouquets of basil—we would barrel down filling up our bags, sometimes stopping for a quick proffered taste of peppery *saucisson* or a sliver of Gruyère that had arrived that morning in a truck from the Haute-Savoie. Wild field greens, arugula, and dandelion leaves, and huge briny barrels of olives—some stuffed with anchovies, others mixed with pimentos, celery, and cracked coriander seeds—occupied the trestle tables farther down toward the harbor. If we were feeling really hungry, and our baskets had gotten too heavy, we would pause for a slice of

Toulonnais pizza, its thick tomato crust studded with shrimp, calamari rings, and octopus tentacles, in homage to Toulon's fishy heritage.

During the war the Allies and the retreating Germans had between them bombed and blown up everything along the water, completely demolishing Toulon's famous harbor. But even worse than this destruction were the buildings that had replaced the ruins in the 1950s. Reminiscent of the most lumpen architecture of the Soviet era, these mountains of gray concrete, now cracked and streaked with dirt, sit there sullenly staring out at the pure blue beauty of the Mediterranean. If you walk down to the end of the Cours Lafayette, to the part where the fishwives preside over their trestle stands, piled high with heaps of shellfish, thick slabs of tuna, and small, fierce *rascasses*, some with half-devoured smaller fish still hanging from their jaws, you can catch a glimpse of the sea in the distance. It is easy to be seduced by the breeze, the boats, the glint of sunshine on the water, but that's where the gulag of concrete begins. Instead we would turn off into one of the side streets off the Cours, and get lost in the rat's nest of dank, crooked alleyways in the old city.

The bombs were interested only in the harbor, so the neighborhood behind, which for centuries had offered hungry sailors all the consolations they craved, had been spared. I loved the way you could leave the wholesome, bright bustle of the market and be transported in just a few minutes into the secret, twilit world of some French film about a handsome criminal—Jean-Paul Belmondo, perhaps—eluding *les flics*, in the sleazy back alleys of a Mediterranean port. Or, at least that was how it felt to me. Not a glimmer of sunlight filtered down onto the fetid streets, and outside one bar I swear I saw a deep brown stain on the sidewalk that could only have been dried blood. The fishwives' younger sisters— with the same peroxide hair and stocky legs but much shorter skirts, and every bit as determined to cajole, seduce, or if necessary, bully their customers—loitered about in the doorways. Just like in the movies.

Once, as we were walking past an especially raucous bar—drunken shouts and the noise of crazed pinball machines spilled out through the pink plastic-beaded curtain—my mother offered me twenty francs if I'd go in and ask for a glass of Orangina. "Go on, take a chance," she urged me, eager to promote any form of anarchy, however mild. Like a fool I refused. But I can still hear her words echoing in my ears, and still wish I had done it. "Take a chance"—this was the precept she had always lived by, the impulse that had propelled her forward, the belief she clung to as fervently as any of the pilgrims who worshipped at the shrine of Notre-Dame du Beausset-Vieux, in that tiny chapel on top of the hill, behind our house.

The army surplus store occupied a strategic corner with entrances on two streets and a window full of faded, oddly hermaphrodite mannequins with painted-on hair and hats emblazoned with the names of long-forgotten ships perched on their lifeless heads. Sylvia had instructed us not to bother with anything other than the American navy stuff. And it's true that we weren't much interested in passing ourselves off as British commandos in khaki camouflage, or dressing up in baggy brown wool trousers that tucked into lace-up boots, like Tintin, or wearing silly berets trimmed in leather: What we were after was the genuine sailor look. It was Coco Chanel who had started it all when she was photographed in the early thirties in high-waisted white bell-bottoms, a skimpy little blue-and-white striped sweater, and a revolutionary suntan. The *mode marine* was born, and I was determined to follow in her chic, espadrilled footsteps.

Once inside the store, we went straight for the stack of not entirely clean navy blue pants (could you catch crabs just by trying them on?) with jaunty square flaps, tailored for the snake-hipped, malnourished navy recruits who had once worn them. My mother whooped with delight when she discovered an olive green double-breasted coat with gold buttons, which looked like something Marshal Zhukov might have worn on the eastern front but she claimed was just the same as the one she'd had in the Canadian army. She slipped it on over her jeans and stood there in front of the mirror, narrowed her eyes, raised her right hand in a crisp salute, and started barking out nonsensical parade-ground commands in a heavy Russian accent. So, that, along with several white canvas belts, the pants, and the striped sweaters, had to be added to our pile. The sad-looking man behind the counter, already alarmed by my mother's Zhukov impersonation, hurriedly stuffed everything into a couple of crumpled paper bags, scribbled *l'addition* on a corner of the newspaper he was reading, and went back to the sports page, relieved to be rid of these noisy foreign women who had disturbed the calm of his dusty shop.

Fired up with the success of our shopping expedition, and in no mood to stop spending money anytime soon, my mother announced that since we were already in Toulon, it would be criminal not to visit a few junk stores. Contemptuous of luxury and extravagance and congenitally incapable of paying full price for anything, she nonetheless had an extraordinary eye for quality. A full-length black, backless cashmere dress (missing one pearl button), shocking pink kid gloves from Italy (slightly soiled), one half of a pair of Georgian silver candlesticks (a bit dented), a majolica teapot (spout chipped), an eighteenth-century Baroque gilded mirror (glass cracked): All these had been bought for a fraction of what they were worth and restored to something approaching perfection. Whereas "junk," in her vocabulary, back home in England, could be stretched to cover anything from a market stall selling old plates and mugs to a real antique store, in France it was altogether different. In their mania for Cartesian order and hierarchy, the French made a clear distinction between *brocante* (junk that an *antiquaire* was too snobby to touch) and *antiquaire* (a better class of junk that could be passed off as Louis XV, Empire, or whatever, and sold for a ludicrous amount of money). Some objects could slide from one category to another, like the rusty wrought-iron bedstead I once saw leaning against the wall of our favorite *brocante* on the outskirts of Toulon that reappeared a couple of weeks later, painted white and tricked up with embroidered linen pillows, in the window of the *antiquaire* on the boulevard Strasbourg. But then again something like the early nineteenth-century pine grandfather clock in our kitchen, with the curvy, pregnant bulge in the middle, where the brass pendulum swung lazily from side to side, could only have come from an *antiquaire*. In the end, of course, none of this mattered; my mother just kept her eyes open (and taught me to do the same), skipping promiscuously from one shop to another, to truffle around for treasures in among the rubbish.

"Okay. I say we go see the one-armed bandit first, and then we can swing by that fag who sold Pussy her armoire." It was an itinerary that neatly covered both ends of the spectrum. Roaming around Toulon, trying to find some garage that Monsieur Tricon swore would be able to fix the ailing "station wagon," my mother discovered a junkyard, hidden away behind an abandoned factory. The *spécialités de la maison* seemed to be broken metal objects. Leaky cauldrons, rusting radiators, strange pipes, and mysterious bits of machinery were strewn about, all watched over by a cheerful, emaciated Algerian with one arm. On her first visit my mother had gone mad, ending up with a cast-iron casserole without a lid, a set of mismatched knives, a coffee grinder, and a large enameled green stove. Impressed by her wild extravagance, the Algerian had insisted on throwing in a free saucepan that was missing one of its handles—rather like himself. We were customers for life, or at least for his life. When we dropped by one day about twenty years later and were told he had died, out of loyalty to his memory we never went back.

BOSSY PUSSY WAS NOT interested in trash. Her taste was altogether more conventional, and her standards were high, so when she said Monsieur Renaudin—the Loulou Richelmi of antiques—was the only *antiquaire* in the whole of Toulon who wasn't a thief, my mother listened. Renaudin et Fils occupied the ground floor of a Belle Époque building just off the place des Trois Dauphins. Pierre Renaudin must have been the *fils* part of the business because, with his sky blue cashmere sweaters, white loafers, and the rose-scented pomade that kept his thinning blond hair plastered to his bony skull, it seemed unlikely that he had any sons of his own. But what he did have was very good taste, and since he wasn't a thief, his prices didn't make you scream with laughter. A tinkly, flirtatious bell would announce your arrival in his shop, and he would hurry out of his tiny *bureau*—really more of a wallpapered womb tucked away under the staircase—to welcome you as if you had just come for a cozy dinner. And it is true that his shop looked and felt like an apartment rather than a place where stuff was actually bought and sold. The air smelled of beeswax and lavender, or at least it did at first, but once your nose got used to being there, it snuffled about and quickly detected the unmistakable acrid aroma of cat's piss, lurking underneath the flowery top notes.

It was Monsieur Renaudin who had sold my mother the curvy clock, and as soon as we walked through the door, after our adventures in the one-armed bandit's scrapyard and the army surplus store, he was there to greet us.

"Ah, bonjour, Madame, Mademoiselle," and like the maître d' in a fancy restaurant, he led us quickly through the back of his shop and out into a small bamboo-shaded garden, where one of his incontinent cats lay asleep under a gardenia bush. We must have looked exhausted, because as soon as we sat down, he said we were clearly in need of *une tisane de tilleul.* A few moments later he reappeared with a teapot, three cups, and a plate of—what else?—madeleines. The garden was deliciously cool— the bamboo rustled, water dribbled out of a dolphin's mouth into a stone shell—and our sagging bodies and spirits quickly revived. Now it was time to talk about a particularly fine pair of carved fruitwood armoire doors that he had recently acquired. An old lady had died, her unsentimental children had sold not just the house but everything in it, "même ses vêtements, qui n'étaient pas tellement propres" (Monsieur Renaudin was particularly shocked by this callous offloading of her not-very-clean clothes). And even her cupboard doors, it seemed. As soon as she saw them I could tell that my mother wasn't going to be able to resist. She gave a little involuntary intake of breath and turned to me, "These are really something else. Look at that carving and the sheen on the wood," she said, reaching over and gently stroking one of the doors as if it had been one of our sleek, overindulged cats. It was merely a question of whether they could fit on the roof of the "station wagon." Taking on Freddie's role, Monsieur Renaudin wrestled with the elastic snakes, and eventually got the doors trussed up and tied to the rusty luggage rack.

"LES RIVAUX DE PAINFUL GULCH. Une histoire de Lucky Luke au Wild Ouest."

"No, Dad, you have to read it in *English*. I told you that before."

"Oh, so you did, darling, I keep forgetting. I am silly, am't I?"

"Yes."

"We had better start again. 'The Rivals of Painful Gulch. A Story About Lucky Luke in the Wild West. . . . Lucky Luke rode into town on Jolly Jumper, the cleverest horse in the West. . . . We have some unfinished business to settle. . . . Is that so? . . . I reckon it is. . . . There's only one place to settle this, and that's outside. . . .

" 'So Lucky Luke, quicker than his own shadow' "—

"I'm hungry."

"Darling, what can I get for you?"

"Meringues and mustard."

"I'm not at all sure where one might find such a thing."

Nick was naked and lay sprawled, like a tiny, bored pasha, on an armchair. Freddie was on his hands and knees, scrabbling around in the back of the cupboard, in search of the elusive meringues. And mustard. "What the hell is going on here? We have fifteen people coming to dinner. There are two doors on the roof of the car. And I need to start cooking. Now."

We had arrived back from our adventure in Toulon, and my mother was not pleased. I was always amazed at how she could whip herself up into a rage about something—mainly Freddie—that was not only utterly predictable but was never going to change. Imagine: We had been away all day and Freddie had, incredibly, failed to tidy the house/do the dishes/put any clothes on Nick. Imagine: After they married, Freddie had, unbelievably, gone on sleeping with other women. "Étonne-moi!" But she never stopped being astonished. And very angry.

The best way to calm her down was with furious activity. As soon as the Canadian sergeant major swept through the clackety wooden beads, we all knew she wasn't kidding. She dumped her Marshal Zhukov coat on the table and stomped back out to the car to get the shopping baskets. Everybody snapped to attention and ran after her, eager to help, or at least eager to forestall another serious eruption. The guests were arriving at eight, the kitchen was a mess, and, as she had pointed out, we had to start cooking. Now. Freddie quite sensibly retreated to his *cave,* mumbling about how much work he had to do, Robin swooped down and picked up the naked Nick, announcing it was bath time, and ran up the stairs. So that left me alone with my mother.

At fifteen I'd had many years of practice and had over time taught myself to ignore her temper. It wasn't easy, especially when I was younger and more easily frightened, but I had pretty well perfected my technique by this point. Keep calm, distance yourself, don't argue back, and allow the impassive, slightly bored expression on your face to convey your cool—no, frigid—disdain for the whole crazy uproar. Naturally it didn't always work. The other trick was to distract her or, even better, to make her laugh. Sometimes I'd dredge up some innocuous but faintly idiotic thing my father had said or done (I know, I shouldn't have) and she would giggle and always come up with something even better, like the time he had given her a trout-fishing rod for her birthday. "Jesus, can you believe it? He knew I didn't give a shit about fishing, but that way he got to keep the rod and didn't have to spend any money on a present I might actually *want.*" Which allowed us to marvel, yet again, at the incomprehensible—and all-too-often reprehensible—ways of men. But that afternoon she wasn't in any mood for jokes about their silly foibles, so I decided to adopt the frantic-worker-bee approach. She stood at the kitchen table, her hair unwashed, sweating not just from the heat and lugging the baskets but also from the exhausting, backbreaking work of shouting. For a moment she looked utterly overwhelmed, and instead of being upset, I felt sorry for her.

My mother carried most—no, all—of the household burdens on her shoulders: She was the full-time chauffeur and cook as well as the part-time, not especially skilled, handyman and cleaning lady; in fact there was nothing she didn't insist on doing all by herself. No wonder she sometimes went mad. After we had put all the food away, I told her I would start on dinner, while she went upstairs and had a bath. "Oh, would you? Could you?" A look of genuine relief came over her face at the thought that she might be able to abdicate her sergeant-major role, if only for half an hour, and she smiled, "Thanks, Gull." With the taste, interests, and obsessions of a fussy homosexual, I was the household's self-appointed sous-chef, party planner, and interior decorator. But, as all artistic people know, when you happen to be blessed with a passion, however hard you drive yourself, it just never feels like work at all. Which was lucky for my mother. When I wasn't fretting, like an old queen, over lampshades and linen napkins, I was a demented fifties housewife in a flouncy little apron, forever scrubbing floors, sewing cushion covers, polishing furniture, and arranging fragrant bouquets of wildflowers. This was my idea of heaven.

All of Elizabeth David's books were lined up on a shelf in the kitchen, along with throwbacks to my mother's New England childhood, like a facsimile of the 1918 edition of the *Boston Cooking-School Cook Book* by Fannie Farmer. Not much interested in recipes for baked scrod, and put off by the dumpy appearance of its unsmiling author, I became instead a rabid disciple of the woman who had taught the English how to make the kind of food she had discovered on her wanderings around France, Italy, Morocco, and the Middle East. Her recipes were wonderfully simple, hardly bothering to specify precise quantities or explain each fiddly step:

She assumed you knew what you were doing. Of course I didn't. But in my role as sous-chef, I was constantly in the kitchen, and between watching my mother, hanging around with Sylvia and Pussy, and devouring every word Elizabeth David wrote, I eventually learned how to cook.

Although I was happy to read about things like *"Cou d'Oie Farci,"* which begins, "When the confits of goose are being prepared, the necks of the geese are stuffed and cooked at the same time. The skin of the neck is turned inside out like the finger of a glove and the inside removed . . . ," or indeed the long and complicated confit recipe itself, which ends on a slightly dispiriting note: "This is only really worth doing for those who have their own geese and a dry airy larder in which to store the jars," I knew they were not for us. Instead my mother and I concentrated on dishes like grilled mackerel: "make two incisions on each side of the fish, into these put a little butter, parsley, salt, pepper, fennel, and a few chopped capers. Grill for 7–10 minutes and serve with a squeeze of lemon." Or, even better, a "Salad of Sweet Peppers" that consists of "cold cooked red peppers (or mixed red, yellow and green) with oil and vinegar dressing."

The menu, on the day we got back from Toulon to find Nick and Freddie caught up in Lucky Luke's adventures out west, wasn't wildly ambitious, which was probably just as well: *pâté de campagne* and cornichons to start, grilled sardines and *tomates à la Provençale*, a salad of wild greens, and two cheeses—a soupy Reblochon and a gamey Époisses—all of which we had gotten in the market that morning. Sweet things were never part of my repertoire. And, as long as the magnificent Patisserie Antoine, just off the place Mirabeau, stayed in business, they didn't need to be. We had bought the biggest *tarte au citron* they had, and that—along with some crème fraîche and a basket of figs so ripe their purple skins had started to split open, threatening to reveal their juicy, red, pornographic interiors—would be dessert.

The guest list was a bit more complicated. What had started out as a simple dinner with the usual suspects like the Deakins and the Guireys had somehow grown into something bigger and therefore much more fun. Freddie and my mother adored parties. She was fearless when it came to mixing people up, ruthless in eliminating bores, and would say *anything* to ignite the conversation. She would also *do* anything, like the time she decided on the spur of the moment to have a blue butterfly tattooed on her shoulder, in the days when only drunken sailors and bikers indulged in such things. Sometimes saying *anything* was a disaster, not that she would ever have admitted it. "Never apologize, never explain" was her most cherished precept—one she stuck to with ferocious fanaticism. Once, during a discussion about the mysteries of marriage, why some worked and most didn't, she turned to one of her guests—a nervous lady in her sixties, who late in life had married a crazed, intermittently violent alcoholic who had stolen most of her money before running off to Spain—and asked her, "Jane, you're not very good at being married. What do *you* think?" Jane looked as though she would rather be dead, if that was okay with her hostess. Freddie and Mummy were both show-offs who loved and needed an audience: No wonder they thrived in the public eye. As guests they were entertaining, and as hosts they knew how to entertain. The food was important, the wine essential, and the fussy queen/fifties housewife always made sure the long marble table looked beautiful, but in the end it was all about the people sitting around it.

Not long after we had bought the house, my mother sold the vertical shed glued onto the back, to an old friend, Francette, who lived in a rambling apartment on the Île Saint-Louis in Paris. As with so many of their friends, the connection to Francette could be traced back to one of Freddie's love affairs. Just after the Liberation he had been posted to the British Embassy in Paris (where he had, memorably, met Monsieur Maurice's friend Jean Cocteau) to work in the intelligence section. The ambassador, Duff Cooper, had written to the Foreign Office in London that he was "extremely anxious to have Ayer back in France . . . he is regarded as a first class political observer," but when Freddie arrived, the job turned out to be a bit of a joke, so, as he wrote to e. e. cummings, "As I had no work to do, and plenty of government money to spend, I had a pretty good time." And part of this good time was passed, quite naturally, in the company of various ladies. According to his autobiography, "I spent most of my time with a French girl of Turkish origin whom I had got to know in Algiers. She was employed by one of the French Intelligence Services, but when we were together we put our work aside." Presumably he also put his work aside when he was with another girl, named Nicole Bouchet de Fareins. Brought up in Normandy, she and her younger sister, Francette, had been in the Resistance during the war, acting as couriers and, in an act of heroic lunacy, hiding a group of seven British airmen from the Nazis in their farmhouse. They and their children survived, but Francette's husband, Georges, was not so lucky: He was caught and tortured to death by the Gestapo. After the war the two sisters often invited Freddie to stay in that same farmhouse, and in Paris he became part of their social circle. And when he mentioned that he would like to meet André Malraux, whose novel *La Condition Humaine* had made "a strong impression on me," Francette arranged a dinner party to which she also invited Camus, "whose work I had just discovered." The party was not a success. Malraux was intimidating, and his habit of sniffing made him appear "disdainful." He also "gave the impression of having little regard for anyone who had not been an active combatant in the war." Freddie inexplicably failed to tell him about his role in the liberation of Saint-Tropez.

Francette was a woman of extreme intelligence, warmth, and courage, but her great weakness was dogs. She had a succession of them, none especially appealing. They were always big, usually smelly, and ridiculously overconfident, suffering from the sad delusion that the entire world must love them just as much as their besotted *maman*. Her current one was called Sorgue, after some local river, and every time he trotted, uninvited, across our kitchen floor, his tail wagging with misplaced optimism, he would be met with shouts of "Fuck off! À la maison!" a greeting he quite clearly misinterpreted as some special term of endearment. But if you wanted Francette to come to dinner—and we always did—her dog was part of the deal. Sorgue reminded me of some unkempt half-witted husband who farted, tried to fuck his hostess's leg, and ate with his mouth open but was tolerated only on account of his wife's charm and vivacity. That evening Francette and Sorgue were the first of our guests to arrive.

Next came the entire, gigantic—there were six of them, and they were all huge—Carr family from Oxford, who were camping, in considerable squalor, down in the valley. When the Deakins had graciously invited them to pitch their tent on some land they owned, not far from Le Castellet, Pussy had made it quite clear that she wasn't having any of them in her house. Never mind that Raymond Carr was a distinguished professor of history and his family old friends and neighbors in Oxford. "They are absolutely filthy," she complained to my mother. "Have you seen the children's hair?" And, with no place to wash, they became even filthier, the children's hair even more matted, until my mother begged them to come for a shower whenever they wanted, and stay for dinner.

Her generosity toward people in trouble was one of her most appealing characteristics. When her old friend Margie Rees, who had been with her at Nick's birth, was dying of cancer, she did everything she could to help. Goronwy wrote my mother a letter a few days before Christmas in 1975:

> You always were the kindest person in the world. I feel I must write and thank you not only for the marvelous smoked salmon, but for your extraordinary thoughtfulness in sending all these things [wrapping paper, tape, labels, and ribbon] which once Margie would have been able to buy for herself, but now cannot. She just spent a very happy evening using them all, which is what she loves doing.

Margie died a few months later. Sometimes my mother helped with money—always giving more than she could really afford—and other times it was something much more public, like taking up in her newspaper column the cause of some helpless, hapless victim trapped inside the government's bureaucratic torture chamber, and forcing the big shots to back down. Her empathy and sense of justice fueled her politics, turning her into a lifelong socialist who always identified with the people at the bottom of the heap. The ruling classes might give better parties, but not so deep down she hated them for their complacent, self-serving obliviousness to the unrelenting shit and suffering that most people in the world are forced to deal with.

Of course there were always exceptions to this rule, but only she was allowed to decide which particular members of the upper class deserved to be saved and which were to be cast into everlasting damnation. Not unlike Karl Lueger, the famously anti-Semitic mayor of Vienna in the 1900s who was once asked why he chose to hang out with quite so many Jews, and replied, "I'll decide who is a Jew," my mother took a similar view of posh people. In London during the fifties and sixties there was one particular member of the ruling classes, Lady Pamela Berry, who was known for the glittering parties she gave every election night. Married to the proprietor of the conservative Telegraph newspapers, the imperious Lady Pamela prided herself on the ecumenical nature of her address book and also knew, as London's most successful hostess, that a social occasion could only benefit from a whiff of barely suppressed antagonism in the air. And so my mother and Freddie were always invited to these carefully orchestrated events, along with a sprinkling of other Labour Party supporters, mainly journalists and writers, to add the required frisson to the party. On election night I would sit on my mother's bed and watch, fascinated, as she pouffed up her hair with strategic back combing, layered on her makeup, stepped into her long black velvet dress, slipped on her sapphire and ruby rings from Burma, and finally sprayed herself all over with Arpège. If, as was all too often the case, a Tory victory looked likely, she would bring out her waterproof mascara, bought especially for the occasion, and as she sat in front of the mirror sweeping it onto her eyelashes, would hum the "Internationale" and mutter defiantly, "I'm not going to let those bastards see me crying. No, they're damn well not going to have that satisfaction."

Admittedly the Carrs were hardly members of the huddled masses, but they were without any question in desperate need of soap, hot water, and a hairbrush, so that summer they qualified for rescuing. Freddie and Raymond sat under the lime tree, drinking pastis and smoking, talking about the Spanish civil war or some convoluted Oxford scandal, while the kids and I lolled about with a stolen bottle of wine up in my room, in an idle, slightly drunken adolescent torpor.

IT MAY HAVE BEEN SYLVIA who introduced my mother to Busch, I don't recall. A small, round woman, with crinkled, ice blue eyes, and wayward gray hair, she had skin that looked like very old stained brown leather—which I suppose it was. She had first come to this part of France in 1930, with her then-husband, Julius Meier-Graefe, an eminent German art critic. Sensing, with unusual clairvoyance, that the situation at home was headed in the wrong direction for Jewish intellectuals like themselves, they had left Germany, and bought a house near Saint-Cyr, not far from Les Lecques. They soon became the nucleus of a group of German and Austrian exiles, which included Thomas Mann, Stefan Zweig, Joseph Roth, and Franz Werfel along with his femme-fatale wife, Alma Mahler. Sybille Bedford, who lived in nearby Sanary at the time and wrote the brilliant autobiographical novel *Jigsaw* about her life there, described Busch as Meier-Graefe's "very young third wife—he had her elope with him straight from Swiss boarding school, pursued by telephone and police." After her husband's premature death, "she specialized in famous writers and artists as well as Greek ship-owners—concurrent with a discreet affair with one of their sons." When France fell Busch escaped to America, where she married, true to form, Hermann Broch, one of the superstars of the German intellectual diaspora. In 1950 she returned to her house in Saint-Cyr, leaving Broch behind in Princeton, and lived there alone, surrounded by both her husbands' books and a dazzling collection of German expressionist paintings, until the day she died.

It probably hadn't occurred to my mother when she invited Busch to dinner that she would come with her own large, ill-mannered, and halitosis-afflicted "husband." As soon as their car pulled up, he leaped out rather rudely and, barging ahead of his wife, dashed straight into the kitchen, eager to meet all these exciting new friends. Even though he clearly wasn't Sorgue—he was twice as big and looked more like a bear than a dog—the automatic greeting of "Fuck off! À la maison!" welcomed Clovis into our home.

"Jesus, what's *with* these ladies and their dogs?" my mother hissed in my ear, but then decided, rather uncharacteristically, to look on the bright side, adding, "Well, I guess they're better than extra men, because at least they won't get drunk, and we don't have to set more places at the table. Or talk to them."

The truth is that she was always much more forgiving of animals than people. And the only reason she bothered to shout at Sorgue was to provoke Francette, which for some reason always cheered her up. Her sympathy for the underdog—or the underwasp, underant, undercat, undersnail, underbird, underspider, undermouse, undergecko, undercentipede—was limitless. In the depths of a gloomy London winter she would trudge to the park with a bag of snacks—stale bread specially sautéed in drippings—for the poor freezing seagulls and ducks. At the height of a Provençal summer she would fill a shallow bowl with water, put it on the terrace, and watch, transfixed, as the poor thirsty wasps hovered just above the surface to take a restorative sip or two. Dogs and cats slept in her bed, baby birds were fed warm milk with eyedroppers, spiders were fished out of baths, and a colony of red ants, which feasted on honey and scurried around inside a special box with a glass lid, lived on the kitchen table in London for many years. The only creatures she ever tried to harm were the giant hornets that lurked inside a dead olive tree in France, and were capable, she always claimed, of killing a baby with a single, murderous strike. Francette said you could catch them by filling glass jars with sugar water and hanging them from the trees, and although we followed her instructions faithfully, I'm not sure a single hornet was ever silly enough to fall into one of these jerry-built traps.

THE SARDINES HAD BEEN decapitated and arranged on their funeral pyre of fennel, ready for the grill; the tomatoes had been sprinkled with breadcrumbs, garlic, and parsley; and a long column of candles marched down the center of the marble table, casting a forgiving, flickering glow across the kitchen. I turned off the lights and drew the curtains Alvys had sewn by hand—her glasses balanced on her elegant retroussé nose that first summer, before she left to meet her lover and die with him on the mountain road above Ravello. Poor beautiful Alvys. But now her son, Adrian—the same nose, the same blond curls—was upstairs with all the other guests, who were jabbering away, drinking wine, wolfing down the pâté, and about to come down the stairs to destroy my meticulously arranged still life.

Since there was nobody to flirt with, Freddie had decided to do the right thing and place himself between Busch and Pussy at the end of the table. My mother made sure she had Azamat and Bill, while everybody else was allowed to sit wherever they could find a chair, and a companion who amused them. Sorgue and Clovis, who had discovered they actually had quite a lot in common and got along surprisingly well, settled down under the table, on top of their "wives' " feet. I flitted about making sure the breadbasket was full, mixing the vinaigrette, spooning the crème fraîche into a bowl, transferring the *tarte* to the big blue-and-white plate with the pomegranate in the middle, and passing little morsels of cheese to the patient, drooling "husbands" on the floor. Too young to really join in the conversation, I was quite happy in my waitress/Mademoiselle Lévi-Strauss role, listening, watching, and learning how to be a grown-up.

After dessert and before coffee I slipped, unnoticed, upstairs to bed. Apart from an almost imperceptible breeze ruffling the leaves of the lime tree, the night air was soft and still, and the sound of laughter and individual voices drifted up from the terrace, like some play you might listen to on the radio just as you were going to sleep. "Yes, I *do* actually believe in

God." Amanda, the lovely, polite ex-deb who had been foolhardy enough to sign on as Nick's minder for the summer, was talking to Freddie about God. Oh dear. Father d'Arcy she was not. I could hear her incredulous, nervous voice going up an octave as it dawned on her that she was actually talking to, working for, *living* with an atheist. It was clear the underdeb needed rescuing. "Lay off, Fred," my mother told him, laughing—but she meant it. Amanda had become one of the freezing seagulls in Regent's Park, and there was no way she was going to be allowed to starve.

"Monsieur Zancanaro makes this marc himself. I'm pretty sure he squashes all the grape skins and pips with his own feet, and I'm telling you it is just what one needs at this point in the evening." Prince Azamat always arrived with a bottle of this terrifying moonshine and amazingly usually found quite a few takers. The beads clacked, the glasses clinked, and Azamat proposed a toast, to whom or what I couldn't make out. "No, Raymond, I will not go back to Spain until that man is dead," Freddie was taking a stand against Franco—something I knew *all* about. Only a couple of months before in London, I had been sent off to a Spanish-themed party, dressed up as a protesting peasant, in a baggy skirt held up with a bit of rope, proudly carrying a hand-painted sign that proclaimed "Abajo Franco." Nervously I had pressed the bell of some fake Tudor toad of a house in Hampstead—all gables and dark leaded windows—and was greeted by my classmate Vivien, the birthday señorita, and her squealing entourage, flouncing about in flamenco dresses, tap-dancing shoes, and sticky red lipstick, with matching roses tucked behind their ears. *Muchas gracias*, Mummy and Freddie, for coming up with *that* idea.

My mother was teasing Azamat about his friend Bendor Drummond, and the mini-Cooper he kept on his yacht for little spins ashore when they stopped off in Capri or Portofino. "Where the hell do you *find* these people, Az?" But, thank God, he did, because the very next week she and Freddie joined the Guireys on Bendor's smooth-as-suede teak deck, all of them happily slurping down Veuve Clicquot and nibbling on minia-ture squares of toast and *foie gras en gelée* while the yacht bobbed about in Bandol harbor. "Was Mann a homosexual? I'm not sure I know the answer." Busch was back in the German literary world of Sanary in the thirties. "Espèce de con . . ." was the man who had refused to back up for Francette on the road that morning. Franco, Monsieur Zancanaro, God,

Bendor Drummond, the rustling leaves, and the opportunistic drone of the mosquitoes—they all became an incoherent, dreamy miasma inside my head as I slipped over the edge of sleep, comforted by the sound of familiar voices, and knowing that nothing could ever go wrong so long as the grown-ups were laughing.

L'Amour

ONE OF THE MANY THINGS my mother loved about Freddie was his past affairs. He adored the company of women. Sometimes they were just friends, but mostly he slept with them. Never classically handsome—his nose was too big and his face too narrow for that—he wasn't tall, and he looked a lot better in one of his neatly tailored three-piece suits than in a bathing suit; but none of that seemed to matter. His appreciation, enthusiasm, and, yes, love of women had a way of making them feel the same way about him. And truthfully, one other factor should probably be added to the equation: Our shameful susceptibility to a man's reputation. We tend to judge a man by the company he keeps. In Freddie's case the company was rather appealing. Who wouldn't want to join a group of beguiling, talented, and often dazzlingly beautiful women? Admittedly it was not a small club, but despite its capacious size it still managed to be classy and exclusive. Once you had paid your membership dues the doors opened, and you were part of a magic circle, a sorority made up of the kind of women you wanted to be with, and be like. Hold up a mirror to their wit, style, and sex appeal, and, if you held it at just the right angle, you could see yourself reflected in it too.

Growing up, I was used to being told by my mother, after I had met one of these delightful creatures, that she was "one of Freddie's old girl-friends." Some men collect old masters, my stepfather collected young mistresses. Or at least they must have been young when he met them, because that was a long time ago, and now he was married to my mother. It was just one of those things about Freddie, like his Coca-Cola-colored eyes, the silver chain he twiddled when he was working, the softness of his hands, his sweetness, and the way his hair curled into the nape of his neck when it got a bit too long. And since I adored him, it made perfect sense to me that all those other girls had too.

Although my mother liked hanging out at her "club"—she loved Liz von Hofmannsthal's dinner parties, Jocelyn's portrait of Nick, and Sheilah Graham's stories about Scott Fitzgerald—she wasn't at all enthusiastic about allowing any new members in. It is even possible that the membership was closed for a while after they married, but somehow I doubt it. As a concept fidelity made very little sense to Freddie. What precisely was the *point* of it? Where was the rhyme or the reason? Or the *logic*? He was, after all, the Wykeham Professor of Logic, and a great admirer of Jeremy Bentham, who famously came up with the "felicific calculus," a splendidly logical system for measuring the moral status of any action. Freddie once explained it to me, and as far as I could gather, it allowed you to do all the things that made you happy, as long as you didn't hurt anybody else. The connection between morality and sex had always eluded him. In a 1966 interview he explained his point of view:

> I have always thought that morality has very little to do with sex . . . compared with the questions of whether or not to drop the atom bomb, what one thinks about the war in Vietnam, what one thinks about racialist questions, the question of who goes to bed with whom is surely only of the faintest interest.

What could be more sensible than that? Even as a very young child I recognized, and loved, his voice of reason, which rose above the crazy cacophony of senseless rules and discipline—"Because I say so"—that most parents seemed to believe in. I liked the sound of this Bentham man, and was suitably impressed when Freddie told me—he was wearing black tie and looked especially dashing—that he was off to University College to have dinner with him. But the best bit was that my new hero *had been dead since 1832*. In his autobiography Freddie described how he came to be dining with a corpse: "Bentham had not held any belief in personal survival, but wishing to have some semblance of an after-life, he had made arrangements in his will for his body to be mummified in a seated position, and expressed the hope that it should sometimes be admitted to the company of his friends." So once a year Jeremy got lucky, and was wheeled out from the lonely glass-fronted cabinet he lived in, seated at the head of the table, and listened, with a beatific smile on his wax face, as his friends raised their glasses and drank a toast to the man who had created the logic of happiness.

The obvious flaw in Freddie and Jeremy's scheme was that people *did* get hurt. And even though Freddie was the kindest, gentlest man on earth, the Aspergian side of his character meant that he was sometimes oblivious to the pain he caused. The fact that he had gone off to spend Christmas in Paris with his then-wife, Renée, and her lover, Stuart Hampshire, and had returned to London after only a few days, alone and miserable, should have taught him something about the supremely illogical human heart. But it didn't seem to.

FRANCETTE HAD KNOWN FREDDIE longer than any of us, and having never been his lover, probably saw him with clearer eyes. She once told me what he had been like in Paris, just after the war, when she and her sister, Nicole, had first met him. "The thing that made him so attractive and charming was his curiosity. He was alert and eager to experience new things, and also thoughtful about other people—bringing eggs to people who couldn't get them. Everybody loved him." But she felt that he had become more "insular" and selfish over the years, and much less open to the feelings of those around him. She was also critical of his cavalier approach to women.

"He thought he was Don Giovanni, boasting about how many girlfriends he had: 'One for breakfast, one for lunch, one for dinner.' I didn't like that." When Alvys, the couturière of curtains, finally left him for a Frenchman and went to live in Paris, Freddie had gone to Francette, complaining, "But I loved her." He was probably surprised by the reception he got from his old friend, "No, I was not very sympathetic. He had treated her so badly, what on earth did he expect?" As his stepdaughter I, of course, saw none of this. In his Benthamite desire to reconcile his own pleasure with the necessity of not causing pain (and the mother of all explosions with his wife) he was incredibly discreet. I suppose all that wartime work for His Majesty's Secret Service must have paid off. But those tricky Nazis had nothing on a precocious teenager's curiosity about the tempestuous affairs of the heart.

When I saw the piece of paper lying there on his desk, I picked it up, wondering what those two columns, running like long, thin ladders from top to bottom could possibly mean. Maybe he had been adding something up? But looking more closely, I saw that the minuscule squiggles were initials, not numbers. Initials meant names. Perhaps he was planning a surprise birthday party for my mother? And perhaps Jeremy Bentham would be joining us on Bikini Beach tomorrow? A long list of people, so familiar that he knew them by their initials—I got it. Quickly testing my theory I found LvH (Liz von Hofmannsthal) about two-thirds of the way down, JR (Jocelyn) not long after her, and there was DW (my mother) quite a few rungs from the bottom. The club had clearly admitted some new members. Not particularly upset or shocked, I thought no more about it. As long as my mother and Freddie seemed happy—and they did—all was well in my solipsistic little world.

A COUPLE OF YEARS after I had found the not-so-mysterious list I turned eighteen. The summer of 1969. And love—or rather, a frantic, unfulfilled, *desire* for love—was in the air. Excruciatingly aware of what I was missing, I mooned about, reading trashy French magazines, *knowing* that if my hair were blonder, my breasts bigger, my skin browner, my lips fuller, my eyelashes longer—I wouldn't be mooning about reading trashy French magazines. Instead I'd be inhaling great gulps of that elusive (and, as I later discovered, highly addictive) narcotic, which floated about in the hot rosemary-scented air, perpetually beyond my grasp. In a desperate attempt to transform myself from Mademoiselle Lévi-Strauss (thin brown hair, blotchy porcine complexion) into Mademoiselle Barbie (see above) I would smear my body with olive oil, soak my hair in lemon juice, and lie on a towel for hours on end, broiling myself under the merciless Provençal sun. Just like one of Elizabeth David's chickens.

"To roast your chicken successfully, the first requirement is that the bird be young and well fed." *Oui. C'est moi.* "Season the chicken inside and out with salt, pepper and lemon juice. Inside put a large lump of butter and a piece of lemon peel." *Non. Je ne pense pas.* With burned brown skin and bleached hair—the lips, eyelashes, and breasts had refused to grow—I waited impatiently for my real life to begin.

I was going on nineteen and, shamefully, had never had a boyfriend.

Convinced of my own unattractiveness, this situation didn't surprise me too much, and I just retreated further into my books and the forgiving cocoon of the adult world. Objectively I wasn't *that* bad looking, but since I lacked all objectivity, how could I have known? Not that I was a total fantasist: My skin was clearly a disaster area. It had started misbehaving when I was about fourteen, and over the next few years had turned from petty crime to full-blown criminality.

Despairing, I tried every cure I could find on the shelves of Boots the chemist, drank gallons of water, avoided anything fried or sweet, and even went to see an old crone on Sloane Street, who charged me a ludicrous amount of money for a jar of her patented cure for acne, made from the finest Bulgarian snake oil. Nothing worked. Apart from my distressing complexion, the other problem was that I went to an all-girls school, so I didn't actually know any boys. If only I'd had a dashing older brother, who could have taken me to parties and introduced me to his friends; but what use would that have been, unless he also happened to be a prizewinning dermatologist?

I may not have been a thing of beauty, but at least I wasn't dumb. And with my strict but futile diet, at least I wasn't fat. Even though I didn't learn to read until I was six—my mother had learned at three, and thought I must be retarded—once I got the hang of it, she made sure I had an endless supply of books. Sometimes they were way too grown-up—was there any point in giving an eleven-year-old *A Handful of Dust?*—but even if I didn't understand every single word, they became the constant friends who kept me company, comforted me, amused me, and taught me about the bizarre ways of the world. Books were my nuclear weapons in the never-ending war against loneliness and boredom. I worked hard and got good grades, so school was never a problem. Unless you count my anarchic delight in breaking the rules, which, of course, my mother never did. I suppose this tendency toward anarchism reminded her of herself, but my headmistress was less indulgent, and I was constantly being summoned to Miss Burchell's office, where she would try to reason with me. "Now, Gully, what would happen if *everybody* behaved like you do?" But they *didn't;* that was the whole point. Miss Burchell did not share Freddie's love of logic.

Bereft of all the normal teenage distractions, I would sit for hours on end in my serene blue bedroom, surrounded by the treasures that my mother and I had found in various London junk shops, and read, and read, and read. The result was that I won a scholarship to Oxford. The Acne Scholarship in Modern History. It was a thrill, but having proved that I could do it, I now had nothing to do with my mind or time other than to obsess about that rather large, missing part of my life.

Paris. That was the answer. With six months to fill before I went up to Oxford, why shouldn't I study *la civilisation française* at the Sorbonne, and "perfect" my schoolgirl French? My mother called Sylvie Boutet de Monvel, a friend from her days at the embassy in Paris, whose lovely, ivy-covered house off the boulevard Saint-Germain we had visited many times, but "Hélas" she couldn't have me. However, her desiccated, recently widowed cousin—"Pauvre Bernard, c'était tellement triste"—who lived alone and was only about eighty and perpetually short of cash—would be delighted to have a paying guest. But the week before I was to set off, without much enthusiasm, and install myself *chez* Bernard, something quite extraordinary happened: I was asked out on a date.

We met at a debutante dance in Berkeley Square. Not at all the kind of thing I usually went to. The hostess was some idiotic American friend of my mother's, who had decided that she wanted her daughter to "come out" in London—so much classier—rather than in New York. Or maybe it was as well as, I don't recall. The point was that a large, stiff, creamy invitation, with my name, "Miss Alexandra Wells," written in blue-black ink in the upper left corner, arrived in a large, stiff, creamy envelope, requesting the pleasure of my company at a dance, to be held at Annabel's, 44, Berkeley Square, Mayfair, at ten o'clock in the evening. Of course I had never been inside Annabel's, but knew all about it from the glossy magazines I pored over at the hairdresser. When Prince Azamat and Bendor Drummond weren't playing backgammon at White's, they were dancing at Annabel's or gambling upstairs at the Clermont Club with friends like its founder, John Aspinall, and Lord Lucan, who famously disappeared after his nanny was found bludgeoned to death. It wasn't the Gypsy's kind of place at all, and it seems that Azamat used to go there with half-witted girls in very short skirts, or so Sylvia told my mother. It sounded like heaven. And it was.

Annabel's was as dark as a cave, but a very civilized cave—whose discerning owner had decorated its walls with luminous paintings of silken racehorses, with doll-like jockeys perched on their backs—and the air was infused with the intoxicating scent of lilies and cigar smoke. Waiters patroled the room with silver trays crowded with champagne flutes, and in the distant, sexy bowels of the cave I could hear Mick Jagger singing appreciatively about the honky-tonk woman who had blown his nose (didn't sound very nice) before she'd blown his mind. Peering through the gloom, I realized I didn't know a single person there, so, slipping into my Mademoiselle Lévi-Strauss role, I plopped myself down on a chintz-covered banquette to observe the primitive mating ritual of the English debutante and her eager, noisy suitors.

The sad thing is that I can't remember his name or what he looked like. All I know is that he suddenly appeared—with two champagne glasses, one for me and one for him—and sat down beside me on that cozy flower-strewn banquette. And, since I introduced myself as Alexandra (why spoil everything by admitting to a name as ludicrous as Gully?), he called me Alexa, because he said my real name was much too formal, and anyway it reminded him of his grandmother. He worked for his family's brewery, and, at the end of the evening, he asked for my number. The very next day the Brewer called and invited me to dinner: a real live date. We met at an Italian restaurant in Chelsea, which, thank Christ—my skin had gone on a crime spree during the night—was just as dark and cavelike as Annabel's, and after we had finished our warm, foamy zabaglione, we smooched slowly around the dance floor.

The Brewer's flat was conveniently—and maybe not accidentally—located a few blocks from the restaurant. I followed him up several flights of stairs; he opened a door and showed me into an enormous, staggeringly messy room with a skylight and an unmade brass bed at the far end. After a few more ill-advised glasses of wine, I did what Bob Dylan told me to and lay across his big brass bed. But even though I could hear my mother's voice inside my head urging me to take a chance, just as she had outside that bar in Toulon, I didn't dare. The Brewer was a gentleman, and gentlemen don't insist, so a few hours later we got dressed, went down the stairs, and he put me into a cab. As he kissed me he slipped a twenty-pound note into my pocket, which either made me a cheap—and none-too-satisfactory—hooker, or him even more of a gentleman. Or both. It was all too confusing. I flopped back onto the seat and closed my eyes as the cab gurgled and chugged its way through the deserted

London streets in the washed-out predawn light. Stunned, I still couldn't believe that I had actually met a man who wanted to sleep with me. And if there was one, then it was only logical to suppose—I knew Freddie and Jeremy Bentham would agree—there might be another.

A couple of days later I was in Paris. Madame Boutet de Monvel had spoken the truth. Poor Bernard—or Monsieur Bretiane, as I called him—was indeed "tellement triste," and so was his apartment. Silent, musty, and dark, it snaked its way along the top floor of a gloomy nineteenth-century building on the rue de Rennes. My room was at the end of the long narrow corridor and looked out over a laundry-festooned courtyard. That evening, and for many more to come, Monsieur Bretiane and I sat across from each other at the table, set with stained, yellowing lace placemats and mismatched silver—the vestiges of a wedding gift from the Marquis de Lamarthe, he told me, sniffing sadly—trying to make conversation as we waited patiently for the Spanish maid to serve us. Monsieur poured me a thimbleful of acrid Bordeaux, offered me some stale bread, and Señorita Mañana finally came crashing through the swinging door with a tureen of unidentifiable soup, which she ladled into our bowls. It could not have been worse.

Eager to learn all about *la civilisation française*, and to meet up with my fellow students, I arrived early for my first lecture at the Sorbonne. Sitting alone at the top of the huge, crowded auditorium, I looked down, dizzy with vertigo, as Monsieur le Professeur began his incoherent musings on *le grand siècle*. I could scarcely *see* him, never mind hear what he was saying, but every now and then I would catch a word and cling to it like a life raft, in the desperate hope that it might illuminate what came next. "Richelieu" drifted up from the lectern below, and then, "l'Académie Française," and then a date and I was lost. What's with the French and numbers? Whose brilliant idea was it to translate 1697 into "one-thousand-six-hundred-and-four-times-twenty-and-ten-seven?" Oh never mind, the professeur had moved on,

"Elle devait nettoyer le français des ordures qu'il avait contractées dans la bouche du peuple." Right. "She needed to cleanse the French of the garbage that had settled in the mouth of the people." Maybe "she" would care to take on my mother next? It was hopeless. And even more hopeless were my dreams of easy camaraderie with a carefree group of fun-loving attractive young students. How could I possibly have turned up at the Sorbonne twice a week for three months and failed to speak to another person? Well, I did.

Instead of wasting my precious time lounging about in cafés, flirting, smoking Gitanes, and drinking wine, or smooching in the back rows at the movies, or going dancing in a French *cave*, or having dinner at that place off the rue Mouffetard, lit only with candles, or going for late-night walks along the cobbled *quais*, or slipping between the sheets of any unmade brass beds—instead of any of that nonsense I began a love affair with the city of my birth. And, since we both had all the time in the world, nothing between us was ever rushed. I would wander for hours on end, crisscrossing the Seine, exploring the Marais (long before it was cleaned up and made chic), admiring the seventeenth-century *hôtels particuliers* around the place des Vosges, and Madame Récamier's seductive sofa in the Musée Carnavalet. Sometimes I would walk from the rue de Rennes down to the Île de la Cité where I would gawk at the heartbreaking perfection of the Sainte-Chapelle. Then I'd cross the footbridge to the Île Saint-Louis and hang about in Francette's kitchen, drinking coffee and watching her cook—and later helping her eat—the best blanquette de veau in the world. I loved those islands, and would spend days, weeks, idling around like a true *flâneuse*, getting to know every alleyway, every little shop, every church, until I couldn't take another step. Then I would collapse on a bench along one of the *quais* and just sit there in an exhausted trance, mesmerized by the beauty that surrounded me.

Although that megalomaniac town planner Baron Haussmann had destroyed the whole center of the Île de la Cité—a maze of medieval streets, ancient tenements, the Jewish quarter, and the brothels in the Val d'Amour—he died before he could launch his planned attack on the place Dauphine, at the western tip of the island. Secret, dark, and leafy, it is surrounded by dignified old brick houses, with shops and cafés at street level and a shady garden in the middle. One hot spring afternoon, loitering aimlessly about as usual, I found myself in the *place*, and in the window of a dilapidated building saw a grotesque, Botero-size cat sprawled in a patch of dusty sunlight on top of a pile of leather skins. Inside, an elderly man was seated all alone at a long wooden table, carefully tapping away with a tiny hammer at the spine of a book. The sign above the door said, "Mors Doré, maison fondée en 1876." I longed to go inside and talk to him about his books—look at them, touch them, smell them—but instead of listening to my mother's voice and taking a chance, I walked on by.

Forty years later I returned to the place Dauphine, no longer the least bit young or shy, and found the Mors Doré still there, completely unchanged, and finally had the conversation I wished I'd dared to have at eighteen. Another elderly man sat at the same table, and told me, with obvious pride, that he had been in the bookbinding business his entire life. "We still fix our gold leaf with egg white and heat. Nothing much has changed since the Middle Ages." He was working on a piece of cobalt blue leather, which he flipped over, inviting me to admire the quality of the goatskin, encouraging me to touch the fur. Or do goats have hair? Who, I wondered, stroking the pelt, would want a book covered in bright blue fur—or hair—with a Schiaparelli-pink spine? But then I read the title page, and saw that it was a first edition of *À Rebours*, Joris-Karl Huysmans's malevolent tale of fin-de-siècle decadence—a title that positively cries out (in pleasure) to be bound (tightly) in electric blue leather.

The place Dauphine was my refuge in the city, a secret place I could escape to, far away from the laughing crowds. And although this bosky triangle, with its narrow passage that sliced through the houses at one end, may have been an oasis of calm for me, for two of France's great twentieth-century men of letters it represented something far more enticing. In a book about André Breton, which Francette had lent me, I learned, among other things, that he had gotten into a fistfight with a Russian who had accused all surrealists of being pederasts, that he'd had a violent argument on a boat off Martinique with Lévi-Strauss about the definition of art, that he had lived with Trotsky on an island in Mexico, and that he had declared of the place Dauphine: "It is without doubt the sex of Paris which is outlined in this shade." Returning the book to Francette, I quoted Breton's pronouncement, and she roared with laughter. *"Malraux a dit la même chose. C'est la vérité."* Even sober, serious André Malraux, she told me, whom nobody had ever accused of being a sex-crazed surrealist, agreed with Breton and had written about the place Dauphine's "triangular formation . . . and the slit which bisects its two wooded spaces." Francette poured herself some more pastis and smiled. *"Breton, Malraux, Freddie, ils sont les hommes. Qu'est-ce que tu veux?"* Which I translated as, "What do you expect? All men are sex maniacs."

One evening, when *triste* Monsieur Bretiane and I were having one of our customary *triste* dinners, the telephone rang, and Mademoiselle Mañana appeared through the swinging door and said, "C'est pour Mademoiselle." "Pour moi?" I excused myself and ran to Monsieur's dusty study—could the Brewer have called that idiotic woman who had given the party, tracked my mother down, *begged* her for my number in Paris and, at this very moment, be gazing out at the place Vendôme from his room at the Ritz? No. He had not. Instead, I heard Raymond Carr's booming voice (he was calling from Oxford, so naturally he had to shout) asking if I would like to have dinner with some friends of his when he arrived in Paris next Friday. Of course I would. I was in love with the whole Carr family, but I loved Raymond the most. He was completely mad, and exuberant, and outrageous, and he made me pee with laughter. He also happened to be a brilliant historian. What more could a girl who had been awarded the Acne Scholarship in Modern History want?

We met on the terrace of the Café de Flore, where he was reading some Spanish newspaper, drinking whiskey and soda, no ice ("Can't stand wine. Never could."), and puffing away on an evil-smelling unfiltered cigarette ("Ducados, dear girl. I get them in Madrid. They're so much better for you than those filthy English ones. Help yourself."). After another drink or two ("I think we have time for just one more, don't you?") we walked down the rue de l'Université, turned left onto the rue du Bac, passed Deyrolle et Fils, where my mother bought her butterflies and beetles, and finally arrived at a honey-colored building at the end of a leafy cul-de-sac.

I wish I could remember the conversation at dinner, but all I recall were the people and the apartment. We were greeted at the front door by our host, Julian Pitt-Rivers, an English anthropologist working in Paris, who was one of Raymond's oldest friends. (It was his brother, Michael, the handsome, gay, ex-convict gentleman farmer—married to Sonia Orwell—I had fallen for at my mother and Freddie's wedding lunch.) His wife, a tiny dark-haired Spanish lady with a glossy pink smile on her lips, click-clacked across the parquet floor, took us both by the arm, and showed us into a large sun-dappled room. Flowering jasmine plants stood on either side of the marble fireplace, and above it an oval mirror in a gilded frame reflected the impressionistic swaying leaves and pink blossoms of the chestnut tree outside: a living, breathing Monet.

Madame poured me a glass of rosé and led me out through the French windows onto a wide, flagstoned terrace, where I was introduced to a man who looked just like one of the glass-eyed, intellectual stuffed owls I had seen in the window of Deyrolle on our way there. His name was Theodore Zeldin, and he taught French history at Oxford. But not the kind of history Monsieur le Professeur droned on about in that vertiginous auditorium at the Sorbonne. *La gloire* and the names of those vainglorious men—thieves, liars, and murderers for the most part—who had swaggered their way through the centuries and onto the pages of the history books were not what Professor Zeldin was interested in. Instead he looked at the French through the prism of their emotions, their desires, the books they read, the music they listened to, the food they ate, the jokes that made them laugh, and the men and women they loved—and hated. All of this I had learned from Freddie, who was rather old-fashioned in his own view of history and wasn't at all sure about this newfangled approach, but had conceded that "Zeldin is a very clever young man. I am told he went to London University at fifteen and had graduated by the time he was your age now." Far too terrified to talk to the brilliant, precocious Owl, I stood there listening as he and Raymond gabbled away, until another older gentleman came over to join us. He was wearing glasses and seemed shy like me, so, feeling a bit sorry for him, I summoned up the courage to introduce myself, and in reply he quickly bowed his head and said, "*Enchanté, Mademoiselle.* Claude Lévi-Strauss." I didn't say another word for the rest of the evening.

But that night in bed I went over every single detail: the scent of the jasmine, the bitter chocolate on top of the profiteroles, Raymond's laugh, the living, breathing Monet, the sparkle in the Owl's eyes, the conversation between our host and Lévi-Strauss (what they actually said had floated way above my head and up into the warm summer sky), the surreal perfection of it all. Would I, could I, ever hope to live like that?

A week later I said *Au revoir* and *Merci beaucoup* to Monsieur Bretiane, took a taxi to the Gare de Lyon, and boarded the overnight train to Toulon.

Le Coiffeur

THE SUMMER BEFORE I WENT UP to Oxford my mother rented Francette's vertical shed to the chancellor of the exchequer. The shed was even more primitive than our house, and a great deal smaller, with a grand total of three rooms and a bathroom the size of a coffin. Why Roy Jenkins would wish to spend his vacation there—along with his wife and two teenage children—was something of a mystery. Admittedly Roy was an old friend and, as home secretary, had been Freddie's ally in the campaign for homosexual law reform and the repeal of the death penalty, but he was also famously partial to the finer things in life, like very good claret, very grand houses, and very pretty duchesses. Francette's shed seemed unlikely to offer him any of these pleasures.

I suppose it never occurred to my mother, with her wonderful American enthusiasm, her uncontrollable appetite for mixing people up, her scorn for convention, and her New England disapproval of *luxe et volupté*, that the shed and Roy might not be an ideal coupling. She just thought it would be fun to have her friends next door. Then again, maybe they were short of money. But how could a man who was in charge of the entire British economy be *quite* so hard up? It wasn't terribly reassuring. But whatever the origin of this ill-fated plan, the chancellor did not last long at La Migoua. About two days after they arrived, an urgent message from the prime minister's office summoned him back to London. Or that's what he said. I've always suspected it might have been an urgent invitation from Marietta Tree in Tuscany or the duchesse de Douceur in Deauville that snatched him so cruelly from his dear friends and the cozy bosom of his family. At any rate he took off—with a far-from-enigmatic smile on his face—in a slick, black chauffeur-driven car early one morning, leaving behind his wife, Jennifer (who was immune to the siren song of dukes and Haut-Brion), and their children, Cynthia and Edward.

Shortly after the chancellor's departure I, too, received an urgent invitation. Actually, it wasn't especially urgent and had come about through one of Freddie's innumerable old girlfriends. During the war he had taken up with a particularly attractive American correspondent named Polly Peabody. (Why had the war been quite so much fun for the lucky few? I would often hear Englishmen of that generation say, with admiration and just a twinge of envy, "George had an *incredibly* good war." Freddie even said it of himself.) It turned out that Polly now had a daughter my age who also happened to be going up to Oxford that fall. Of course we had to meet. Serena was even prettier than her mother, tall and slim, with robin's egg blue eyes, ludicrously long legs, and satiny blond hair. And, as if that wasn't bad enough, she was also clever, funny, and extraordinarily sweet. What could she do? I knew it wasn't her fault, and flattered myself that with my natural sensitivity and deep psychological insight I was able to see through the exquisite wrapping paper into . . . her equally delectable interior. We became close friends immediately. Which is how I found myself, in early August, staggering down a swaying gangplank into the blazing noonday sun of Ibiza's harbor.

Life at Polly's *finca* was altogether different from the scene at La Migoua. From the moment she woke in the morning—around ten, when the maid brought her breakfast in bed—to the moment she laid her weary but still amazingly lovely head on her downy Frette pillow at night, Polly devoted all her strength and energy—often exhausting herself to the pursuit of pleasure. Her project was neither selfish nor solitary, so you could say she lived for others, since everyone around her was invited to join in the task she had set herself. Like Prince Azamat, she made it all seem effortless, as if her only desire in life was to make sure that her guests enjoyed themselves just as much as she always did. At the beginning of each day Serena and I would sit out on the terrace, in the shade of the grape arbor, drinking our *café con leche* and eating *churros*—deep-fried sausage-shaped pieces of dough oozing grease and sugar—with nothing more demanding to do than discuss which sublime beach we might want to visit later on. A picnic lunch would be prepared by the cook, and around noon the four of us would set off: Serena, her boyfriend, a good-looking young Englishman named Ed, myself, and Sean, the other houseguest, whose complexion, I noted with evil satisfaction, was possibly even worse than my own. Some beaches were so remote that they could be reached only after abandoning the car and following a narrow, scraggly goat track through the scrub—the boys lugging the picnic baskets, Serena and I mincing on ahead—until we finally arrived at a secret deserted crescent of sand. It was a long way from Monsieur Maurice and Bikini Beach. Tired but happy, we would return home in the late afternoon for a well-deserved siesta in our cool, darkened rooms and then awake, fully restored, in time to get dressed up for the long night ahead. It was a routine I adapted to with terrifying ease.

The only thing Serena and I ever competed over was the length of our skirts and the size of our bikinis. And since this was the summer of 1969, the only pressing question was how high and low did we dare go? On one of my marathon walks around Paris I had discovered a boutique on the rue du Cherche-Midi that specialized in the tiniest bikinis known to man. Standing there on the sidewalk, I dared myself to actually open the door, walk into the shop, brave the predatory witch behind the counter, and emerge with one of these creations wrapped in tissue paper inside an appropriately minuscule bag. If I could just do that I *knew* that my life that summer would be transformed. So I did. And it was. No matter that I had spent a good portion of the rent I owed Monsieur Bretiane on a "garment" that was considerably smaller than the handkerchief he used for blowing his nose and for smearing around soup stains—after he'd spat into it—on his tie. It just had to be done. As soon as I arrived in Ibiza it immediately became clear what a wise investment this had been.

As I was determined to liberate Mademoiselle Barbie once and for all, and to relegate the tiresome Mademoiselle Lévi-Strauss to the library where she belonged, the bikini acquired a talismanic importance way beyond anything it deserved. It was after all just a few scraps of gauzy fabric, tied at the sides and back with bits of string, but for me it was pure magic. Whenever I put it on men couldn't take their eyes off me. Or so I imagined. And since wearing it was the equivalent of going naked, it was probably true. Their gaze may have been entirely confined to my body— I don't recall any of them bothering to linger too long above the neck— but what did that matter? It had delivered on its side of the bargain. Even Serena, who had her own magical bikini—tiny white triangles joined together by three golden hoops—was impressed enough to ask where it came from. I was thrilled to be able to reply with a bored shrug, "Oh, it's just something I found in a little shop on the Left Bank."

Never before had I uttered quite such a dazzlingly sophisticated sentence. Serena barely nodded and went on basting her long bronzed legs with almond oil.

EVERYBODY ELSE WAS still getting dressed for dinner when I walked out onto the terrace just as the sun was setting. The heat from the smooth flagstones seeped through the thin leather soles of my sandals, and the scent of the chamomile plants that somehow survived in the arid chinks of the terrace wall hung in the warm evening air. I stood there wallowing in the peculiar sensation of having absolutely nothing to do—no picking basil or looking after my baby brother or decapitating sardines or setting the table or washing pots or telling Sorgue to fuck off—when I heard Polly's little geisha footsteps tip-tapping across the living room tiles and turned around to see her standing in the doorway. With her absurdly tiny waist, flouncy skirt, and off-the-shoulder white blouse, she looked exactly like the ballerina that twirled around on top of the musical jewelry box my father had given me for Christmas when I was six.

"Darling, where are those boys, and why on earth haven't they brought you a drink yet?"

Polly was convinced that all men had been put on this earth to do things for her. It was a concept I had slowly been groping toward myself, but I had never actually met a true believer before. She flirted, she flattered, she charmed, and men responded by making her life even more agreeable than it already was. Maybe she was onto something. Maybe if you didn't shout at them, tell them what fools they were, and make it clear that anything they could do you could do better, they might be more likely to concentrate on giving you a good time. A novel notion, and one that I was determined to try out just as soon as I could find a man to experiment on. But the instant this heretical thought floated into my head, I heard my mother's voice snorting in my ear, "Sure, be my guest, go ahead and let me know where it gets you."

"You just watch me," I hissed back.

Evenings chez Polly started out with cocktails and tapas on the terrace, followed by several more drinks, and then it was time for the boys to drive us—yet another novel notion, make men do the driving!—to some quaint, seaside restaurant where a toothless old fisherman's wife made the "best *camarones a la plancha* in the whole of Ibiza." Polly's world was populated with wonderful little men and women whose lot in life was to supply her with goods and services for a fraction of what they should have cost. The "little" lady around the corner who would run up curtains/ transform an old Dior dress/copy a new one, all for a pittance, or the "little" man who would fix the lawn mower/dishwasher/car, for practically nothing: an army of happy, busy midgets whistling while they worked. Politics was not necessarily a subject you wanted to explore with my hostess. Franco—who really *was* little—had saved Spain from the Communists and was, thank God, still firmly entrenched in power in 1969, and the Guardia Civil, his enforcers, were those "handsome gentlemen with patent-leather typewriters on their heads." She was actually quite right: Their hats *did* look like shiny black typewriters, and some of them were kind of cute, in a thuggish sort of way. Polly's views of El Jefe and his fascist regime may have seemed a bit outlandish to a well-brought-up, radical-chic girl like myself—how could I ever forget that peasant costume and the "Abajo Franco" sign?—but I knew that only boring prigs allowed things like that to interfere with friendship. So I never did.

After we had stuffed ourselves with the charred tentacles of an extended octopus family, an entire nursery of baby squid, the gigantic grilled *camarones*, and way too many bottles of *vino tinto* (known as *vino tonto* because *tonto* was what it surely made you), we all knew that there was no choice about what had to happen next: dancing. Dancing at a terrifyingly noisy discothèque with seizure-inducing strobe lights. That was what we needed. My recollections of the rest of the evening—and all the other evenings, because they tended to follow a similar pattern—are a bit hazy after forty years, but I do remember what happened when we staggered back to the house a few hours before dawn. Polly went to bed and the four of us settled down to play strip poker.

Cards—along with jigsaw puzzles, backgammon, charades, dominoes, and every "bored" game ever invented, as well as all sports, from hopscotch to hockey—have always been a mystery to me. Not unlike Freddie's attitude to fidelity, I've just never been able to grasp what the *point* is. The consequence was that I had absolutely no idea how to play anything, least of all poker, which I'd never even encountered before. Patiently, through a miasma of *vino tonto,* with quite a bit of repetition, rambling segues, and several conflicting interpretations, the rules were explained to me and I nodded obediently, pretending to understand. Was I ready to start playing now? "Oh yes." I smiled, horrified. It soon became clear that Serena had no more idea of what was going on than I did, because within half an hour we had both lost most of our clothes, and shortly after that our little group had been transformed into some tacky, twentieth-century version of *Le Déjeuner sur l'herbe.* How could this have happened? Were Sean and Ed secretly professional poker players? Could they have fiddled about with the cards? Unable to figure it out, I sat there in silence, mesmerized by the astonishing shape and size of Serena's breasts—softly rounded, gravity-defying torpedoes that projected straight out from her slim torso—and by her total insouciance at being stark naked. Contemplating my own poached eggs along with my pathetic embarrassment, I had an epiphany. If I didn't get on with doing that thing that people do, I would be a sad, lost soul forever more. And more specifically—whether I liked it or not—the job had to be done before I went up to Oxford. There was only a month left.

THE DAY AFTER I arrived back from Ibiza, my mother announced that we were going on our annual pilgrimage to Saint-Tropez. Which sounds a great deal more glamorous than it was. This outing had very little to do with lounging about at Senequier sipping pastis in the company of Bardot's discarded lovers, or shopping for see-through crocheted minidresses, or even revisiting the scene of Freddie's wartime exploits, when he had liberated the tiny fishing village: It was all about having lunch with their friends, the Kaldors, who lived in La Garde-Freinet about twenty miles from the coast. Born in Budapest, Nicky Kaldor was a brilliant Cambridge economist who was now one of Prime Minister Harold Wilson's advisers on how best to revive the wheezing British economy. Who knows what fantastical schemes he came up with, but Freddie had once told me that Nicky was the genius behind the "famous cobweb theory" of economics—he had even made a futile attempt to explain it to me—so whenever I saw the Kaldors, all I could think of was spiders.

The journey to La Garde-Freinet was the usual farce of upside-down maps and swearing, but we finally arrived at their rather grim house, on a snaky backstreet of the medieval village, just in time for lunch. There was nothing remotely spidery about our host, who was bald as a melon, fatter than the Michelin man, and sweeter than a baby. My mother and Nicky had met through Robert Neild (her boyfriend before she ran off with Freddie the menace), and they adored each other. (I'm not at all sure Mrs. Kaldor shared her husband's enthusiasm.) Inside their hot dark kitchen, set out in the middle of the dining table, was a large, brown platter of braised meat encased in a jiggling mountain of urine-colored jelly. Which is all I remember about our meal apart from the startling sight of Professor Kaldor falling asleep and snoring, sitting upright in his chair, fork halfway to his mouth, just as he was about to start on his second helping of this disgusting dish. Nobody paid the slightest bit of attention.

Refreshed by his little nap, Nicky woke up about half an hour later, finished off the remains of his congealed lunch, and, smiling brightly, said, "Now, who wants to come with me in the boat to Saint-Tropez?"

I thought he'd never ask. An alarming drive on a narrow zigzagging road down through the hills followed, with the roly-poly professor pinioned behind the wheel of their ancient Mercedes—would he have another one of his narcoleptic spells?—and the next time I dared look out the window we were in the suburbs of Saint-Raphaël. From there it took us about the same amount of time to crawl through the tourist-clogged streets until we reached the marina where the boat was docked. A quick change into our bathing suits, and we were all lined up and ready to go— Nicky in his "grape smugglers," me in the magical bikini, Freddie in his billowing "shorts," my mother in an innocuous black number, and Mrs. Kaldor in something she must have spotted while window-shopping in Zagreb. The boat turned out to be—appropriately enough—a luminous orange floating version of a Michelin man, with just enough space for Nicky and one other person to squeeze into the cavity, and an outboard motor the size of a hairdryer glued onto the back.

"So, I am the taxi driver. First I'll take Gully, and then I'll come back and fetch the rest of you." A strategy worthy of the brain behind the famous cobweb theory. Dangerously low in the water after the chauffeur got on board, the hairdryer spluttering, we set off—waving merrily to our friends on shore—for Saint-Tropez, just visible through the shimmering afternoon haze on the other side of the bay. The boat swerved and bounced around, I held on tight, and Nicky swore loudly in Hungarian at assorted Frenchmen who—unable to understand our wildly erratic course—were in constant danger of crashing into us.

"Et voilà, on est arrivé."

The relief of actually making it across the water must have inspired Nicky to launch into his rather shaky French as he steered the boat into the harbor and tied it up.

"Et maintenant nous allons à la plage."

Walking along the boardwalk all I could think of, in my shameful narcissistic way, was what we must look like together. I needn't have worried. Why would anybody even bother to glance at us, when all they would see was a mirror image of themselves? The entire place was a seething mass of overtanned girls in practically nonexistent bikinis and their fat, old, bald companions. They all seemed perfectly content in each other's company, so I told myself, quite sharply, to snap out of it.

After about ten minutes Nicky suddenly stopped and pointed at a crudely painted sign—palm trees, parrots, turquoise water, yellow sand, and the words "Bora Bora"—nailed to the side of a wooden hut.

"That's our place. Follow me."

It was a replica of Bikini Beach: the same blue-and-white striped parasols, the neat rows of canvas-covered mattresses, the deck chairs, the cabanas, and the same shack selling Pschitt and slices of stale cake in cellophane wrappers. The only thing missing was Monsieur Maurice. Instead of an ancient hunchbacked queen with a yellow plastic nose guard and literary pretensions, "Bora Bora" was ruled by a sullen decidedly unbookish prince who looked like a young—*very* young—Alain Delon. Busy smoking and entertaining his harem of giggling girls with a filthy convoluted joke involving several sheep and a *saucisson*, he wasn't about to forgo the punch line, and so he ignored us.

"Excusez-moi, monsieur."

Nicky repeated his greeting in a slightly louder voice, and the prince swiveled around and sauntered toward us.

"Oui, monsieur?"

"Bonjour. C'est très simple." Nicky smiled, the prince didn't.

"Je voudrais une maîtresse. Mais seulement pour l'après-midi."

It certainly was very simple: All poor Nicky wanted was a nice, comfy, canvas-covered mattress for the afternoon. Not a mistress. Because he clearly already had one of those. Which the baby-faced smirking Alain Delon look-alike was quick to point out.

"Il semblerait que vous avez déjà trouvé une."

And he winked at me.

"Mais si vous en avez besoin de deux, suivez-moi."

Nicky's French wasn't quite as shaky as I had thought. He had caught the drift of this exchange and started to laugh, delighted at the thought of having two mistresses and by his own sudden burst of fluency in this perplexing foreign language.

"Oui, tout à fait. J'ai besoin de deux maîtresses."

Nicky left me lying down on top of his other mistress while he went back to the boat. My love affair with the sun started before the age of consent and has, I'm vaguely ashamed to admit, outlasted all the others. Exhausted by the boat trip, still reeling from the *boeuf en gelée*, and blurry from the wine at lunch, I positioned my body so that it was in the direct gaze of my lover, turned over onto my stomach, discarded my bikini top, closed my eyes, and sank into the sounds of the beach. Baby waves slurping against the sand, a child's indignant shriek as her mother tried to put a sun hat on her head, the hoarse baritone of a man hawking roasted nuts and *France Dimanche*, the lazy *put-put* of a small airplane high above, the murmuring of two women exchanging secrets, the barely audible laughter of the prince's harem—they all slid together as I was gently lulled toward sleep.

It sounded as if the couple beside me were making love, except every now and then they would interrupt their sighing and moaning and start singing to each other. Her voice was high and delicate, tinged with an English accent; his was smoky and deep and oh-so French. "Je t'aime, oui je t'aime, oh mon amour," she began, which was understandable enough; however his reply, "Moi, non plus [Me neither]," was a little confusing. But then again what did I know about the sensual, enigmatic vocabulary of the French male in love? *Rien du tout.* Sadly.

This was followed by lots more moaning as he told her, "Je vais et je viens entre tes reins," which sounded sexy except that I happened to know that *reins* were kidneys, which are not, in England at least, the most obviously alluring part of a woman's body. Must be another French thing. Finally I gave up and stopped listening to the words and just lay there in the sun, mesmerized by the pure unadulterated pornography of this intoxicating song. As it turned out, "Je t'aime, moi non plus" was the song of the summer of 1969, and everywhere I went I was tortured by the sound of Serge Gainsbourg and Jane Birkin breathlessly coming and going between each other's kidneys, reminding me that I had only three weeks left.

IN ADDITION TO THE ÉMIGRÉS from England and America, my mother and Freddie did actually have some French friends, mostly neighbors and people they had met through Francette. The closest, at least in terms of geography, were the Tricons, who lived two houses down, at the other end of the tiny hamlet of La Migoua. But however often we saw them—which would be several times a day—and however friendly we all were—which would be very—the relationship necessarily always retained its quite proper element of French formality. It must have taken at least ten years to progress beyond Monsieur and Madame to Marcel and Jeannine, and in all the forty years we knew them, we would never have dreamed of switching from *vous* to *tu*.

Conversation revolved in cozy, concentric circles around the business of La Migoua (septic tanks, the scourge of hornets, the lack of rain), sometimes stretching as far as Le Beausset (the iniquities of the mayor, a well-known *espèce de collaborateur* during the war, the new fountain in the *place*, the opening of an American-style *supermarché*), and always included a quick résumé of important events that had happened during the past year (Georges was doing his military service, Madame Tricon's mother had died, Monsieur Tricon had expanded his business into canned snails). Jeannine was a good if not great cook, and knew how to make all the Provençal classics like bouillabaisse, *pistou* (a Niçoise vegetable soup, which my mother naturally called "piss stew"), and aioli, but her true talent was as a winemaker. The recipe had come from her grandmother and called for white wine, Seville oranges, eau-de-vie, sugar, cinnamon, and vanilla, all combined in what proportions I never discovered, bottled, and left for a month or so, to transform itself into a nectar called *vin d'orange*.

The nectar was always served at the annual Ayer-Tricon *pétanque* tournament, played on the dirt road that ran in front of both our houses. Freddie, who was the most competitive man I have ever known (the galaxy of girls must have been about more than mere love or lust), never met a game he didn't need to win, whether it was a debate on television, decimating my boyfriends at chess, or beating poor Marcel Tricon on his home turf. It's just what he did. And he usually did it in such a guileless, childish way, taking such obvious delight in his victories, that it was hard to hold it against him. In some curious way he never stopped being the precocious little boy he once was, and I suspect that the origin of his absolute determination to succeed in life, whether it was socially, in his work, with women, or in games, lay in his lonely and rather bleak childhood and in his feeling that he was an outsider.

His father was descended from Swiss Calvinists and his mother from Dutch Jews, and even Freddie, the Aspergian snail, recognized it was not a happy marriage. An only child, he was packed off to prep school at six, followed by Eton at twelve—all bankrolled by his maternal grandfather, after his father's catastrophic bankruptcy. For a physically small, wildly intelligent (he had won a scholarship) Jewish boy with a funny last name who didn't excel at sports and had very few friends, life among the ferociously snobby boys at Eton must have been pretty good hell. But he always had his brains. And, like my mother, he used them to escape the dreary, constricted world of his family and fly away to the sunlit uplands of Oxford, pretty ladies, and intellectual and social triumph.

My mother told me she felt he looked at the world with "big desiring eyes," and even after he had succeeded in achieving so much of what his eyes had desired, that underlying insecurity still lurked in the shadows of his psyche. Anthony Grayling, who was his last graduate student at Oxford, told Ben Rogers, Freddie's biographer, that after a few drinks Freddie had once confessed, "You know, I always think that one day someone is going to point a finger at me and say: 'You are a fraud. You got into Eton and to Christ Church, you were an officer in the Welsh Guards, you became Wykeham Professor at Oxford and you secured a knighthood. But underneath you are just a dirty little Jew-boy.'"

Which may go some way toward explaining why the "little Jew-boy" had to beat the shit out of the mild-mannered flan salesman from Toulon at *pétanque*. Of course he didn't always win, but when he did a beatific smile would spread across his face, his big, desiring Coca-Cola eyes would light up, and we would all gather on the Tricons' terrace to celebrate with yet another round of Jeannine's celestial *vin d'orange*.

About halfway up the hill between Le Beausset and La Migoua lived some very different French neighbors. Unlike the Tricons, André and Nicole Padula were not locals, they were not bourgeois in the least, and it was *tutoyer* from the day we first met them. They seemed more American than French with their openness, warmth, and easy informality, which must have been what drew my mother to them in the first place. In addition to their many other charms, they also had an adopted son, Frédéric, who was exactly Nick's age, and the two boys were told by their respective mothers that they loved playing together, and did so frequently, whether they wanted to or not. (But forty years later, with all the parents long gone, they still have regular playdates, so maybe there is something to be said for arranged friendships after all.) André, who was an architect, had decided to build his dream house on an idyllic stretch of hillside, where, if you stood in exactly the right place and squinted a bit, you could actually see a glittering patch of the Mediterranean in the distance. The long driveway was guarded by cypress-tree soldiers lined up on either side, and the house itself, with its sliding plate-glass windows, open-plan kitchen (with a dishwasher!), and exposed stone wall and fireplace, also felt curiously American. Ranch style, it had a huge living room (with speakers hidden in the roof beams!), an avocado bathroom (with a sunken tub!) and looked just like something from a *House Beautiful* feature, circa 1964. It was the perfect house for parties.

I HAD BOUGHT THE DRESS on another one of my marathon walks around Paris, and in its way it was every bit as magical as the bikini. Floor length, made of the same blue-and-white stripey cotton jersey as Coco Chanel's little sweater, cut like a bathing suit, it had a deep décolleté back with crisscross straps, and pulled off the sly trick of being both childish and sexy at the same time. Of course I had never actually dared wear it. But what had been the point of bankrupting myself, just to have it sitting there in the closet, reproaching me for my extravagance and, far worse, for my timidity? "Take a chance," my mother always said, and so that night I did. Standing in front of the bathroom window, looking out at the sunset—one of the many oddities of the house was the fact that this was the only room with any real light or view—I propped up a mirror and set to work on my face. Six weeks in the sun had incinerated the top layer of skin and with it all the acne, so that was good. All I needed to do now was pile on the makeup: deep copper foundation, blue mascara, shimmering peach blush, sparkly silver highlighter, lots of kohl around the eyes, mint green shadow, brown lip liner, sticky pale pink gloss. Had I gotten carried away? Maybe piled it on a bit too thick? Mixed too many colors in one palette? I studied my face in the mirror again—dispassionately, objectively, disinterestedly—and was forced to admit the truth, there was just no way around it. How could I tell a lie? I looked gorgeous. Several strategic blasts of Miss Dior—didn't the magazines tell you to put perfume where you expect to be kissed?—some savage back combing of the bleached straw on my head, and I was ready to slip into the magical dress. With a back like that, a bra was clearly out of the question, and with the clingy fabric, the panties had to go too, but who wears underwear with a bathing suit anyway? My mother shouted up the stairs in her best New York accent: "Okay, Gloria, enough already with the bubble bath and the potions. Put on your rhinestones and let's go."

I descended the staircase slowly, careful not to trip on my long dress, and stood in the doorway of the brightly lit kitchen.

"Jesus, you look like Tricia Nixon! If Tricia Nixon had graduated summa cum laude from hooker school."

"Darling, don't listen to your mother. You look lovely."

We got into the car and headed down the hill to the Padulas' party.

Tiny white lights twinkled on the terrace, Johnny Hallyday—France's peroxide-blond approximation of Elvis—was on the sound system, smoky torches illuminated the cactus garden, the swimming pool glowed like a gigantic turquoise kidney, and a battalion of wine bottles was lined up on the sideboard beside a mystery dip encircled by a multicolored necklace of crudités. My mother put on her party face, Freddie looked appalled, and I knew instantly that this was the night. Noisy, hot, and crowded, it wasn't the kind of social occasion where Freddie's famous wit and intellect could sparkle quite as brightly as he would have liked, so he decided to fall back on his skills as a francophone Don Juan. He claimed that he was constantly being mistaken for a Frenchman, so brilliant was his command of the language (it may even have been true), and his special way with the ladies was such a self-evident fact that even he had given up boasting about it. Out of the corner of my eye I watched him patrol the room and pick out a pretty woman in a slightly too-tight black dress and then settle down happily beside her. Maybe this wasn't quite such a bad party as he had first thought. My mother's French was a much more haphazard affair, but so what? She just barreled on, throwing in as many English words as she needed, entertaining everybody with her faultless franglais. It never failed, and I could see her on the other side of the kitchen, with André Padula, waving a cigarette around and laughing out loud, probably at one of her own jokes. I wandered about, chatting with old friends, complimented Nicole on her onion-and-sour-cream dip—"It tastes so American." "*Vraiment?*" She beamed—and made frequent trips to the avocado bathroom to reapply my lip gloss and back comb the straw.

It was just like the movies. That enchanted evening I—finally—saw a stranger across a crowded room. Handsome in a French B movie kind of way, charming (or at least eager to charm me), older (probably twice my age), he handed me a glass of wine and smiled. Would I perhaps care to sit down? *Mais oui,* of course I would, how did he know? Sensitive, perceptive, intuitive—he had read my mind and, pointing to a daybed in a particularly dark corner of the terrace—he led the way through the crowd and I followed.

The plot of this particular movie may have been utterly predictable— I never doubted for a moment how it would end—but it was no less thrilling for being so. He knew his lines (could he perhaps have played this role before?), and yet after all these years the only words of his I can recall are "Que tes pieds sont jolis." Looking down at my feet—stuffed into high-heeled sandals, tightly trussed up with silver laces, the nails polished a lurid pink called Kiss and Tell—I whispered, "Merci." Maybe I would like another glass of wine? Or three? He made a foraging sortie into the house and returned with an amphora-shaped bottle of Ott rosé, some cold pizza, and a bowl of olives, and—just as we were going to continue our conversation about my "jolis pieds"—I spotted my mother making her way toward us. Oh please, no. Snappy wisecracks in franglais were not part of this script at all.

"*Pardonnez-moi,* Gloria, for interrupting your *intime tête-à-tête,* but *il est très tard* and we gotta go *chez nous immédiatement.*"

Was she insane? I glared at her, but maybe she couldn't see my eyes through the gloom, so I stood up, took hold of her arm, and propelled her firmly back into the house, where Freddie was saying goodnight to André and Nicole.

"Pas de problème," Nicole reassured my mother. "We will make sure she gets home safely."

"Okay, but just keep her out of the clutches of that rapist friend of yours out on the terrace."

"Je t'aime, oui je t'aime, oh mon amour." It was that song from Bora Bora beach, and the rapist and I danced all alone on the terrace. Just as I had imagined we would when Nicky had left me dozing in the sun on top of his other mistress a week before. All the other guests had finally left, and even our party-loving hosts seemed quite relieved when he—I still hadn't quite caught his name, Jean-Marie, Jean-Pierre, Jean-Something—announced he would be more than happy to drive me home. Home? I didn't think so. And nor did he.

I had never been to the beach at night. Cool, dark, and deserted it was a completely different place, vaguely menacing, smelling of the sea, with only the sound of the waves breaking on the sand. He ran ahead of me, naked, and plunged into the water. What had possessed me to abandon my underwear on the bathroom floor? How could I possibly take my clothes off in front of a man whose name I didn't know? And so I went swimming in my long blue-and-white striped magical dress. The first streaks of light had appeared in the sky as we drove back on the familiar road from Les Lecques to Le Beausset, headed up the hill toward La Migoua, past our house (everybody asleep in their nice cozy beds. I must be mad. What was I doing?), and up a bumpy track I didn't even know existed. Not so much a house as a plywood cabin—slightly smaller than Madame Carrère's shack, slightly bigger than the double bed it contained—I stood there shivering and allowed a man whose name I didn't know to undress me.

Was that *it*? I suppose it must have been because about half an hour later I was back in my sodden dress and being driven, very fast, down the track, to find myself deposited in front of the lime tree on our terrace. The sun was shining, Monsieur Tricon waved at me, Sorgue started barking, and I could hear Freddie's voice in the kitchen reading to Nick, "Faster than his own shadow, Lucky Luke rode into town. . . ."

Neither of them even bothered to look up as I came clattering through the wooden beads and ran up the stairs. Thank God, my mother was still in bed. But no, there she was in her nightdress, coming out of the bathroom with an evil smile on her face,

"Well, Gloria, you sure look BEDraggled. Where've you been?"

BIKINI BEACH WAS just the same as ever. Monsieur Maurice was trolling around for candy wrappers and cigarette butts with his rake, Teddy St. Aubyn was taunting Nick, Sylvia lay on her mattress smoking a cheroot, Freddie was in his deck chair doing *The Times* crossword, Prince Azamat was building a sand castle with his son, Sagat, and Madame Carrère was dispensing overpriced bottles of Pschitt from her shack, which was only slightly larger than the cabin up the hill behind our house. I, on the other hand, had been transformed. How odd that nobody noticed. Surely they could tell just by looking at me? Even my mother seemed to have forgotten all about our encounter on the stairs. I lay down on a towel and began replaying scenes from my recent adventure inside my head, amazed and thrilled by my own chutzpah. I'd taken a chance and met my deadline. Now I wouldn't be a sad and lonesome creature forever more. Leaving my bikini top on the sand, I slowly walked into the sea.

Francette was the concierge of La Migoua. She knew everybody and she knew what everybody was doing. That evening, as the sun was going down, I wandered around to the vertical shed and found Francette and my mother sitting at her kitchen table cackling away like two old *tricoteuses*. Did I know that my new boyfriend was married, that his wife was pregnant, that he was my mother's hairdresser—"Yeah, I thought he looked familiar when I saw him sitting there"—and that he was a rabid supporter of Jean-Marie Le Pen's fascist Front National? No, I certainly did not. As best as I could recall there had been no mention of "ma femme enceinte" nor of "le coiffeur de ta mère" nor any rousing call for "France pour les Français!" But so what? It wasn't as if I was ever going to see him again. Which wasn't strictly true, because one day many, many years later a bandy-legged, wizened, thieving old man in a rusty truck stole my parking spot in the village. "Fuck you," I said, before realizing that I already had.

Londres

WHEN NICK WAS ABOUT SEVEN YEARS OLD he came home one afternoon after playing with a friend who lived around the corner, and told me about the picture that hung above the fireplace in Tom's house. His description was somewhat confused. As well it might have been, poor little chap. It was a lady's face, he said, and she had curly dark hair, not too long and not too short, but her eyes were funny because they were huge and round, like tennis balls that bulged right out of her face, and he opened his own eyes very wide and tried to make them stick out. And then there was her mouth—a dark triangle that didn't look like a mouth at all—and he squidged up his own lips as tight as he could to demonstrate. "What was her nose like?" I asked, and he had to think for a moment, conjuring up the image of the strange lady inside his head, and then said that she didn't really have a nose, just a little hole that looked like a belly button. I laughed and said she sounded like a very funny lady indeed and Nick nodded in agreement. "She is funny, but I like her."

The lady in question belonged to Tom's dad, George Melly, and had been painted by René Magritte in 1934. It was called *The Rape*. Maybe at seven Nick didn't understand what made her look so odd—or why he found her so fascinating—but when he got to be just a bit older he realized that her startled-looking face was composed of "all the naughty bits," which can only have added to her already considerable allure.

George had discovered the surrealists in London as a young man in 1944, on leave from the navy. He once told me that the recruiting officer had looked a bit surprised when he said the reason he wanted to be a sailor was because "the uniforms are so much nicer" and was deeply disappointed when he was assigned to some boring desk job and didn't get to mince around on deck in a pair of bell-bottoms.

George never lost his taste for flamboyant clothes, and by the time I got to know him he tended to favor the thirties gangster look with a dash of Harlem pimp—dark shirts, loud ties, pale double-breasted suits, and a fedora. A brilliant jazz musician and blues singer—his heroine was Bessie Smith, whose voice he imitated perfectly and whose "avoirdupois" he acquired—George also never lost his taste for anarchy, subversion, and the louche side of life. Warmhearted and extremely funny—he wrote an autobiography called *Rum, Bum and Concertina*—no wonder he and my mother were so fond of each other. (And, as a true friend and soul sister, he sang the blues at her memorial service almost forty years later.)

George was married to the beautiful Diana, having left the sailors and bell-bottoms behind long ago, and they lived in Gloucester Crescent, a leafy enclave of solid Victorian houses that curved around behind Regent's Park Terrace, where our house was. I always thought of the "terrace" as being Freddie's territory—our neighbors were respectable people like V. S. Pritchett, a couple of judges, and Ralph Vaughan Williams's widow—while the much more raffish "crescent" was my mother's domain.

At the back of our house we had a long, dank garden kept in permanent shade by two huge trees, where a few etiolated plants eked out some kind of sad existence but were far too depressed ever to produce a single flower. My mother didn't really do gardens—witness the gravel-strewn parking lot in front of the house in France—so the space became a bucolic bathroom for our two dogs, when they could be bothered to use it. Usually they found it much more comfortable and convenient to relieve themselves indoors on the carpet, and the only times my mother ever went near the garden was when she was screaming and beating them with a rolled-up newspaper while shoving them out the back door. This happened about twice a day. Her difficulties with house-training pets was nothing new, and she told me that in Burma she had adopted a monkey who was no better behaved than our dogs, so she would hit him on the bum and throw him out the window—they lived in a bungalow—until the clever little creature quickly learned the correct routine. First he'd pee or shit on the floor, then he'd smack himself, and then he'd jump out the window.

The garden's only other purpose was as a shortcut for Jonathan Miller's sons, Tom and William, to use when they came over to play with Nick. Actually Tom, who was older and much better behaved than his younger brother, mostly took the more conventional approach, and would walk around on the sidewalk and ring the front doorbell. But William thought it was quicker and much more fun to climb over the garden wall, run up the steps, and come through the door at the top. Which would have been fine if the door hadn't opened into the bathroom. Freddie was an old-fashioned gentleman who liked to have a quiet breakfast—tea, toast, and *The Times*—in his pajamas and dressing gown and then retreat for a long ruminative soak in his bath afterward. What he *didn't* like was to have "that bloody William Miller," as he understandably called him, burst through the door and dash by on his way upstairs to see his son. Or, more likely, his wife.

My mother adored William, and the more he teased and tormented silly old Freddie, the fonder she grew of him. And William adored my mother because she was wicked, glamorous, funny, opinionated, unpredictable, and ferociously rude. His own mother, Rachel, had many qualities, but these were not among them. Who wouldn't fall for a woman who, when you said you were bored, bound your hands in Scotch tape until you begged to be released? Or who suggested you dial a telephone number, and when the voice at the other end answered with a crisp "Buckingham Palace," told you that the cops were coming to get you? (This was an old trick of hers that had terrified me—every time—when she used to play it on me.) Or, when you were a bit older, gave you a marijuana plant, all your own, to take home and keep on the windowsill in your room? There was no end to the fun they had together. But it was fun that excluded her son. At the beginning it was scarcely perceptible—she just behaved in the same hilarious and outrageous way with William as she did with everybody else—but gradually, as the years passed, it became more noticeable. Of course none of this was William's fault—he was just a young boy— but how about the other boy who watched while his mother amused herself with his friend? What was she doing? And why? Forty years have gone by and I still have no answer.

William was so taken with my mother that he soon started talking like her, which caused some consternation at his school. His parents were a bit surprised to get a call one day from his teacher, who said she was "very disturbed" by William's language, and perhaps they would like to come in and discuss the problem. Were they aware that his ever-expanding vocabulary included "fuck off," "goddammit," and "son of a bitch," and where did they suppose he might have picked this up? Only one place, they said, and promised to wash out his mouth with carbolic soap just as soon as they could lure him home from that well-known den of sin around the corner.

FROM ABOUT THE MIDSIXTIES to the midseventies the Ayer-Wells den of sin was just where you wanted to be. No wonder "that bloody William Miller" was constantly barging through Freddie's bathroom. And plenty of other even-more-scintillating guests used to barge through the front door for lunch, drinks, dinner, and big parties, where people would spill out of the drawing room and spread out all over our five-story house. Politicians like Roy Jenkins or the foreign secretary, Tony Crosland, would find themselves sitting around the table with Sue and Basil Boothby from Burma, newspaper editors like Charles Wintour, writers like Kenneth Tynan, Stephen Spender, or Alan Bennett (who lived in the crescent opposite the Millers); and then there would usually be a few Americans to remind my mother of home. Sometimes a certified superstar like Norman Mailer—fame was always her great *faiblesse*— would be produced; sometimes it was an old girlfriend like Colette Douglas (who had been a bridesmaid at her wedding to my father) or Anthony Lewis, the *New York Times* man in London. Once it was a visiting American Indian chief from South Dakota. Honestly. Hey, it was the sixties! And bliss it was to be alive in that extraordinary time, but to be young--or at least in your midforties, like my mother—was very heaven.

I don't now recall how Chief Spotted Eagle came into our lives, but he seemed to hang around for an awfully long time. The Bernsteins had their Black Panthers and my mother had Spotted Dick—as I called him. (spotted dick is a leaden Victorian pudding, full of suet and dried fruit, that was served under a thick blanket of lumpy Bird's Custard at school.) A man of few words, he was a tall laconic Lakota Sioux, who had come to London for a benefit—organized by my mother and other guilt-ridden expatriate Americans—to benefit the tribe back home on the reservation. The date chosen for this festive event was the anniversary of the massacre at Wounded Knee. Sadly I missed the party (maybe I was in Oxford) but that didn't mean I missed Spotted Dick, who had settled into our spare room and was soon quite at home in London, showing no sign at all of missing the wide-open spaces of his native land. He had long black hair and favored tight jeans, colorful shirts, and necklaces made of shells, beads, and teeth that looked as though they might once have belonged to a mountain lion, or a shark. Or possibly just an extremely large dog. Not averse to the odd cocktail, Spotted Dick was particularly fond of firewater from Bordeaux, having found a case of claret in the cupboard in Freddie's study—"That bloody Indian has drunk all my best wine. Really, it's too much. When the hell is he leaving?" But what he liked best of all was radical-chic pussy, of which there was an endless supply in London at that time. He managed to have his wicked way with several of my mother's friends, starting with, a hirsute poetess who lived in Hampstead, and then moving on to several other adventurous ladies *d'un certain âge.*

IN ADDITION TO HER HUMANITARIAN concern for the Lakota and her energetic social life, my mother was also busy with her work as a journalist and, increasingly, as a regular guest on television talk shows. Imagine getting paid—and paid very well—to argue, shock, hector, and harangue your way into millions of living rooms across the country, when it was something you had been doing all your life for free! It was too good to be true. My mother "knew from talk," as they say in New York, and she was a television producer's dream booking for the same reason that William Miller found her so fascinating. Clever, rude, witty, and above all opinionated, she sparkled even more brightly in front of a television camera than around the dinner table. Fame may be the ultimate aphrodisiac, but it also has a strong autoerotic component. I think being on television made her feel sexy—and powerful—at a time when she was beginning to worry about the horror of approaching middle age (which enveloped you in its sweaty menopausal grip a good decade earlier than it does now).

Just after Nick was born she started appearing five nights a week on a program called *Three after Six.* The format could not have been simpler: Invite three journalists into the studio and switch on the camera while they yacked on about that day's news. It was live, which gave it an added frisson, and the producers tried to goad the guests into an argument—never a problem with my mother—by mixing hard-core Tories with permissive society socialists. My mother's instinctive mistrust of authority made her deeply suspicious of all cops, and I remember watching her one evening—just after some Goya had been stolen from the Duke of Wellington—let fly on what the police would do next: "What they want is to get this poor hopeless little nut into the station and beat him up and let him fall down a couple of flights of stairs, and then say: 'Well, we've dealt with that ruffian.' In that splendid police way."

Three after Six was a straightforward chat show, but *Not So Much a Programme, More a Way of Life*, on which she also appeared, was rather more ambitious. Hosted by the ubiquitous David Frost, it combined satirical skits, music, and appalling one-liners—especially written for Frost by his tame hacks—with the guest yackers. It was on this program that Freddie had made a total fool of himself one Valentine's Day, discussing the mysteries of love with a flirtatious Eartha Kitt, who had cooed in his ear—"Oh, Professor"—while he droned on about the troubadours. Between their frequent television appearances, her newspaper column, and Freddie's persona as a public intellectual, they became surprisingly well known. Instead of writing about other people my mother was now the one being interviewed and profiled in magazines and newspapers. I suspect that she liked it much better that way.

Freddie must have been vaguely aware that the times they were a changing, but actually not too much changed for him. He spoke up against the Vietnam War, supported all the usual liberal causes, believed people should do whatever they wanted so long as it didn't hurt anybody else, and had always slept around: So what did the sixties have to teach him? As a respectable gentleman of sixty who was *au fond* part of the Establishment, he loathed any form of chaos, and had no interest at all in any of the wilder aspects of that thrilling epoch. Not so my mother. She felt that the world had—finally—come around to her way of thinking. Boats were rocked, royals mocked, rules challenged, satire boomed, the Labour Party ruled, skirts shrank, students revolted, and everybody got high. The satirical review *Beyond the Fringe*, which our neighbors Jonathan Miller and Alan Bennett had written and performed with Peter Cook and

Dudley Moore in the early sixties, was part of the same wave that created *Private Eye* magazine and its general piss-taking of . . . the Establishment. The dreariness and conformity of the fifties had been swept away by a whole new set of attitudes *Time* magazine conveniently shoved under that capacious psychedelic umbrella it called "Swinging London."

Within the dynamic of my mother and Freddie's marriage, the sixties had a lot to answer for. Increasingly she started viewing him as an uptight old fart stuck in the past, while he began to see her as a loudmouthed harridan swept up in the idiocies of the present. And neither of them was entirely wrong.

In her novel *Jane*, which she started writing in 1970, she describes the heroine's posh boyfriend, Anthony, like this:

In bed he was lovely. When not in bed, he was too English. He never helped do the dishes. He never carried things, not even potatoes. If Jane started the *Times* crossword puzzle and put it down even just to answer the phone, he'd finish it. In ink.

If he took a shower he always let the curtain hang outside the tub and couldn't understand why it made her cross. If he took a bath he'd leave his facecloth unwrung-out and folded in a neat square on top of the soap, where they fused in a cold slime. He used her toothbrush, too. But this could have been a genuine cultural difference; she had known enough Englishmen to know by now that they all used whatever toothbrush happened to be there, even if it was a wet one.

Anthony's other main drawback is that he is emotionally remote. Detached from, and not really interested in, other people's feelings, he is hardly any more familiar with his own. And, having gone through the usual upper-class mill of nannies, prep school, and Eton, he has never begun to solve the impenetrable mystery of what goes on between women's ears, as opposed to their legs.

After long stretches with Anthony you got the feeling you'd been playing tennis against a brick wall. The ball came back each time you hit it—sure—and right there that's more than you can say about playing tennis with people. But when you play a wall the only energy in the game is your own. You have to begin it. You have to keep score. You have to

decide when the game is over and who, if anybody, won. And it's only
you that gets sweaty and tired.

What you can say in favor of playing with a wall is that it never says
no or complains. And it never plays any better or worse than the time
before; you know where you are with a wall. The catch is, though, that
the wall never really gives a damn. It's like children who go all limp and
dull-eyed and say, "I don't care," when you ask them if they want an
ice-cream cone. Except with them it's probably a primitive hedge against
the possibility that the offer of the ice-cream cone may not be genuine.
The wall, alas, really means it.

This was, of course, a portrait of Freddie, the Aspergian snail. Freddie's shell was always his work, and when he was writing, his ferocious
powers of concentration meant that he noticed absolutely nothing of what
went on around him. But even when he wasn't working, he didn't notice a
whole lot more. That was how he had been when she first fell in love with
him, and that was how he remained when she fell out of love with him. He
didn't change, and why should he, even assuming he could have? She may
have found this exasperating, but Nick was clever enough to spot what a
huge asset this character trait could be in a doting father.

The routine on Saturday mornings went like this. Freddie would have
his tea, toast, and *The Times,* followed by his customary session in the
bathroom—enlivened by William's all-too-fleeting appearance—and
then he would settle down to work in his study. Sitting at a big round
table, his back to the window, twiddling his silver chain in his silken
hands, he would get so carried away by the question of ontology and
relativism, the relation between experience and theory, and the extent to
which what counts for us in the world depends on our conceptual system
that he wouldn't notice that his son had been standing beside him for a
good five minutes. Nick wanted his pocket money and he'd quite like it
now, if his father didn't mind.

"Oh darling, I'm so sorry," and Freddie would hand over a five-pound
note, without taking his eyes off the piece of paper—covered in his own
inimitable and incomprehensible blue-black squiggles—in front of him.
Ten minutes later, Nick would be back.

"Oh darling, did I forget to give you your pocket money? Forgive me,"
and another note would change hands. Twenty minutes later—better give

the old fool plenty of time to get lost in that crazy maze inside his head—Nick would reappear. This would be repeated at regular intervals—I think the record was four, or was it five?—with Nick's tone becoming increasingly aggrieved with each visitation.

"Dad, it's almost lunchtime and you still haven't given me my money."

"Darling, are you sure? I thought I had. I am silly, am't I?"

Finally Nick, the ever-artful dodger, recognized that the game was up and that he couldn't go on gaslighting his poor old dad any longer, and then he'd retire to his room with a pile of five-pound notes, and have lengthy pornographic fantasies about all the candy, Action Men, and comics he would be able to buy with his ill-gotten gains.

MY MOTHER WAS DEFINITELY going off Englishmen. And the longer she was away from America, the more attractive the men there looked. Even my dear father, who got only more handsome as he aged, was completely rehabilitated. Whatever crimes he may have committed—all she could ever come up with was that he was a bit tight with money, and that she'd gotten bored with being married to him—were forgotten, and his many, and varied, qualities were constantly remarked upon. Was there any man in the entire world better at planning a trip? How about that journey to the Shan states in Burma, where they had met that prince who ate live monkey brains? Or an impromptu party? What about that time they had drunk vodka until dawn, with those Russians who lived near the Palais Royal? Nobody was better at hooking up an outdoor shower. Or building a log fire. Or charming his way into a château that was closed to the public. Or fixing a furnace. Or cleaning up dog shit. He was also extraordinarily gifted at doing the dishes, driving a car, and carrying potatoes.

A few other American men also had their own special place in her heart. Larry Adler was famous (always a plus), had been hounded out of the country by McCarthyism (a double plus), adored my mother (even better), and played the harmonica rather well. Harvey Orkin, a TV and screenwriter, was another favorite, who made up for not being famous with his wit and sweetness. S. J. Perelman (famous and funny) made a brief appearance. As did Julian Bond, the civil rights activist (liberal, good-looking, and black, a triple plus) who dropped by once for a drink with his sad sister (underdog, in need of rescuing), who lived in London and so was invited round all too frequently.

As luck would have it, David Bruce, who had given my mother away at her wedding to my father, was the American ambassador in London at the time, so embassy parties were always a happy hunting ground for new American friends, as was any gathering at Tony and Linda Lewis's house. One summer I remember her coming back from a lunch party chez Lewis, giddy with delight. Guess what? They'd had hamburgers and hot dogs in the garden—could it have been July Fourth?—and lots of kids were running around on the grass, and Bobby Kennedy had been there, making ice-cream cones for the children. With *sprinkles!* Sprinkles were always big with my mother. The kitchen cabinet was full of jars of tiny silver balls and technicolored sprinkles that lurked at the back gathering dust, waiting to decorate the cakes that were never baked. Sprinkles represented America, the summer, her youth, and the drugstore in New Bedford that she used to hang around in with her brother. They were decidedly not English. But it was the image of Bobby in the blue button-down Oxford shirt that matched his eyes, sleeves rolled up, forearms tanned, handing out the cones—did she have one too?—that had enchanted her. So relaxed, so Massachusetts, so (newly) liberal, so Kennedy—he was everything she missed about America. He was everything Freddie/Anthony was not.

Less than a year later he was dead. I came home from school that afternoon in June 1968 and found my mother in bed, the curtains drawn, so depressed she could not get up. I had never seen her like this before, and it took weeks for her to slowly heave herself out of this deep black hole. Kennedy had been shot—again. Martin Luther King had been shot. Maybe America wasn't quite so wonderful after all. Thirty years later in France, as we were sitting around under the lime tree, I finally understood why she had taken to her bed. Yes, she had seen him again after that sunlit party, with the hot dogs and the ice cream and the sprinkles. How often she didn't say, and I never asked. My mother had actually met Bobby Kennedy once before at his house, Hickory Hill, outside Washington in 1962. Arthur Schlesinger had invited Freddie to an informal symposium, hosted by the Kennedys, where the subject under discussion had been—what else?—God. Somewhat ill-advisedly, Ethel decided to take on the infamous atheist, and as she sank ever deeper into the quicksand of Freddie's intellect, Bobby finally put an end to her floundering and told her to "Drop it, Ethel." Naturally enough this was one of my mother's favorite Freddie stories, and, one assumes, made even more privately delicious after her secret affair with Bobby.

As my mother soon discovered, she had married a man firmly set in his ways. Freddie wasn't about to start doing the dishes, or carrying potatoes, or picking up dog shit, and he never did learn to drive. And he certainly was not about to stop sleeping with other women. Who knows when or with whom he resumed this lifetime habit, or when she found out, but she did tell Ben Rogers, Freddie's biographer, that she had gotten used to his disappearing in the afternoon to play "chess" with various lady friends, or simply going off to his club to "sit and read." I don't imagine she liked it at all, but so long as they were old girlfriends or casual new ones, maybe she felt it didn't really matter that much. In any case there was nothing she could do about it.

Like all sensible wives she also made a clear distinction between a fling and a real love affair. We like to think we can cope with the first and come out the victors. After all we have the house, the children, the shared friends, the shared money; and husbands on the whole seem reluctant to see their entire lives—and bank accounts—go up in smoke. If it's just a fling he's bound to get bored with her eventually, or at least that's what our girlfriends always tell us. Odd, though, how perfectly sane and intelligent husbands can sustain an interest in mad and stupid mistresses for surprising lengths of time. And even odder how that first type of affair often mutates into the second—and once that happens the only victory a wife can ever hope for is the kind that King Pyrrhus brought back from Heraclea in 280 BC.

Just before he married my mother, Freddie had become the Wykeham Professor of Logic at Oxford, which meant that he spent the middle of each week, during term time, in New College. He would set out for Paddington Station with his neat little overnight bag on Tuesday morning and return on Friday afternoon just in time for tea. He had had his doubts about this arrangement, and in a letter to Marion Cummings had wondered whether it might strengthen or weaken his forthcoming marriage. But there was no way my mother or Freddie could have lived in Oxford full-time—they were both far too attached to the bright lights of the big city—so they decided commuting was the solution. Maybe they also felt that this weekly break—like the crisper drawer in the fridge—would keep things fresh longer. It wasn't as though Freddie had been frantic to get married—rather the opposite in fact. The siege had been lengthy, and fortress Freddie had withstood five years of seduction, cajoling, persuasion, and hoodwinking before finally admitting defeat and signing a peace treaty at St. Pancras Register Office. I imagine he was rather relieved to have a bolt-hole in Oxford to escape to. And as bolt-holes go, it wasn't bad.

EVERYBODY KNOWS THAT New College is one of the most beautiful colleges in Oxford, and everybody at New College knew that Freddie's set of rooms was probably the most delectable piece of real estate in the entire place. They occupied the corner of a beautiful eighteenth-century quad, built from that honey-colored Cotswold stone that glows in the sun—when the English sun can be bothered to put in one of its tantalizing appearances A paneled drawing room overlooking the gardens, a small bedroom, a study that doubled as a dining room, and an enormous drafty bathroom with a fire-breathing water heater: It was an apartment that cried out for company. Freddie, that most social of men, entertained his students there for sherry parties, his friends for luncheons, and his mistresses for *cinq-à-sept* assignations. He may have thought he was being discreet, but he was surrounded by prurient undergraduates and fellow dons who were all too aware of what he was up to. Some of them even trained their binoculars on his windows to see what they could see.

One of the many reasons I loved being at Oxford was because Freddie was there. I had always adored his company, and with him at New College, I felt instantly at home. He let me charge books to his account at Blackwell's, he took me to dinner at High Table, and if I was feeling a little hungry around lunchtime, I would just turn up at his rooms, and then we would wander across the quad together for some comforting nursery food in the college dining room. One day I found myself sitting in the Radcliffe Camera, a monumental circular library loosely modeled on the Pantheon, struggling with the bloodthirsty but still amazingly dull doings of some medieval king, when I started daydreaming about steak-and-kidney pie and rhubarb crumble. I looked at my watch, I looked at the cute guy across from me, I gazed out the window, and finally I gave up. It was almost one o'clock. I abandoned King Ethelred the Unready, son of King Edgar and Queen Elfthryth, husband of Queen Elfgifu, to his endless tribulations with the Vikings, and decided to continue my research into early English history at New College. I walked through the medieval gateway, built in 1379, during the reign of Richard II, passed the cloister where the monks used to hang about until Henry VIII got rid of them—I've always been a great believer in history by osmosis—climbed up an oak staircase (circa 1750), and knocked on Freddie's door.

My stepfather was not pleased to see me. Not at all pleased. He stood there, looking wild-eyed and completely mad, blocking the doorway, and finally mumbled something about this not being "an ideal moment." Apparently. A little perplexed, I backed away and went down the staircase again, crossed the quad, and, as I was going out through the fourteenth-century gateway, bumped into a reincarnation of Queen Nefertiti. Tiny, with inky black hair, flawless cappuccino skin, bitter-chocolate sloe eyes, this exotic vision was dressed, somewhat incongruously, in a childlike flower-sprigged cotton dress with a high waist and little puff sleeves. It was as if the Egyptian queen had decided to have a little something run up by Jane Austen's dressmaker. And since I spent so much time at grown-up parties with my parents, I knew exactly who she was. Her name was Vanessa, and she was married to Nigel Lawson (always called "Pig Lawson" by my mother, on account of his Tory politics and his generously proportioned body), who was at the time editor of the *Spectator* magazine. Surprised to see her in Oxford, I suggested that as she happened to have wandered into New College, she should really go call on Freddie, and spent some time explaining to her precisely where his rooms were. She listened patiently, smiled sweetly—God, she was beautiful—and did just that.

The next time I was in London I quite innocently told my mother about the encounter, and she narrowed her eyes, and said, "Oh, really." We both agreed Vanessa must be having an affair with somebody in Oxford. I imagined some handsome Byronic young don, but Mummy came to a different conclusion.

Oxford

Serena and i shared a black leather skirt so abbreviated that the belt—with its big round brass buckle—actually occupied half its "length." The skirt belonged to her, but since we had ended up in rooms right next door to each other, she kindly allowed me to borrow it whenever I liked. And Serena, of course, had reciprocal membership of my wardrobe. Saint Hilda's, like all the women's colleges at Oxford, was ugly and Victorian and, we naturally assumed, full of lesbians intent on getting firsts in chemistry or quite possibly geography. The best things about it were that the Cherwell meandered past the bottom of the garden, and that it was just across the bridge from Magdalen College, so you never felt as if you were stuck in some distant, dank nunnery in north Oxford. The only other good thing was that most of my tutors were in other colleges, so I was hardly ever there.

But back to Serena's skirt. A few days after my mother dumped me in Oxford—a hit-and-run job with no lingering, which was just fine with both of us—Freddie invited me to dinner at New College. Clearly I would have to wear our skirt. Early that evening I carefully laid out my clothes on the bed: first the horizontal strip of leather, then a black chiffon blouse (too diaphanous for a bra), black fishnet tights, and there—lying on the floor like two fearsome dead snakes— the thigh-high suede boots I had gotten at Biba's the week before. In keeping with the witchy hooker theme, I outlined my eyes in kohl, smudged neutral concealer over my lips, and put on the long black academic gown that had come as part of the deal (along with fifty pounds a year) with the Acne Scholarship in Modern History.

I walked out through the gates of Saint Hilda's (locked every night at eleven thirty), crossed the bridge, my gown billowing out behind me like the sinister black sail of some pirate ship, and headed up the High Street. Turning right onto New College Lane, I passed the crenellated remnants of the ancient city walls and presented myself to the porter at the lodge, who didn't even blink at my outfit. And neither did Freddie—maybe the gown had managed to hide the worst of it. Or, far more likely, he just didn't notice. First we stood around in a gloomy paneled room with his ancient colleagues—most of them were probably about my age now— savoring a glass of sweet viscous sherry, and then it was time to form a procession, led by the warden, and slowly walk up the length of the medieval dining hall to dinner. Already seated at their long wooden tables, the rows of undergraduates turned to watch us, and they at least (or, so I imagined in my awful vanity) appreciated the unreconstructed tartiness of my getup. Never mind Freddie and the blind old fool in the lodge; *they* were the men I had dressed for.

Sandwiched between the Regius Professor of Greek and some physicist, or maybe it was the Reader in Divinity and a mathematician, or the bursar and a geologist, when grace was said I thanked God, from the bottom of my heart, for the munificence of the New College wine cellar. The table glittered with elaborate silver candelabra, plates, saltcellars, a grisly depiction of hounds tearing apart a stag, and other shiny loot acquired over the college's six-hundred-year history. The chef's repertoire was similarly indebted to the past. Potted shrimps on toast or smoked trout, followed by hunks of beef, legs of lamb, or—when in season—venison, grouse, and pheasant, accompanied by elderly boiled vegetables. Dessert came next, maybe lemon posset or trifle, or something heavy and steamed, like bread-and-butter pudding served with cream so thick you needed a spoon to winch it out of the jug. After that, cheese: Stilton, Caerphilly, or cheddar (nothing exotic or foreign, thank you very much) with crisp stalks of celery and slightly stale biscuits (never bread) that lived inside several small ornate silver drums.

The finale was always a savory. Just when you thought dinner must be over, some bizarrely named dish would appear, like Scotch woodcock (toast smeared with Gentleman's Relish, topped with scrambled eggs) or Angels on Horseback (bacon rolled around an oyster) or Devils on Horseback (same idea, with a prune instead of an oyster). Whatever made the

English think it is a good idea to serve cheese and a strange canapé *after* dessert? Must be something to do with putting the French—and their misconceived notion of ending a meal with fruit or something sweet— in their place. Angels, devils, or woodcocks all gobbled up, the warden would then lead us out of the hall into another dimly lit paneled room where a bottle of spectacularly old port made its courtly way—*always* clockwise, *never* counterclockwise, or was it the opposite?—around the table. Nuts, chocolates, coffee, and maybe just one more go-round of the port, and it was time for me to thank my hosts and make my mildly drunken way back past Magdalen, across the bridge, and into my — conveniently located—convent, before the gates clanged shut.

WHEN I GOT TO Oxford I knew only three people: Freddie, Serena, and the man who was to become the first great love of my life. Martin Amis and I had met the year before in London. No, it wasn't at some sexy drug-infused party in Chelsea, nor was it at a throbbing down-and-dirty disco, nor at a chic dinner party with some brilliant mutual friends: The embarrassing truth is that we were set up on a playdate by our parents. As I recall, Jane, Martin's stepmother, and my mother met when they were both on some television talk show, yammering away at each other from different ends of the political spectrum. In the green room afterward— on-air disagreements forgiven—they discovered they had kids about the same age, and thought it might be fun if we could meet. They were right. It turned out to be much more fun than they could possibly have imagined. Sometimes Martin and I had dinner at the house in Maida Vale that Jane shared with his dad, Kingsley, and sometimes we went out on decorous dates to the movies, usually followed by a boiling-hot curry at some Indian dive, and then he would take me home in a taxi. I'm not sure we ever kissed, but if we did I have forgotten, so it amounts to the same thing. Maybe he didn't want to? And I would have been the first to understand that. Still trapped inside my Mademoiselle Lévi-Strauss persona, convinced of my own unattractiveness, with zero experience of men, I knew all I had to offer was that I wasn't totally stupid, and could sometimes be quite funny. He, on the other hand, was *very* funny and *very* clever. I was always a sucker for that particular combo—maybe it reminded me of home—he made me laugh and told me things I didn't know. In my prelapsarian state, undistracted by lust and still innocent of the heavenly havoc it causes, I was free just to giggle and chat with the most fascinating man I had ever met.

Our favorite movie theater was the Curzon in Mayfair. It was like going to a fancy private screening room, not that I'd ever been anywhere near one. But Martin had, so I felt I knew. Underground and tiny, it was a plush cave with thick carpets and squashy armchairs that tipped way back—and even more decadently the cave also served real drinks. Off to one side was a cocktail bar, covered in quilted black fake leather, the bottles reflected in a pink-tinted mirror, like miniature skyscrapers outlined against the dawn sky. Never had I been anywhere quite so slick with anybody quite so cool. It wasn't just the way he looked—the skintight black velvet pants, the snakeskin boots, the gossamer shirts covered in swirling jungle flowers, with huge rounded collars and cuffs so long they must have had at least six buttons—it was everything about him. His irony, his wit, the sardonic throwaway remarks that never missed, his wholly original and brilliant vocabulary, his unsentimental view of the world and . . . his sweetness. The way he didn't smile too much—could have been the disastrous teeth, not that I ever noticed anything wrong with them—but loved to laugh, and always extracted the maximum humor from the grisliest situations. The grislier the better, because that made it so much funnier. Then there was his face. The wide mouth, shaped like a crinkle-cut chip (a description he borrowed from me and later used in one of his novels), his infinitely intelligent eyes, the sultry hint of a monobrow. The way his hair was strictly maintained at a permanent five-day degree of dirtiness; the grease making it easier to arrange in an artfully disheveled style. (It was a complicated process that involved a daily wetting, only very occasionally allowing a thimbleful of diluted shampoo anywhere near it.) After a month or two—or was it longer?—I disappeared to Paris, then to the house in France, and didn't miss him at all. In fact I don't think I ever thought about him again until the day I arrived in Oxford.

He was just as I remembered him, but something had changed, and I fell inexplicably, deliriously, desperately, irrevocably, shamelessly, hopelessly in love. Only the most awful clichés could possibly do justice to the way I felt. After the fall my life became a pathetic parody of all the mediocre lyrics of every mediocre pop song ever written. He was always on my mind, he was just too good to be true, I couldn't take my eyes off of him, and I never wanted to let him go. And amazingly it seemed that this guy was in love with me.

In addition to the sexy French kidney business in Serge Gainsbourg's song, Martin introduced me to all kinds of other exciting things I'd only dreamed of. Stuff any normal teenager would have yawned at, like smoking, hanging around in his rooms listening to loud music (T. Rex and Led Zeppelin), getting drunk (on Special Brew, a spectacularly unpleasant beer, whose only virtue was that it made you *very* drunk), and, most daring of all, sleeping over in his tiny single bed. Having a girl in your room after the gate was locked at night was against the college rules (how dull kids' sex lives must be in coed colleges today) but, disappointingly, I never heard of anybody actually being punished for this primal sin. By 1969 the old-fart university busybodies must have realized the game was up, the tide had turned, we had taken over the world, and youth ruled. Or something along those lines. Then again, maybe they were wiser than we knew and just could not have cared less. Well, if they didn't mind sex, what about drugs? They must have given up on that, too, because I never knew anybody who got into trouble over them either. However, drugs were another subject where I had a lot of catching up to do. A slack student, I wasn't especially interested, being quite content with my Special Brew, the odd bottle of vintage port Freddie gave me, and the pretty pink—and very cheap and sweet—Mateus rosé that Martin favored whenever we went to a restaurant. He told me it went particularly well with Indian food, and who was I to disagree? Still, drugs were cool, so whether I wanted to or not, I knew I'd have to get serious about them at some point.

ONE BALMY SUMMER'S DAY we were lolling about in the garden at Exeter College, enjoying a refreshing cup of tea, when Martin's friend Adam loped across the lawn to join us. Even though he was an undergraduate, Adam seemed much more grown-up, partly on account of his age—he was about five years older than we were—and partly because he exuded a sexy, knowing air of world-weariness. He'd been around, he'd *lived*—I think he might even have been to India or Afghanistan on a Harley, or perhaps in a Land Rover. He looked like Jim Morrison, with sideburns the size of small Mason Pearson hairbrushes, smelled of pepper, and I couldn't begin to imagine how many women he must have had. Adam was Martin's best friend—they dressed like twins in the same velvet "strides," cobra-skin boots, diaphanous shirts, tightly fitted velvet jackets, except Adam liked to complete his ensemble with long wispy scarves or one of those chicken-wire Arafat numbers. (Martin and I despised scarves—why I have no idea.) Sometimes Adam would exaggerate or add a little extra embroidery to the truth, but you always knew when he was about to do this because he'd preface the whopper with "virtually," so that was okay.

Adam sat down on the grass and asked us if we'd like to have some fun. I thought I was already having more fun than I'd ever had in my entire life, but apparently I was mistaken. Adam had something in his pocket— he reached in and produced three little cubes, wrapped in silver foil—that was guaranteed to blow our minds. Did we ask what they were? Where he'd gotten them, or what they might do to our brains, apart from blowing them apart? No, we did not. That would not have been cool. Even I knew that. The fate of my teacup was the first clue that the sugar cubes had started to work their special magic. I was standing up, my saucer a long way away below me—it felt like miles—on the grass, so I just dropped the cup onto it. They both broke. Now, that wasn't right, Martin told me gently; people might think I was on drugs. Might be best if we split. A picnic was what was called for in a situation like this. Christ, why hadn't we thought of it before? Special Brew, sausage rolls, Scotch eggs—what more could we possibly want? Music. Can't have a picnic without music. Christ, we weren't thinking straight. Adam and Martin had the records, and I had a small portable, plastic record player—powder blue, I think— that my father had given me for Christmas.

While we had been having our tea the sidewalk on the High Street had, rather extravagantly, been resurfaced with diamonds. Embedded in the concrete, they flashed and sparkled in the sunlight just like Marie Antoinette's infamous necklace, which had been the beginning of her end. Commissioned by Louis XV for his mistress Madame du Barry, the *rivière* became the dazzling centerpiece of a scandal that destroyed the tragic Austrian queen's reputation and . . . I was busy pointing all this out to a bewildered passerby when Martin took me firmly by the arm and nearly pushed us both under an oncoming bus. Christ Church meadows: That was the place we needed to be. Cows, clover, voles, dandelions, rabbits, Queen Anne's lace, mice, birds, cowslips, deer, buttercups, ants, trees, fish swimming about in the river, moles burrowing around under the ground—nature in all its Wordsworthian glory. Martin could recite poetry to me, and I could tell him lots and lots more about poor Marie Antoinette.

Led Zeppelin, Special Brew, cigarettes—bliss was it to be sprawled on the grass (we'd forgotten to bring a blanket), flies buzzing around my sweaty face, but to be stoned, and in love, was total ecstasy. The fact that I had departed this world and would never see any of my family ever again was not a problem. That's just the way it was. Like Alice—it had to be of cosmic significance that we were within sight of Charles Dodgson's college—I'd tumbled into another universe and was quite comfortable there.

Martin and Adam were not so happy. They were not country people and had no idea how to appreciate flora and fauna the way I—especially in my new state—did, and after a while (minutes, hours, days?) they told me it was time to go. Fortunately there wasn't much packing up to be done, since we'd eaten all the Scotch eggs and sausage rolls and had thrown the Special Brew bottles behind a bush. Adam shoved the records into a plastic bag, and Martin picked up my record player. Oddly enough, during our picnic it had been transformed into the kind of vanity case—a mirror embedded inside the top, elastic pouches to hold miniature plastic bottles—that tarts carried their cosmetics around in. He looked like a complete fool. A poofter with a handbag, a slut with her bag of tricks, a transvestite swinging his/her purse around—I couldn't stop laughing. Martin turned round and asked me what was so fucking funny, and— tears streaming down my face and about to wet my pants—I told him. The vanity case had to go. Get rid of it. Chuck it in the river. Now. Which was the end of any music in my sad little room at Saint Hilda's.

I KNEW MY MOTHER would love Martin—clever, funny with a famous name, he was a triple plus. Freddie liked anybody who made me happy and—as befitted the tolerant rational person he knew himself to be—was prepared to give Martin the benefit of the doubt and overlook his dad's abhorrent, lower-middle-class (yes, Freddie was a snob), rabidly right-wing political views. Apart from me, Freddie and my new boyfriend didn't have a whole lot in common, but they used to play gladiatorial chess, and occasionally Martin would give Freddie a ride in his car so he could watch his favorite team play football. Here's his description of my stepfather's approach to puzzling objects—like ashtrays:

> Twenty years ago I drove the late A. J. Ayer to White Hart Lane to support Tottenham Hotspur. On the way Ayer smoked three cigarettes. For his first butt he disdained, or did not see, the obvious—and butt-infested—ashtray, favoring the naked tape-deck with the fiery remains of his Player. (The tape-recorder itself had been stolen, true, but the empty console had the word PHILIPS clearly stamped on it.) His second butt he squeezed into the base of the hand brake, his third he ground out on the speedometer. The high point came with his third spent match, which, with incredible skill, he balanced on the bare ignition key, where it wobbled for at least three seconds before dropping inexorably to the floor.

The first time I slept with Martin at home, he left in the middle of the night—maybe we thought it might be best if he met my parents over the dinner, rather than the breakfast, table—and the next morning my mother had some advice for me. An enlightened parent, she didn't care whom I slept with or where (she never tired of talking about the married, fascist, rapist hairdresser) but she certainly didn't want me getting pregnant, and wouldn't it be a good idea if I went and saw our friend Dr. Slattery? This struck me as a bit odd, since she had never before shown the slightest interest in helping me unravel the mysteries of sex, or the female body.

But I still wish that my mother had thought to tell me what you are supposed to do when you wake up for the first time in a pool of blood and are due to spend the day at some fancy country club, frolicking in a swimming pool, with a school friend and her very stuffy parents. It was not a pretty sight. Even less lovely was the backseat of their Jaguar, after they had dropped me at home. Why would you let that happen to your daughter? It must have had something to do with her own mother's neglect, and the way she had learned early on to look out for herself, because nobody else was going to do it for you. She had gone to the drugstore alone, at twelve, to buy a box of Kotex, so why shouldn't I? As far as Dr. Slattery went I told her not to worry: It had already been taken care of.

FOR CHRISTMAS THE YEAR I went up to Oxford my father gave me a present that was even more fun, and considerably more expensive, than the now-drowned record player. A great believer in the virtue of wholesome outdoor activity (I was never allowed to go to the movies if the sun was shining), he decided to treat me to a skiing vacation in Switzerland. A nice, well-brought-up young man I knew was organizing a chalet party in Zermatt, with some other nice, well-brought-up young people, and invited me to join them. It seemed like a perfectly reasonable idea at the time. How was I to know that it would become totally unreasonable—no, totally abhorrent—within the space of a few months? Of course I had to go, my father had already paid for it, and it was only for a week, and I couldn't let my friend down, but every time I thought of leaving Martin I would start to cry.

I went to sleep crying the night before I was due to go, I cried in my sleep, I woke up crying, I cried in his car on the way to the airport, and we were both in tears by the time we parted at the gate. The nice young people soon realized that they had a deeply disturbed person on their hands. A couple of the girls, softhearted debs with concerned, blinking eyes and furrowed brows, clucked around offering me hankies and sweets, telling me they knew *just* how I felt (how could they possibly? how could *anyone?*). The men busied themselves organizing tickets, being bossy to hapless brown porters, hauling clanking piles of skis about, and steered well clear of the loony. Lost in grief, I huddled in my seat on the plane and cried some more. Things did not improve once we arrived at our cozy chalet. I kept the softhearted deb who was sharing my room awake all night with my sobbing, refused to go skiing, and sat in the chalet crying. The next day I called Martin and said I was coming home, and started to pack, dizzy with joy. When my friends returned from their fun-packed day on the slopes, the loony was dancing about, laughing. The men looked nervous, the girls genuinely relieved, and when I told them I'd be flying back to London in the morning, they all looked extremely happy.

There he was at the airport, standing at the gate; I ran into his outstretched arms and burst into tears. I told him I was never *ever* going to leave him again, and I never did. We drove straight back to Kingsley and Jane's sprawling house in north London, where we holed up in unlawful, unmarried bliss for the next couple of weeks. Martin once described Lemmons, as the house was called, as "a citadel of riotous solvency." And that it was. The marble-shelved larder, the size of a small kitchen, looked like a corner of Harrods Food Hall, stuffed with whole hams, pork pies, homemade jams, sausages, Stilton in pottery jars, rounds of cheddar, *confit de canard, pâté en croûte,* and row upon row of chutneys, pickled onions, and gherkins. These last three items had to be stocked in industrial quantities because Kingsley ate them with everything. Jane was a truly gifted cook, but whatever she made—ethereal blanquette de veau, sublime risotto with wild mushrooms, juicy *magret de canard,* spicy Sicilian bouillabaisse—Kingsley's plate would always be piled high with his palate-annihilating pickles. In addition to the larder, the freezer was packed full of frozen delights—haunches of venison, more kinds of ice cream than Howard Johnson's (served with heavy cream and liqueurs)— and an enormous cupboard off the kitchen was similarly stocked with an array of drinks that would have put the bar at the Curzon cinema to shame.

Like my mother, Jane was married to a man who did nothing but sit in his study all day long and scribble. And like my mother, as the years passed, she became increasingly angry with the same man she had once been crazily in love with. Kingsley (like Freddie) had never learned to drive, so Jane was the chauffeur, housekeeper, chef, gardener, and household accountant; and once she had taken care of all of that, she too sat down to scribble, producing a series of very good novels and short stories. But on Sunday mornings, when it came down to the choice between standing at the kitchen sink peeling potatoes with Jane, or going to the pub and getting pissed on laughter and alcohol with Martin and Kingsley, I went with the boys.

Nearly forty years later I still feel ashamed, but what else was a spoiled and selfish twenty-year-old to do? The trouble was that there were just too many potatoes to be peeled, because the house was constantly full of people, which was what made it so much fun. In addition to the permanent ménage—Jane's brother, Colin, always called "Monkey"; Sargie, a painter; and Jane's desiccated mother, who rarely (thank Christ) left her room—there were endless weekend guests. Kingsley and Jane loved to entertain in the true meaning of that word. It went way beyond the delicious profligacy of her cooking and his skills with the corkscrew; it was about sitting down at a huge round table and knowing that whatever else happened, the next few hours were absolutely guaranteed to be *entertaining*. It was just like being at home, only better—much better—because I was with Martin. We spent the rest of the Christmas vacation in the "citadel of riotous solvency," recovering from the "hell of Zermatt" (what our new friend Christopher Hitchens would call a "tumbrel" remark, as in the cart that dragged poor misunderstood Marie Antoinette to the guillotine) until it was time to go back to Oxford.

L'Été

THAT SUMMER MARTIN AND I WENT to stay with Serena in Polly's castle in Italy. About fifty miles north of Rome, Rocca Sinibalda had belonged to Polly's extraordinary mother, Caresse Crosby, who had converted it into an "artist's colony" (like many rebellious Americans with generous trust funds who fled to Europe between the wars, Caresse had been *mad* about artists), and now that her mother was dead, it was Polly's. Actually "extraordinary" does not even begin to do justice to the wild decadence—and ultimate tragedy—of Harry and Caresse Crosby's life together. They had both been born into haute Boston society—van Rensselaers, Lowells, Peabodys—but when they fell in love they knew it was their destiny to run away, to leave behind that repressed, dreary, philistine world forever.

Paris was where they belonged. What did it matter that Caresse was already married with two children, and that their families were horrified? In Paris, Harry would be liberated, and his true genius as a poet would finally be realized. They would live in a *hôtel particulier* on the rue de l'Université, with their whippets, Narcisse and Clytorisse, where they would entertain other artists of his caliber, like James Joyce, D. H. Lawrence, Hart Crane, and Ezra Pound. They might even start a small press and publish their new friends' work on handwoven paper, with special inks from Japan and illustrations by Cocteau or perhaps Picasso. It was pure madness. And yet some part of the dream came true. The Black Sun Press *did* publish all those writers and artists (as well as Proust), the books *were* exquisite, and the Crosbys' parties were legendary. The genius thing was less easily acquired—no matter how impressive the account at J. P. Morgan.

Although Harry was serious about his poetry, and knew that a great talent should never be squandered, there were just too many distractions—the bar at the Ritz, cocaine, a pretty girl walking down the rue de Rivoli, opium, an impromptu expedition to Venice, absinthe. Like Lord Henry in *The Picture of Dorian Gray*, he believed it was imperative to give in to temptation, otherwise an artistic soul would surely atrophy for lack of stimulation. Happily that was never Harry's problem. The opium was supposed to unleash his imagination—just as it had done for Coleridge and Baudelaire—but as De Quincey pointed out, "If a man whose talk is of oxen, should become an opium eater, the probability is that (if he's not too dull to dream at all)—he will dream of oxen." Harry's dreams and poetry unfortunately never transcended their mad but still oxlike nature. Yet when it came to a night out on the town, there was nobody more inspiring than Harry Crosby. Every summer in Paris, when the art schools packed up for the year, the students and anybody else who was around would celebrate at a huge, bacchanalian party called the Four Arts Ball. In 1926 the theme was the Inca, and Harry came up with one of his typically brilliant ideas. He rubbed red ocher all over his body and, dressed only in a loincloth, wearing three dead pigeons around his neck, he set off with his beautiful wife, Caresse—topless, in a turquoise wig— for the ball.

In 1929 Harry—comparing himself to Icarus—took up flying, which rather satisfyingly combined his twin obsessions with death and the sun. He was punishing his body with oxlike quantities of drugs and alcohol, his fragile grasp on reality became increasingly frayed, and his lifelong fixation with suicide began to take over. He started to look around for a woman who loved him enough to follow him to "the undiscover'd country from whose bourn no traveller returns." He found her in the newly married Josephine Bigelow. (Caresse had already declined to jump from the twenty-seventh floor of the Savoy-Plaza Hotel in New York with him.) The day after his wife's refusal he received a note from his mistress, which ended with the words "Death is *our* marriage." On December 10 he borrowed a friend's apartment in the Hotel des Artistes on West Sixty-seventh Street, where he shot Josephine and then—a couple of hours later—turned the gun on himself. The revolver had a golden sun engraved on its handle.

Devastated, Caresse published various posthumous editions of Harry's oeuvre and eventually moved to Italy, where she died forty-one years later. Which is how Martin and I came to be in a pinball arcade in Rome in the summer of 1970. Unencumbered by anything as dull as a guidebook, or a single word of Italian, or any desire to waste our time gawking at Roman ruins or the Vatican, we headed straight for the Eternal City's tawdry underbelly. Billiards, pinball, cocktails, bar football—what more could we have asked of the one day we had in Rome? Enchanted by our degeneracy—it felt like going to a dirty movie on a sunny day—I eagerly followed my guide into this exciting new world. The improbable combination of dazzling intellect and a profound *nostalgie de la boue*—he could have been Harry Crosby, but with more brains and less craziness—has always been one of Martin's most endearing, and enduring, characteristics. And one that I quite naturally found irresistible.

Rocca Sinibalda—the setting for Martin's most recent novel, *The Pregnant Widow*, in which the hero, Keith (Martin), spends the summer with his pots-and-pans girlfriend, Lily (me), "34-24-34," and, quite understandably, lusts after her tall and lubricious friend Scheherazade, "37-23-33" (Serena)—grew straight up out of the rock like some monstrous medieval prison. This is how he describes it:

> So here was the castle, its battlements kept aloft on the shoulders of the four fat-girthed giants, the four towers, the four terraces, the circular ballroom (with its orbital staircase), the domed pentagonal library, the salon with its six sets of windows, the baronial banqueting hall at the far end of the implausibly and impractically long corridor from the barnyard-sized kitchen, all the antechambers which receded, like facing mirrors, into a repetitive infinity. Above was the apartment (where Oona [Polly] spent almost all her time); below was the dungeon floor, half submerged in the foundational soil, and giving off the thinnest mist of what smelled to Keith like cold sweat.

Way, way down below, the village curled around the base of its massive windowless walls, and the only approach was up a steep, narrow ramp that really should have had a rusty portcullis at the top, but didn't. The gate opened onto a cobbled courtyard, with four Rapunzel towers, and in the main building, an endless enfilade of enormous frescoed rooms culminated in a terrace that jutted out, like the prow of a ship, where we would sit at dusk and watch the swallows swirling around in the sky beneath us. When Caresse had bought the castle it apparently came complete with a title—Principessa—and staying there, I kept thinking of my mother's favorite line in the hymn "All Things Bright and Beautiful"— "the rich man in his castle, the poor man at his gate." "Jesus Christ, no wonder the English can't escape their goddamn class system, if they sing songs like that." Yet she herself had never been averse to the odd weekend in a castle. It was extremely confusing. So much simpler to be like Polly, who knew precisely on which side of the moat she belonged. But since Martin and I would soon be huddled within the all-too-genuine peasant walls of La Migoua, surely a girl was allowed a few days of innocent fun in this palatial citadel?

A few days stretched into more than a week, and then it was back to Rome for more pinball before catching a creaky, sweaty train for Toulon. At La Migoua, instead of our romantic bedroom in one of the Rapunzel towers, Martin and I occupied a corner of Freddie's study. The ground-floor window gave us a panoramic view of Francette's terrace, where she took her breakfast—coffee, Gauloise, and lots of shouting at Sorgue—and the plywood door, which had never closed properly, was all that separated us from the raucous early-morning and late-night chaos of the kitchen. Never lazy when it came to his work, Freddie would read Nick a rousing chapter of Lucky Luke—"Dad, I *told* you to talk in English"—around seven, and then liked to be at his desk tackling the foundations of empirical knowledge no later than eight thirty. Sexy, semi-somnolent lingering in bed was not an option. In any case we had to get ready to go to Bikini Beach.

At Rocca Sinibalda we had been a long way from the Mediterranean, so the question of Martin's seaside wardrobe had not arisen. Used to seeing him in his ubiquitous velvet "strides," diaphanous shirts, and snakeskin boots—or naked—I had never really thought what he'd wear while lounging on one of Monsieur Maurice's blue-and-white-striped "mistresses." Since it was much too hot for velvet and Martin was way too cool for sneakers, here's what he came up with: snug little pale blue shorts, a chiffon flower-patterned shirt, unbuttoned, and the snakeskin boots, unzipped and flapping about to let the breezes in. Heaven. Apart, that is, from the boiling, red Mount Etna of a "big boy" (as he called them) suppurating on the side of his nose; but I can't imagine that was what set Freddie off. Normally the most mild mannered of men, he exploded when he saw Martin standing in the kitchen: "You cannot possibly go out dressed like *that*. That is *not* what one wears to the beach, or anywhere else, for that matter!"

A little odd coming from somebody whose own anything-but-snug pale blue underpants were, at that very moment, extending a good three inches from the top and bottom of his "shorts." Maybe he was just fed up with us sleeping in his study. Martin ignored the outburst and, declining to debate the Wykeham Professor of Logic on the topic of beachwear, we climbed into the back of the car, along with Nick and his inflatable croco-dile, a plastic bag full of buckets and spades, an air mattress, some filthy towels, and the picnic basket.

Even though the French refused to come around to the notion of col-lecting garbage—the dreaded Bandol dump was still an inescapable part of our lives—they were very good at delivering letters. Every morning, you could hear the postman down in the valley, approaching on his fart-ing motorized bike, and by the time he rounded the corner we would all be out on the terrace hopping about with excitement. Since we had no telephone, letters were our only link to the outside world. (Being French, Francette had, through her connections at *la mairie*, managed to get a telephone installed in her vertical shed, but we were allowed to use it only in the most extreme emergencies.) That summer I noticed that Freddie was unusually happy to see Monsieur le Facteur, greeting him by name, and he even assumed the role of Monsieur's assistant, handing out the let-ters with his very own hands. It was quite touching to watch him wrestle with the intractable elastic bands on the package of mail, and then deliver each envelope to its recipient with a cheery smile on his face. He must have decided that this was the one household task that he could master.

The night after the beach-wardrobe assault, Freddie came up with a new plan of attack and challenged Martin to a game of chess. Dinner was over, the marble kitchen table had been cleared—except for the ashtrays and wine bottles—and the chessboard was brought out. Neither of the players was smiling. They each lit another cigarette, filled their wine-glasses, and settled down to plot how best to kill the man on the other side of the table. Did I understand the moves? Of course not. But I could see very clearly what was going on. Freddie reached nervously for his silver chain, the one he twiddled whenever his ferocious concentration went into overdrive, and Martin's right hand started shaking with an almost imperceptible tremor. Their eyes never left the board. As I bustled about—doing the dishes, emptying ashtrays—the only sounds I heard were an occasional groan, or yelp of victory, and whichever one of them had just lost would say in a perfectly reasonable voice, "I think we should have one more game, don't you?" How could the winner refuse? And then the whole murderous testosterone-fueled battle would begin all over again. I have no recollection of how many games they played, or which of them walked away triumphant in the end. But I suspect they were both convinced that they had put the arrogant little shit/vain old geezer in his place, and that the vexed question of who was the grand master had been settled in an entirely satisfactory manner.

Thirty years later Martin found himself sitting in a pub called the "Jeremy Bentham," while his father lay dying in a nearby hospital, and his thoughts naturally turned to Freddie. This is what he wrote about playing chess with him:

> A. J. Ayer was the stepfather of my second great love: the dedicatee of my first novel. He used to play chess with me. . . . And he almost always won. Your only hope was to make it into the endgame with your knights intact. Then you could get him so frazzled by proliferating possibilities that he would disgustedly resign or even throw the whole set in the air.

UNTIL I MET MARTIN I thought that Freddie was the most intellectually—and sexually—competitive man on earth. Apparently I had been mistaken. A bargain-basement shrink might conclude that the sex part is related to the humiliating and terrifying idea that you aren't—and never will be—attractive enough to persuade anyone to go to bed with you. If this notion gets you in its pernicious grip early enough in life, and then if you wake up one day (I suspect that this either happens quite suddenly—or never) to discover, miraculously, that lots of people want to do just that, is it any wonder that you can get a bit carried away? At least that was what happened to me. And once it did I finally understood that long ladderlike list of ladies' initials I had discovered on Freddie's desk so many years before. (As far as I know, Martin's long ladderlike list is safely locked up inside his head, where such things should remain.)

All of which brings me back to Freddie's new job as an assistant postman. One evening that summer, I was in the kitchen enjoying a well-deserved glass of rosé while starting on dinner. I hacked the heads off some mackerel we had bought in the market that morning, slit them open, and yanked the slimy entrails out of their silvery bellies. I chopped up garlic, parsley, and fennel; shoved them inside the corpses; sprinkled them with olive oil, sea salt, and pepper, and laid their bodies to rest inside a nice hot oven. I wrapped the fishy remains in some newspaper, took it out to the shed where the hateful dustbins lived, and was about to throw it on top of a pyramid of moldy artichoke leaves, when I stopped. There teetering on the summit were two pieces of blue paper. If I hadn't been me I would have dumped the mackerel innards, put the lid back, and gotten on with cooking dinner. But I was born evil, so instead I joined the two halves of the paper together and started to read a letter that I should never, ever have picked up. Seemingly written in haste, the words tumbled over one another in their desire to describe the upheaval inside the writer's heart, and every detail of the lovers' last meeting. Intimate, thrilling, pornographic, touching—it was the kind of letter you would want to snatch right out of any postman's hand.

I looked at the signature—a scrawled V. Vanessa. Queen Nefertiti in her Jane Austen muslin dress with the little puff sleeves, whom I had run into that day crossing the quad in New College. Wicked old Freddie, happy old Freddie, clever old Freddie, but old—at sixty—he undoubtedly was. Imagine being in love at *that* age! Freddie never gave up his lifelong dance of romance with women, which was yet another reason why I loved him so much. And yet, as I tore the letter up and shoved the minuscule bits deep inside the mackerel mess, I *did* have to wonder what exactly he had learned in MI6. Weren't you supposed to burn or better still eat incriminating pieces of paper, to prevent the Gestapo's getting their evil hands on them? And talking of the Gestapo, did Freddie never stop to think about the blitzkrieg from hell that would have been unleashed if his wife, instead of his forgiving stepdaughter, had taken out the garbage that night?

Apparently not. Silly old Freddie. *Extremely* lucky old Freddie.

~

WHEN WE GOT BACK TO Oxford that fall, Martin moved with Adam and Kevin, another college friend, into a rose-covered cottage beside a trout-filled stream in a picturesque Cotswold village, about twenty-five miles outside Oxford. He had written to Jane earlier in the year, "The prices are around 12 pounds . . . I'm sharing with two other boys (I can't look far enough ahead about Gully) so that's about 4 pounds each on rent." We had never talked about my joining them, so I stayed in Saint Hilda's and went out to the Old Forge on the weekends and any night in the week when I didn't have an early tutorial in the morning. But quite naturally I dreamed of the day when Martin would finally come to his senses and beg me to come and live with him. (Why is it that when girls fall in love their thoughts—almost inevitably and usually unwisely—become consumed with visions of geraniums on kitchen windowsills and gleaming copper pots and pans?) The house had two big bedrooms upstairs overlooking the garden and the babbling brook, and a small, dark airless one under the stairs. Since Martin and Adam obviously needed to entertain ladies in their rooms and Kevin had no girlfriend, it seemed only fair that he should live in the closet under the stairs. Or at least that's what happened, and Kevin didn't argue. In fact Adam no longer had any ladies to entertain because over the summer he had gotten married (how grown-up! well, not very, as it turned out) to a bossy, histrionic, but presumably sexy woman named Angela. It did not take long for the Old Forge to turn into a madhouse.

The insanity culminated in one unforgettable weekend. I guess drugs must have been involved, sex certainly was, and rock and roll was an entirely innocent bystander. It all started on the Friday when Kevin had become a tad agitated after he'd found some girl he was—unrequitedly and unrealistically—in love with in bed with Martin's best friend, Rob. Here's how Martin described what Kevin did next in a letter to Jane,

Saturday: prolonged loony behavior (stealing my car for the afternoon, spending all his money) followed by a suicide bid (some sleeping pills) us trying to make him sick and keep him awake, and then an 80 mph dash to the Radcliffe [hospital] with me at the wheel. He seemed to be

O.K. and Sunday he returned while only Gully and Angela were here, a scuffle ensued (with Angela) and after this becoming scene she called the police. . . . He went to the local loony bin (where he has since had a *fit*) and Angela has gone to the London Clinic.

He went on to add, "I hope Gully can come soon and live here which would be better in every imaginable way."

So, thanks to Kevin and his opportune fit, my dreams came true and I moved into the madhouse.

ALTHOUGH STILL DEEPLY MIRED in the outrageous doings of my old friends the Tudors and Stuarts, I was allowed some choice when it came to European history, and naturally gravitated toward France and a course taught by Theodore Zeldin, at Saint Antony's College. How could I ever forget that night in Paris with Raymond Carr when I had stood there, not daring to speak, on that shady terrace between Claude Lévi-Strauss and Professor Zeldin, who had looked just like one of the glass-eyed stuffed owls in the window of Deyrolle et Fils? And now I was being invited to study the social fabric of the Third Republic—so different in every way from the dreary litany of great men that Monsieur le Professeur at the Sorbonne had droned on about—with this paragon.

Between Martin and the Owl, I was the luckiest girl in the whole of Oxford.

In his study at the top of a gloomy Victorian house in north Oxford, Theodore guided us through *Swann's Way*, illuminating Proust's inimitable words with asides on the real people from whom the author had taken the disparate strands that went into the creation of his characters. We looked at photographic portraits by Paul Nadar and thought we detected in Charles Haas's birdlike features, slightly quizzical expression, and upturned mustache, clues to Swann himself. When Proust wrote of Elstir's paintings, "The rare moments in which we see nature as she is, poetically, were those from which his work was created," we knew that he must have been thinking of Monet, which took us, in turn, to the impressionists. We saw aspects of Odette, Swann's mistress, one of the grandest of the *grandes horizontales*, in Madame de Benardaky, who had been photographed with an extravagant arrangement of ostrich feathers

Ambassador David Bruce
giving my mother away at her
wedding to my father in Paris
on September 24, 1949

My father and mother
at their civil marriage
ceremony in Paris

My mother—surrounded by men, as usual—at a party in Rangoon in
1953, when my father was first secretary at the American Embassy

Pleased as can be,
I am standing in front of
my father's Triumph
sports car in Vienna

In the summer of 1955 my
father and I took a trip to Italy,
where this sizzling temptress
was staying at our hotel.
I did my best to get rid of her
by dumping her off the pedalo
at sea, but amazingly she
reappeared at dinner.

With my parents in Connecticut in the early '50s, after their divorce. I remember setting up this picture in a pathetic attempt to portray us as a "normal," happy family.

On a trip to Venice my father and I decided to dress in stylish matching lederhosen for a visit to Piazza San Marco

At home in London with my mother and Freddie in our house on Conway Street, shortly after they married in 1960

Freddie, *left*, and Bertrand Russell, *right*, at Woburn Abbey in 1962, with their host, the Duke of Bedford, standing behind them

My brother, Nick, with Freddie and our mother
at the house in France in 1964

What *was* I thinking?
An embarrassing and
ill-advised photograph that
appeared with an item about
me in *Cherwell*, the Oxford
students' newspaper, in 1971.
My tutors at Saint Hilda's
were not amused.

GULLY WELLS

To start smutty summery thoughts circulating in your bloodstream again, I can offer you **Gully Wells** of St. Hilda's 33-24-34, the ONLY girl in Oxford ALWAYS to look stunning in hot-pants, though here she seems to have taken them off.

A lass of enterprise. Her stepfather is Professor **Sir Frederick Ayer**, so she has a head start at Oxford — which she wasted, I am sad to say, on a long friendship with **Martin Amis** last year. Nasty Amis (call him **Hardy**, apparently endurance is his only virtue)

is son of **Kingsley Amis**, who writes books. Martin deserves a worse reference in my column (to which he has long aspired, I hear) than as a friend of the divine **Gully**.

At the end of last term she was hot on the heels of decayed trendy **Lord Rudolf Russell**, which earned her two weekends at Woburn Abbey.

But she's always good for a night out in Oxford if you can get past the vigilant eye of **Tom Sackville**, who keeps her guarded in his flat in the Cowley Road.

Photo: A. Neighbour

Alexandra Wells and Martin Amis . . . bright but different backgrounds

A photo of Martin and
me that appeared in
The Daily Express
gossip column, 1970

Freddie and I gave a garden party together in the cloisters at New College, Oxford, in 1971. Iris Murdoch is on the right and Martin is standing behind her.

Vanessa Lawson, who would become Freddie's third wife in 1982, with her newborn daughter, Horatia, in London in 1967

My lovely stepmother, Melissa, and my father in London in the 1970s. He's in the driver's seat of his old London taxi cab wearing the fur hat that was for some reason part of his chauffeur's uniform.

Our neighbor Francette Drin, whose large and malodorous dogs always accompanied her to dinner at La Migoua

With Tom Burns, my favorite Spanish "tutor," in London in the early 1970s

A view of the front of La Migoua, taken from the vineyards below the house

After our wedding in London in June 1978, my kind and generous father-in-law took everybody to lunch at the Waterside Inn in Bray, overlooking the Thames. Here I am with Peter, my brand-new husband, and our bridesmaid, Sarah Haycraft.

The night of our wedding we had a huge party at a restaurant in Chelsea called Eleven Park Walk. Hylan Booker, my mother's lover; Antonia Fraser; and Marigold Johnson were among the hundreds of guests.

Christopher Hitchens and Anna Wintour at the party after our wedding

Four of the cooler, younger guests—Oliver Haycraft; Selima Guirey; my brother, Nick; and William Miller—loitering on the sidewalk outside Eleven Park Walk

My husband, Peter, in the Virgin Islands just after we moved to New York in 1979

My mother flanked by our
neighbors Francette Drin and
Nicole Padula in the kitchen
at La Migoua, circa 1990

In the summer of 1995 I took my son, Alexander, to La Migoua for the first time.
Here we are on the terrace with Nick and his then girlfriend, Jemima.

Alexander with his sister,
Rebecca, in the main
place in Le Beausset in
the summer of 1996

With our houseguest Christopher Hitchens in
the dining room of our apartment on Bank Street

and pearls perched on her head, and plenty more jewels decorating her expansive alabaster *poitrine*. The subject of mistresses naturally led us to President Félix Faure, who had been lucky enough to expire while entertaining a young lady in his office in the Élysée in 1899. The rumors that flew around Paris claimed she had been giving him a blow job, which allowed Georges Clemenceau, his longtime political opponent, to write, "Il voulait être César, il ne fut que Pompée," a double entendre that could be translated as, "He wished to be Caesar, but was only Pompey" or, far more wittily, "He wished to be Caesar, but was only pumped."

Clemenceau hated Faure for many good reasons, but principally for his support of the guilty verdict against Alfred Dreyfus, in that infamous miscarriage of justice in 1895. The Dreyfus Affair allowed us to study anti-Semitism under the Third Republic, which led us to the novels of Émile Zola, who had launched the campaign to reopen the case in 1898, with his incendiary open letter, "J'Accuse . . . !" The letter was published on the front page of *L'Aurore,* a newspaper owned by none other than Georges Clemenceau, who also happened to be one of Monet's closest friends.

Everything was connected and it was all, quite simply, thrilling.

Less thrilling was our life in the madhouse. Martin was in his final year, and if he was going to get a first (which he did; even better, he got a congratulatory first, meaning the examiners skip the questions and just stand up and clap instead) he needed to work. And work extremely hard in a quiet place a long way from the hysterical atmosphere at the Old Loony Bin. Why we felt compelled to escape in the middle of the night, without telling Adam and Angela, I don't know, but I'm sorry to admit that's what we did. The plan was to find our own flat in Oxford. While Martin battled *Beowulf,* and marveled at Marvell, I would bring him perfectly poached eggs on whole-grain toast and fortifying cups of tea, before we retired to our softly lit bedroom for delights that Félix Faure could have imagined only *dans ses rêves.*

Curiously, over the Christmas vacation Martin stopped calling me. It was so unlike him, what could possibly be wrong? Far too cowardly to pick up the telephone myself, I consulted his friend, Rob, who mumbled and rumbled, telling me nothing, and so I decided—extremely ill advisedly and extremely uninvitedly—to go to the "citadel of riotous solvency" and find out what I should already have known. It was pitch dark when

I arrived, cold, windy, raining, sleeting—the weather had thoughtfully gone out of its way to come up with the appropriate gloomy backdrop for my despair. And Martin did the rest. No, it wasn't some other girl (unless you count Aphra, Jane, and George as my rivals, which of course they were), he just needed to move back into Exeter College and get a first. He didn't want the eggs, he didn't want the bacon or tea, and he most certainly didn't want me. What he did want was to walk into that room and watch those examiners stand up and clap. He wasn't heartless or cruel, but that was how it had to be.

I couldn't go on sitting around in his room crying, and I was much too sad and exhausted to get on the train and go home, so I went downstairs in search of comfort. Jane was busy in the kitchen cooking dinner, but not too busy to give me a long hug, a large glass of wine, and a little Byron— "Man's love is of man's life a thing apart, / 'Tis woman's whole existence." Yes! Yes! Had anything truer ever been written in the whole history of love? I sat there nodding and sniffing as she told me all about the first time her heart had been broken. It had mended, been shattered several more times, and now here she was standing at the kitchen sink, scrubbing potatoes, married to a man who no longer wanted to make love to her.

The man in question was sitting in his study, dark velvet curtains muffling the sound of rain slashing against the windowpanes, holding a glass of whiskey that was illuminated like stained glass by the cozy glow of the lamp on his desk. Of course he already knew the whole story—"Christ, Dad, what am I going to do? She says she's getting on a train and will be here in an hour"—having lived through the same scenario himself more times than he cared to recall. I imagined that he might have calmed Martin down with some story from his own past. Who knows, maybe he had even made him laugh? Because Kingsley was incapable of *not* making you laugh. But with me he didn't say anything at all, just folded me in his arms, poured me some whiskey, patted my hand, and listened with endless patience. Which was all he could do, and all that I needed.

Dinner passed by in a blur of misery and embarrassment and surprisingly, nobody seemed at all eager to linger at the table. Butter pecan ice cream with hot fudge sauce? Port? Brandy? Coffee? There were no takers. I suppose I must have helped Jane wash up as best I could, and then, horrifyingly, it was time for bed. Where all Martin longed for was the oblivion of sleep and an end to the nightmare. And you might have thought I would have felt the same way. But oh no, I had an entirely different plan in mind for how we might best pass the hours until dawn. It involved a great deal more talking, not acrimonious of course, just deeply emotional, combined with stroking and kissing, which would culminate in the most profound act of lovemaking that either of us had ever experienced in our entire lives. But even I realized that this was probably a long shot, and I was prepared to compromise and settle for an all-night session of cuddling, a long heartfelt conversation, and a few totally innocent kisses. As soon as we got into bed it became clear that not a single part of either of these scenarios was ever going to happen.

Where was the man who was going to put his arms around me and kiss my tears away? Martin was *not* a candidate. He had been banished from my life. Forever. (History had already been rewritten, and I was now the one doing the banishing.) I was never, ever going to see, or speak to him again. But what about dear Kingsley? He had always liked me, he had been so kind to me that evening, and personally I had absolutely nothing against (extremely) older men. What if I slipped into his side of the bed? Even with my diminished sanity I knew that was nuts.

Which left Monkey.

Colin—always called "Monkey"—was Jane's funny, sweet, handsome brother, who, along with their considerably less appealing mother, was a permanent fixture in the Amis ménage. Monkey did something complicated with electronics and hi-fis, was rather partial to the tanning bed, and with his absurd good looks was a huge hit with everyone. He was also one of my favorite men in the entire world, and I'd always liked to think that this affection was reciprocated. Monkey had a big heart—you had only to look into his beautiful eyes to see that—and I knew he would understand what I was going through. So I got out of bed, wrapped a towel around me, tiptoed across the passage and silently opened his door.

The room was pitch dark and freezing cold, but there in the corner was a mountain of blankets, and from beneath it came the sound of Monkey's gentle, decorous snoring. I dropped the towel on the floor, lifted up the edge of the mountain and snuggled up close to his lovely warm—vyella-pajama-encased—body. Poor Monkey. Not at all what he had expected or wanted or needed to find in his bed in the middle of the night. But I'd been right about his good heart. He *did* put his arms around me (asking him to kiss away the tears would have been pushing my luck), he calmed me down, and eventually (Christ, he must have been relieved!) I was able to creep back to Martin's room.

The next morning it was still dark when I left the house, punch-drunk from Dr. Kingsley's patent medicine and my turbulent night, and stumbled onto the train back to London. "'Tis woman's whole existence." How *could* that Byron have known what was going on in my heart? He must have been just like Martin. The brilliance, the dangerous sex appeal, the carefully arranged filthy hair, the constant scribbling—a man who needed to keep his love apart from his life. And if a girl interfered with those poems, she would have been bundled into a carriage at dawn and sent on her way through the swirling early morning mist. Leaving her whole existence behind her. I pressed my throbbing head against the cold glass of the train window and started to cry all over again.

L'Amant

SOMETIME IN THE SUMMER OF 1971 my mother's sister, Bee-goonie, gave a lunch party in her London garden. This bucolic expanse, full of fat pink roses, delicately scented phlox, teetering hollyhocks, sky blue delphiniums, espaliered pear trees, raspberry canes, and drowsy drunken bees in no way resembled the outdoor dogs' toilet that was our garden. An idealized vision, captured in overenthusiastic color by some modestly talented Edwardian lady painter, it was the perfect setting for a delicious *déjeuner sur*—its meticulously maintained—*l'herbe*. And what made it even lovelier was the *déjeuner* itself.

An entire wild Scottish salmon would be gently poached in fish bouillon, and while it cooled, my aunt would dribble olive oil, brought back from La Migoua, into deep orange egg yolks in a stone mortar, whisking them by hand into a miraculous, unctuous mayonnaise. Next, cucumber slices—so thin you could put them over your eyes and still read the headline in that morning's paper—would be arranged, overlapping like pale green fish scales, along the entire length of the salmon as it reclined on its enormous blue-and-white platter. The day before raspberries and red currants from the garden had been briefly heated with sugar, placed in a bowl, lined with a crazy patchwork of slices of white bread (crusts removed), and left—a heavy weight compressing this celestial mess together—in the fridge. Overnight the mess would have been transformed into a summer pudding that was served—turned upside down onto a plate—along with a jug of double cream and a silver spoon, because cream that thick really cannot be expected to move without assistance.

My aunt always kept in touch with old friends—and old boyfriends—

from New York, and that day the visiting American belonged to the second category. Andrew Arkin was a charming, elegant gentleman who worked in that least charming, gentle, or elegant of professions—the Seventh Avenue *schmatte* business. Andrew's romance with Beegoonie had assumed a fairy-tale aspect in my young, impressionable mind after a visit to New York, when he had taken us both for a ride in a carriage through Central Park, followed by dinner at the Colony, there being no more chic restaurant in the entire city. How I envied my aunt her glamorous life: breakfast at Tiffany's, lunch at La Grenouille, dinner at the Colony, moving from one to the other in a velvet-lined carriage, drawn by a prancing glossy black horse, with this dapper gentleman at her side. As it turned out, Andrew stayed on Seventh Avenue and my aunt moved to England, but they remained close friends and on that particular—momentous, in retrospect—day, he arrived at lunch with a friend, an American dress designer working in London.

No, I wasn't there in the garden, but over the years I heard about it so often from the central actors in the drama that ensued that I began to feel as though I might have been. Hylan Booker had been born in Detroit into a large family, and after finishing high school had joined the air force because that was probably the only way that a young black kid from his kind of background could fly away and fashion the kind of future he dreamed of. (Just as my mother had signed up with the Canadian army to escape from her own very different family so many years before.) The air force took him to England, and when he got out his talent for drawing and design led him to art school, first in Swindon and then a few years later to the Royal College of Art in London. By the time Andrew brought him to lunch, he had just been awarded the Best British Designer prize by the American press at a glitzy ceremony at the Plaza in New York (maybe he had even gone for a ride afterward in one of those romantic carriages?) and was about to be signed up by the House of Worth to design its couture collection. He was a long way from Michigan.

Soon after that lunch my mother—wrestling with the guest list for one of her many dinner parties in Regent's Park Terrace—found herself staring at some names scribbled on the back of an envelope and realized she was facing every hostess's nightmare: too many single ladies. What is it with women? Why do they keep misplacing the men they were once attached to? What particular black hole do they disappear into? Well, she had no time to get into that, but she did suddenly remember that nice young—he was thirty-three at the time—dress designer she had met at her sister's house, so she picked up the telephone and asked if by any remote chance he might possibly be free to come to dinner next Tuesday? Informal, eight for eight thirty. Wonderful! She would see him then. Not too surprisingly Hylan was quite popular with her lady friends—he even had a brief fling with one of them—and after several more of these parties, being the well-brought-up gentleman that he was and still is, he sent my mother a large bouquet of yellow roses with a thank-you note. Many years later he told me what happened next:

"You must understand I knew nothing of her life, nor was it a concern from my perspective since I had met Freddie at the dinner parties and found him quite charming in that cool English way. But the yellow flowers were a kind of turning point, since from then on our relationship moved in an entirely different sphere."

AFTER THE DEBACLE with Martin I went back to Oxford, miserable and homeless. But two kind friends, Anthony and Tom, who shared an unspeakable dump halfway up the Cowley Road, gallantly came to my rescue, and offered me a room in their flat. It was quite possibly the most awful place any of us had ever seen, let alone *lived* in. My saviors had met each other at Eton, but they could not have been less like the drunken Christ Church louts whose antics Evelyn Waugh immortalized as "the sound of English county families baying for broken glass." Waugh must have been thinking of the time in 1927 when the high-spirited members of the Bullingdon Club got so carried away after one of their festive dinners that they went on a rampage, smashing the glass in all 468 windows in Peckwater Quad. And don't think that their grandsons—some of whom had been at school with Anthony and Tom, and were now at Oxford—were much better behaved in the early seventies.

The dump occupied the cramped ground floor of a squat semidetached house a long way from the center of Oxford. It consisted of two bedrooms at the front, where Tom and Anthony were lulled to sleep by the sound of trucks and buses grinding their way up and down the Cowley Road, another room at the back (soon to be my boudoir), a frightening kitchen, and a bathroom of sorts, both of which were crammed into a flimsy unheated addition that stuck out into what might once have been a garden. Anthony's dog, who slept in his bed, whether or not his master happened to have company, completed our cozy little household.

As well as being scholars, my saviors were forward-thinking entrepreneurs, specializing in the secondhand-bed business. They had invested in a clapped-out Land Rover for pickups and deliveries, and the inventory—mainly iron bedsteads that looked as though they had done good service in some prewar mental institution—was stacked up against every available wall in the flat. As far as I can recall the beds were so content living with us that they rarely if ever moved out. We, on the other hand, tended to go out a great deal.

One evening we ended up in New College, where the haunting sound of Mick suggesting we spend the night together escaped from an open window, beckoning us up a twisty staircase and into somebody or other's rooms. Flagons of cheap Spanish wine were lined up on a table, alongside a sweaty arrangement of cheeses and hunks of bread, while in the other room Mick had moved on to the exciting, forbidden flavor—"How come you taste so good?"—of brown sugar. And there in the dark I could just make out two figures: one, an extremely large and energetic woman, and the other an elflike man with wispy hair, swooping wildly around to the urgent deafening beat of the music. It was Iris Murdoch and her husband, John Bayley, out for a night on the town.

Raymond Carr, the warden of Saint Antony's College and my old friend from Paris, gave the best parties in the whole of Oxford. Like my mother, he knew that the key was to mix people up—academics, students, a few interlopers from London. Soon after I moved in with Anthony and Tom, we all turned up one evening chez Carr, and I remember standing by the fireplace and watching an excitable visiting professor from the University of Salamanca—an expert in the iconography of early Renaissance religious art—as he tried to strike up a conversation with a tall girl in astonishing violet suede hot pants and matching high-heeled boots. She was so stoned that she had to clutch his arm to steady herself. His fractured English quickly disintegrated into gibberish—his *mujer* back in Salamanca probably didn't dress up like that too often—and when the girl, bored with his chatter, said "Let's dance," I saw a look of entirely misguided masculine bravado (*Qué hombre, qué cojones,* no wonder she wants me!) spread across his pudgy features. On the other hand she was *very* stoned, so even he might have gotten lucky.

That same night I, too, met somebody who asked me to dance. While I was sitting with Isaiah Berlin, talking about the only thing we had in common, which would have been my disreputable stepfather, whose way with the ladies Isaiah neither understood nor approved of, a young man he seemed to know walked over to join us. Which allowed poor Isaiah to escape, and us to join the excitable Spanish professor and his new friend on the dance floor. One thing led to another—some smooching in the garden, lots more dancing, a few more champagne cocktails, some undercooked sausages with Raymond in the kitchen just before dawn—and instead of going home we went upstairs. On the top floor we found a deserted bedroom where, exhausted, we fell asleep.

"Ah, my dear girl, you and your friend are just in time for breakfast." It must have been around three in the afternoon, and Raymond, in a frayed stripey dressing gown, was back at the stove, using last night's encrusted frying pan to make bacon and eggs and thick greasy slices of fried bread. And baked beans, if anybody wanted them. The entire Carr family, as well as a couple of other stragglers, were slumped in a catatonic state around an unbelievably messy table. It was home. Just like our kitchen in La Migoua. I was even wearing my magical backless dress, the one I'd gone swimming in with the married fascist hairdresser, after he had admired my "jolis pieds" at the Padulas' party. We found a couple of chairs, sat down at the table, and, for the first time since my disastrous visit to Monkey's freezing bedroom, I realized, to my astonishment, that I was actually happy.

DANIEL REES, whose parents, Margie and Goronwy, were my mother and Freddie's oldest, dearest friends, had been staying in our house in London. And one fine day he decided to come and see me in Oxford. As we sat in some fetid pub that stank of beer and cigarettes, and was festooned with horse brasses, plastic holly, and winking tiny white lights, he filled me in on the news from home. Apparently my mother had turned into a caffeine- and nicotine-crazed dervish who didn't even bother to get dressed or wash her hair anymore and spent all day in her nightdress

at the desk in her room. She was writing a novel. Later on, after it had
become a huge success, she claimed, totally disingenuously, that she had
started it because "I was idle and had a perfectly good typewriter and half
a box of paper." A likely story.

She had always been a writer, first of long, funny letters and after
that of newspaper articles, but she knew perfectly well that *real* writers
wrote books. Almost everybody around her did, so why shouldn't she?
She would show them that anything they could do she could do better.
Although she would never have admitted it out loud—weakness and insecurity had to be locked away behind wit and aggression—I don't think
my mother ever quite came to terms with the fact that she had skipped
college. Her brothers and sister had gone to Swarthmore, Harvard, and
Radcliffe respectively, but her rebelliousness and delinquency, vis-à-vis
anything so dull and regimented as school, meant that her education had
been a total mess. So she packed it all in at seventeen. "I just said I was
through with schools forever and my family didn't dare argue with me,"
and went off to join the Canadian army.

I suspect she probably felt sorry for herself ever after. Instead of long
afternoons in the Widener Library and long nights in a Harvard dorm,
lying in the arms of Walker Mortimer IV, she found herself freezing her
ass off at eight in the morning on some parade ground in Ontario, surrounded by half-wits. But there was one shining exception—one fellow soldier, who was most certainly not a half-wit. V. R. "Bunny" Lang
was a brilliant, outrageous poet and playwright from Boston, who was
to become my mother's closest friend. (My Mother's novel, *Jane*, was
dedicated to Bunny's memory. She had died in 1956, and even though
I was only five at the time, I can still remember the awful day when my
mother got the news.) It was Bunny who had written the poem about my
grandmother, the cat murderer, and it was to Bunny that she wrote a letter
describing what had passed for her education:

> I did not go to school very often as I didn't like it . . . and when I did
> go, I never took books home and neither did, nor handed in any home
> work [*sic*] assignment. I smoked in the girls' toilets and drank brandy
> from those tiny bottles you get on trains, in the back row. Not only did
> I hate the school and the school hate me, but I hated everyone in the
> school and everyone in the school hated me. I went less and less.

It being wartime, there were a few unfortunate children who had been evacuated from England and France in her class, and much as my mother despised these unappealing outcasts, she discovered they had their uses:

> When it came time for final exams I had some disquieting moments and it was only then I realized how really bright and well-informed the refugees were. I took every exam and passed by the simple system of copying their papers. But now I was terrified that the war would end and then the refugees would undoubtedly go home, and I would have to do my own homework, and pass or not pass exams on my own hook.

But thanks to those brave young Japanese pilots who came dive-bombing to my mother's rescue on December 7, 1941, she was able to relax, safe in the knowledge that the refugees wouldn't be going any-where for a very long time.

The novel my mother was writing, so Daniel told me, was about a clever, sexy American journalist in her midthirties, who has a soft spot for animals and underdogs, lives in a loft in Covent Garden, and keeps herself busy—when she isn't reviewing movies—juggling three boy-friends, none of whom know about one another. When it came to men, Jane isn't one of those safe, predictable women who always seem to gravitate toward the same model. Oh no, that would not have been her style at all. In fact this trio of gentlemen callers have absolutely nothing in common beyond their shared, and totally understandable, passion for Jane. The first, Anthony, is a cultured, ineffectual aristocrat, dominated by his witch of a mother, scarred by his loveless childhood and a session of trau-matic buggery at Eton, who has never gotten it together to do anything at all.

The second gentleman, Franklin, is equally posh and handsome, except he's American and black. An ambitious, high-powered, Yale-educated law professor, he wears monogrammed shirts, was the tennis champion of southern New England, and dances and makes love better than any man she has ever known—"No wonder white men are so scared of them. They have every reason to be."

The third man, Tom, is really no more than a boy. "He was even younger than she'd thought. Eighteen? Twenty-two? Tall for fourteen? At thirty-four she was no longer sure of anything about the young." Tom is a burglar who happens to be going about his business one rainy night on her roof, when he slips and crashes through the skylight, landing on her bed in a shower of wet leaves and broken glass. The gash on his hand is so deep that she feels the least she can do—before sending him on his way—is to give him a glass of brandy and stitch it up. But after she has done her Florence Nightingale bit, she makes the mistake of looking up at his beautiful face.

Already hooked, I needed to know what happened next, but Daniel had no idea because she was still hunched over her typewriter and refused to give away any more.

However, he did have one other thing to tell me about my mother. She had a lover. Daniel didn't seem to know where she had met him, but he came around all the time (Freddie was safely in Oxford from Tuesday to Friday) and was a black American dress designer named Hylan Booker. I was too old to be surprised by anything my mother did (appalled sometimes, but never surprised), and I trusted her taste. Had she not married my two favorite men in the entire world? So I didn't doubt for a moment that this improbable but amazing-sounding creature was a good thing.

Daniel had to tell me everything about him, immediately. Well, he was tall, very dark, and extremely handsome, probably about ten years younger than her, had a daughter Nick's age who lived with him, and he had transformed my mother's life. As only a new lover can. She was ridiculously happy; she had lost weight, her skirts had gotten shorter, she drank champagne and giggled, and when they went out at night, she wore Hylan's creations, with swirling capes and crazily patterned stockings. They gave small dinner parties and Hylan would make Chinese food from scratch. The fridge was full of fermented black beans, water chestnuts, sea cucumber, and lotus roots, and one evening Daniel had even seen a couple of live crabs crawling around the kitchen floor. Instead of dessert they served their guests perfectly rolled, calorie-conscious joints. I could not wait to meet him.

After my mother found out about Freddie and Vanessa, she was much unhappier than I ever knew at the time. She sensed this was the real thing, unlike any of his other affairs, and Freddie knew it too. In 1968 he had told his old friend Marcelle Quinton, "I have just met someone I am absolutely in love with." Marcelle felt that he and Vanessa loved each other "in the way people do when they think it is their last chance." Vanessa was a geisha. She was beautiful, she whispered, she was tiny, she sat at his feet (figuratively and literally), she didn't argue, she didn't work, she didn't shout or swear, and most important of all, she adored him. It would be hard to imagine any woman less like my mother.

Freddie had found somebody who made him truly happy, but I doubt that he ever thought seriously about divorce. He had always been accustomed to having more than one woman simultaneously. Freddie was not the kind of man who falls violently in love and overturns everything in order to commit himself to the object of his passion. With his deep, visceral aversion to confrontation and upheaval, he just wanted to be left alone to get on with his work and sleep with whomever he pleased. Surely that wasn't too much to ask? He didn't think so. Of course he loved Vanessa, and he undoubtedly loved going to bed with her, but in many ways he was quite content being married to my mother—at least on the weekends. She provided him with a comfortable home, cooked the kind of food he liked, amused him, organized their social life, and above all she was the mother of his adored son.

My mother was less easily pleased. And she became spectacularly displeased when she found out about Vanessa. Her disenchantment with her husband spilled over into a disenchantment with England. She missed America and was increasingly angry about the whole stuffy, uptight, class-ridden system in this bizarre country she seemed to have landed in. Except that the anger was within her, and had always been there. She lashed out because that's what she had been doing her entire life, and I often thought that it was really just target practice—the sniping made her feel alive and kept the dreaded boredom at bay. In any case the bizarre country was changing fast. And about fucking time too, as she would have said. The Labour Party was in power, and all the usual high-minded liberal reforms had been pushed through Parliament: no more hanging, no more corporal punishment in schools, no more throwing nice—or even not nice—queers in jail. The kind of admirable stuff Freddie had campaigned for all his life. But there was so much more to be done—and so much else going on.

Diana Melly had a boyfriend, and he really *was* a boy, the son of some British diplomats my mother had known in Burma. Of course Diana still had the kids and George at home in Gloucester Crescent, but she had also acquired a cozy love nest nearby with an enormous water bed that made you feel seasick if you so much as perched on its edge. Who knows what it must have been like after a couple of joints, when you started rolling around on top of it? One could only imagine. Sylvia had gotten rid of Prince Azamat, sold their huge house in boring old Chester Square, and had moved on to a new life in exciting young Chelsea. She favored futons over water beds, Barcelona chairs over her mother's Louis XVI fauteuils, and became a connoisseur of both the finer vintages of marijuana and of London's more attractive experimental artists and poets.

Around about this time my mother decided that she too needed to make some changes in her living arrangements. She left Freddie behind in their cavelike bedroom on the ground floor—decorated in her signature medley-de-*merde* color scheme—and moved two flights up, where she created a dimly lit womb of her own. She hung a jewel-colored beaded curtain across the doorway, papered the walls with bloodred fabric, draped the windows in heavy jungle-printed curtains, and converted her bed into a kind of Ottoman divan, with kelim-covered bolsters and cushions. A series of nineteenth-century oil paintings of obscenely overweight cows, their spindly little legs scarcely able to keep them upright, stared down with bovine wariness from their place above the mantelpiece.

I can't now recall my first meeting with Hylan, but it scarcely matters because it soon felt as though I had known him forever. The thing about him was that he really liked women.

"They don't even have to open their mouths for him to know what they're thinking or feeling. He just *knows* what they want. And not just in bed. Even in restaurants he knows what they want. . . . I don't have to finish sentences with him. Sometimes I don't even have to start sentences with him." This is her description of Franklin from *Jane,* but I bet she was thinking of Hylan when she wrote it. Or then again maybe she met Hylan after she had written it, and had a blinding moment of *déjà-écrit* in her sister's garden when she realized that here was the man she had already imagined. The other thing about him was that he was American. She was fed up with Englishmen, nostalgic for home, and missed that warm, wide-open, cheerful spontaneity that she associated with her fellow countrymen. Look at the way Bobby Kennedy had rolled up his shirtsleeves at Tony Lewis's party, and made ice-cream cones with sprinkles for all those shrieking kids. Look at the way my father had surprised her in Paris when she was too pregnant to shop or cook by coming home from work one day with a tub of caviar from Fauchon and ice-cold vodka. Look at the way Hylan had made minced squab with bamboo shoots, wrapped in crispy lettuce leaves, and had served it on a tray, so they could eat dinner lolling on the Ottoman divan. Look at the way Freddie had welcomed her home from a week in the hospital: "Oh dear. I don't imagine you are up to cooking, I suppose I'd better dine at my club."

Hylan didn't have a club. He was an outsider, something my mother could understand and identify with. Even though she was Mrs. A. J. Ayer and, through Freddie, the ultimate insider, knew every interesting person in the whole of London, if you arrive in a new country as an adult, it is probably impossible to ever feel truly at home there. You can always make a virtue out of this: You may imagine you perceive things more clearly than the complacent, accepting natives; you may have deep affection for the place and grow accustomed to its funny ways; you may even decide to stay there forever, but still you will always be a foreigner. Another thing about Hylan was that he was black and beautiful—two words that had not necessarily been conjoined before—which was entirely incidental and yet curiously fortuitous. My mother had started writing the book before she met Hylan, but by the time the book came out, she and Hylan had become an established couple, which only added to the gossip swirling around the novel—and them. It was a publicist's, and a betrayed wife's, dream scenario.

Freddie had old-fashioned ideas about mistresses: Clearly love affairs were an essential and delightful part of life, but a married gentleman— or lady—should never flaunt the relationship in public. A little light luncheon (an *omelette aux fines herbes* and a nice bottle of claret) at their special corner table in a favorite restaurant (La Sorbonne, in Oxford), followed by some stolen moments in his rooms at New College (spied on by his binocular-wielding fellow dons) was the way he thought these things should be conducted. Not entirely discreet, but those were his rules. To arrive at a party accompanied by your mistress instead of your wife was not something that would ever have crossed his mind. It would have been . . . vulgar.

My mother had no such inhibitions. In fact, vulgar and inhibition were two concepts she never quite got to grips with. She was in love and wanted her friends—who were also Freddie's friends—to meet this fascinating new man. At home there was always a thicket of stiff white invitations propped up on the marble mantelpiece in the drawing room, requesting the pleasure of the company of Professor and Mrs. A. J. Ayer at some fancy party or other. Often these glittering occasions were in the middle of the week, when Freddie would be otherwise occupied in Oxford, but no matter: His delightful, lively wife was certainly available. And so was Hylan. I suspect that more than one London hostess was a little startled to find herself welcoming not a famous elderly philosopher, but rather a much younger talkative black gentleman in a perfectly cut white suit— flared pants, wide lapels, daringly unbuttoned shirt—into her lovely home. (In a roundup of the Parties of the Year in 1974, *Harper's Queen* magazine spotted my mother at "Thea Porter's black and white party in her black, white and silver flat in Mayfair. . . . Dee Wells came in black with a black man in white.") But the hostesses were instantly charmed— women liked him just as much as he liked them—and who cared if some of the more conventional husbands were harrumphing away in the background? Harrumphing out of masculine loyalty to Freddie or because my mother was having too much fun? Or harrumphing because they feared their wives might be inspired by the example of their outrageous, subversive American friend to have too much fun themselves?

The Ayer/Wells ménage acquired a certain pleasing symmetry with Hylan's arrival in Regent's Park Terrace. He restored a sense of balance to the marriage, and the household settled down into a carefully choreographed and surprisingly peaceful routine: Freddie left on Tuesday morning, Hylan arrived that evening, and moved out on Friday when Freddie returned from Oxford. My mother lived upstairs, Freddie lived downstairs, and the floor between them—the drawing room and his study— was an elegantly appointed DMZ. Except that hostilities seemed to have ceased, and when the two sides met in the middle on the weekends (minus their allies) they actually got along much better than they had in a long time. It was a logical, pragmatic, oh-so-Benthamite arrangement. But how, you may be wondering, did the fifth player fit into this new regime? Ah yes, Nick. What about little Nick?

Le Frère

ONE DAY SEVERAL YEARS AGO Hylan came to lunch at my apartment in the Village. It was early summer and we sat outside on the terrace, shaded by an ancient wisteria vine that was slowly, deliberately choking the house—and would be murdered soon after by my landlady, who cared far more for the value of her property than for its thick jungly foliage or the ethereal scent of its dangling purple flowers. In a fit of nostalgia for La Migoua, I had cooked ratatouille and left it outside on the table to keep warm in the sun while I poured him a glass of wine and then disappeared into the kitchen to poach a couple of eggs. As soon as the whites were set and the yolks still runny, I made a little nest in the mound of ratatouille on each plate, plopped them in, and picked a few leaves of fresh basil from the bush by the door to scatter on top. A salad of lambs'-tongue lettuce, jazzed up with a handful of peppery nasturtium flowers—the greenflies flicked off when Hylan wasn't looking —bread, some almost liquid, extremely smelly Époisses, and that was it.

After lunch we sat in the sun and he started to talk about that time, so long ago, when he had first met my mother: "She was my bad girl, and I think all of us innocent guys want that. She was like those fearless New York literary women—Dorothy Parker, Lee Miller, Lillian Hellman. She was cocky, insolent—almost masculine--worldly, funny, but underneath all that her heart was made of mush."

But she was always careful to hide the mush away behind her bulletproof armor, so most people never even knew it existed, and those of us who were closest to her were allowed only the occasional glimpse of this tender, elusive aspect of her character. Mush might be too easily confused with sentimentality—something she despised and scorned above all else: "The soft nature of human foibles made her impatient, as if it were mere trickery." I knew exactly what Hylan meant.

But animal foibles were an entirely different matter. Spiders were rescued from baths, caterpillars carefully put back on their leaf of choice, and no dog or cat of hers was ever allowed to eat anything from a tin. No fast food for them, oh no. Instead regular trips to the butcher yielded the ingredients for a fragrant ragout of fresh lamb's hearts and kidneys that was kept bubbling away on the back of the kitchen stove—the yellowish gray scum boiling over, the *parfum d'abattoir* permeating the whole house—just like the special from Chez Macbeth.

Animals were powerless, vulnerable creatures that needed to be loved, protected, and rescued. Just like children. Or so you might have thought. And yet it didn't necessarily work out quite that way. Hylan poured us both some more wine, turned his chair to face the sun, and told me about one particular evening, early on in their relationship. He had arrived at the house straight from work to cook dinner for his new girlfriend (conjured up in a smoky wok from the adventurous ingredients in the fridge) and afterward, when they were sitting around enjoying a joint—or maybe just some illicit fattening coffee ice cream—they suddenly remembered Nick. Alone in his room two floors below, he would have been eight or nine at the time.

HYLAN BROUGHT OUT the best in my mother. He calmed her down, made her laugh, and was probably the only person who knew how to tame the fire-breathing furies inside her. At least some of them, some of the time. He fed them a steady diet of Szechuan shrimp, chilled Vouvray, funny stories, sad stories, stem ginger drowned in heavy cream, Acapulco gold, a little music (they favored early Sinatra), and endless amounts of warmth, sympathy, and above all, love. The furies gobbled all these things up—greedily, but also gratefully—and sometimes asked for more, but usually they just curled up and went to sleep. Until they got hungry again. With Hylan there, life at home became much less fraught—he kept things steady and consciously or not became a buffer between Nick and his mother. "Buffer" is my brother's word, not mine, but I know precisely what he meant, and why he chose it. Once, many years ago, somebody who knew my mother quite well described her to me as "a most alarming woman," which deeply upset me at the time, maybe because it was the truth.

As a small child Nick, I think, was truly alarmed by his mother, and understandably so. Sometimes she wasn't there at all—she was working, she was at a television studio, she was out at a party—and when she was around, you could never be entirely sure if she was going to cook lamb chops and peas and make you laugh, or whether it would be the furies who needed feeding far more urgently than you did. No wonder Nick was so eager to welcome the Buffer into the bosom of our family: "At the time I thought I had the best of both worlds." His lovely dad doted on him at the weekends, and cheerful Hylan kept his mum happy during the week. Even better, the Buffer soon started bringing his daughter, Alex, with him, so the kids would hang out in Nick's room, giggling, stuffing themselves with potato chips, revolting sweets, and Coca-Cola. At a remarkably precocious age—maybe around ten—Nick added cigarettes to his well-balanced diet. He had started out by pinching them from Freddie or our mother but quickly tired of the taste of Players Navy Cut, and before too long graduated to Marlboros. His equally precocious sense of design inspired him to glue the empty packs to the walls of his room, and since he smoked so much, he was soon able to create a kind of red-and-white-patchwork-quilt effect that cheered up his surroundings no end.

The patchwork nature of Nick's education was sadly less of a success than the nicotine wallpaper. His father's view was quite simple: Send your children to the best private schools, encourage them to work hard, buy them lots of books, engage them in lively conversations, and watch them sail off to the best universities, where they would get first-class degrees. Just as he, and everybody he knew, had. But poor innocent well-meaning Freddie hadn't taken into account the two whirlwinds swirling around him. The first was the confusing, fuck-the-Establishment times he found himself living in, and the second was the anarchic, fuck-the-English attitude of his wife. Together they made a perfect storm that ended up sabotaging his son's education. My mother was theoretically in favor of schools, despite her own fractured and largely hostile relationship with them, and she never lost her admiration for that highly educated crème de la crème of intellectual society that lived in some paneled library full of first editions. And yet she expected people to be naturally, effortlessly brilliant, to reach the clouds without sweating, and had nothing but contempt for what she called "greasy grinds"—those dreary, conventional kids/adults who worked too hard at school/jobs and were pathetically bereft of all glamour, fun, and wickedness.

At this stage in their marriage stuffy old Freddie had only to suggest something for his contentious, increasingly wild, and ever younger— in spirit if not in body—wife to disagree. Jesus, why the hell would she want her son to end up like every uptight, out-of-touch, private-school-educated, misogynistic, insensitive Englishman she had ever known—or been to bed with? No way was she going to subject little Nick to that. Most of her friends, enlightened left-leaning people like Jonathan and Rachel Miller, Sylvia, George and Diana Melly, had long ago come to the conclusion that it was wrong, and a waste of money, to send your children to fee-paying schools. Never mind that these same people had all gone to nice private schools and Oxford or Cambridge themselves: This was the dawning of a new age. Get with the program, Fred. How on earth could there ever have been any kind of social justice if one privileged class continued to pay for education while everybody else was forced into the state school around the corner? And Freddie called himself a socialist! Back home in America, everybody went to the same local school (no, not really) and had an equal chance of getting into Harvard (no, not at all), and that was the only way for any sane country to run its educational system. Well, she had always known the English were nuts. And don't think this was just idle chatter—my mother and her friends put their children where their mouths were.

Little Nick's patchwork experience started out somewhat inconsistently at a private nursery school in Hampstead with a pretty garden at the back, geraniums in the window boxes, and the reassuring onwards-and-upwards name of Stepping Stones. His father's fuddy-duddy idea was that he should graduate from there—summa cum laude—and move smoothly right along to prep school, which would in turn prepare him for Westminster (founded in 1179), where Freddie's hero and occasional (dead) dining companion, Jeremy Bentham, had gone. But this was not to be. Instead Nick followed his friends Tom, William, and the Melly kids to Gospel Oak, the local state school. Not altogether a bad place, but with thirty-odd kids in each class, its harried teachers didn't have the energy, time, inclination, or training to take on Horace, the finer points of the Peloponnesian Wars, trigonometry, Aristophanes—or whatever fuddy-duddy rubbish you had to know about to pass the entrance exam for Westminster.

As far as extracurricular activities went, there was lots of smoking and regular, energizing fights in the playground, and quite soon visits to the Tavistock Clinic in Belsize Lane were added to Nick's busy after-school schedule. Why our mother had decided a shrink might be a good idea wasn't entirely clear. Maybe she had noticed that Nick seemed unhappy, or maybe it was because the Millers and the Mellys were sending their kids there, or quite possibly it was just another way to annoy Freddie, who had no patience at all for the good doctor Freud's exotic excavations of the psyche. The mind was a wondrous thing, extremely useful for solving problems of a verifiable nature, but was there any point in rummaging about in its nether regions to see if one might have forgotten having had sex with the gardener at the age of seven? Freddie didn't think so. Nick's recollection is that he had cut himself accidentally fiddling about with his father's razor, and when he appeared at school festooned in Band-Aids, his obviously concerned teacher had called his parents to alert them to his possibly suicidal tendencies.

Either way, or more likely both ways, Nick now found himself twice a week sitting in a room full of toys he didn't want to play with and books he didn't want to read, opposite an earnest gray-haired lady in Birkenstocks he didn't want to talk to. But talk he must. That's why he was there. "Now, Nick, what are you thinking about?" Not a lot. In fact nothing at all. His mind was a blank, all he wanted was to go home, watch the telly, and have a much-needed cigarette. But he didn't feel he could really say that, and so he remained silent. She asked him again. And again. Finally, in despair he said he was looking at the screw in her chair. Aha! *Now* at last they were getting somewhere. Screw. The miasma had started to lift: Nick was thinking of screwing. Whom did he want to screw? His mother? Her? The gardener? (If only we'd had one—then the dogs' toilet could have been transformed into a lovely bijou garden.) The poor child looked mystified, but at least he had ignited some kind of conversation; the only problem was he had no idea what she was talking about. The kindly lady had suddenly become animated—far too animated— and had taken off on an embarrassing riff about that thing that people do.

At ten Nick certainly knew all about that, but what did it have to do with the screw in her chair? He fell silent again, and then, thank God, his time was up. Perhaps Freddie wasn't such a fool after all.

HYLAN HAPPENED TO BE precisely thirteen years older than me and thirteen years younger than my mother, and far from acting like a buffer between us he actually brought us much closer together. My friends all loved him. At a party he'd hit the dance floor with a whoop of joy, hands clapping, sweeping you along in his wake, spinning wildly like a fifth top—and it wasn't just that he knew the moves, he was *from* Motown, for God's sake. In our sheltered, snobby, white Oxford world, he was probably as close to the real deal as any of us would ever get. And as for his acid-tongued, wickedly funny girlfriend, nobody, I was proud to say, had a mother remotely like mine. What had been alarming to a young child and embarrassing to a teenager were the exact same qualities that kept my friends (and me) entertained in our twenties. I had always inhabited her world, gone to grown-up parties from a ludicrously young age and hung about with her guests, and now, newly rejuvenated by Hylan, she was more than delighted to return the favor. Sometimes we even went away for the weekend together.

Ever since it was founded in 1823, the Oxford Union has suffered from an advanced case of *folie de grandeur,* fancying itself as *the* prep school for Parliament. The few times I went there as a student, it seemed to be full of self-regarding bores, whose voices were too loud and predictable opinions too strident, but amazingly a few of these windbags did actually make it into the House of Commons. So I guess as prep schools went, it wasn't a total flop. Mostly a debate in the Union consisted of often-drunk undergraduates haranguing one another, but every now and then, just to add a bit of class and celebrity sparkle to the occasion, they would invite guest speakers from the real world to come and join in. One day my mother was the lucky recipient of such an invitation. Who knows what the debate was supposed to be about, but since she could always fashion an argument out of thin air, it really didn't matter—what mattered was having fun. And what could be more fun than a little mother-and-daughter outing to a hotel in Oxford, accompanied by our respective boyfriends?

Even though I had made it quite clear to Martin several times—first during the hysterical night at his parents' house, then in a stream of letters—that I would never have anything whatsoever to do with him ever again, it seems he didn't believe me. And nor did I. He wrote in his memoir, *Experience,* that "we had started going out together when she came to St. Hilda's to read history in 1969, and it lasted in its intermittent way about as long as the average marriage. Ten years?"

Was it really that long? I'm not so sure, but it still makes me oddly happy to think he remembers it that way. At any rate, when the Oxford Union came calling we were in one of our on-again phases, and since Hylan and Martin got along so well (and still do) and my mother adored Martin (and always did), the four of us set out for our double date at the Randolph Hotel full of excitement.

Our hosts—a couple of eager young men with troubled complexions and misguided notions of the depth and range of their own wit—had laid on dinner in a pub as an entertaining [*sic*] prelude to the great debate. Clearly they knew that their guest speaker, Dee Wells, could be relied upon to stir things up, but I wonder if they expected Mrs. A. J. Ayer to come to her husband's home turf with her lover? Probably not. At the time this aspect of our expedition never crossed my mind, and yet, looking back, it must have been on my mother's the entire time. If Freddie could take Vanessa to La Sorbonne for discreet lunches, then just watch me take Hylan to the Union for an indiscreet showdown. Not only would she destroy the Conservative opposition with her glorious swift tongue, but she would prove to all those greasy grind undergraduates what a sexy, desirable woman she was too. And it worked: She won the debate, she looked sensational in one of Hylan's creations, and most satisfying of all, she must have generated enough gossip to keep the greasy grinds jabbering away for at least a week.

After her triumph the four of us sailed back to the Randolph in search of a celebratory drink. But this was Oxford, not London, and at eleven o'clock its cryptlike lounge was deserted. The crypt's elderly, irritable keeper was eventually persuaded to bring us four small glasses of whiskey and a bowl of melting ice cubes—"Jesus, what *is* it with the English and ice."—and then we sat about making much too much noise, having much too good a time, before stumbling off to bed. The next morning, after breakfast in the silent dining room—"Jesus, what's wrong with the English. Why don't they talk when they eat, like normal people do."—it was time to say good-bye to the dreaming spires and head back home. My mother and Martin went to the front desk, Hylan and I collected the bags, when suddenly there was a little yelp, not a real one but a funny one, when she discovered she was apparently being charged a pound more than Martin for her equally miserable double room. She examined her bill more carefully, she examined his and then, with a smile on her face, turned to the girl cowering behind the desk: "Oh I see. You charge extra for niggers. Well, you know what? They're *worth* it!"

And with that she produced her credit card and snapped it down on the counter. It was the perfect ending to a perfect weekend. I should add a postscript here. Nick, who had adored Hylan from the very beginning, soon took to using that very same word rather freely—always with great affection—following his mother's example. The poor child was understandably a bit confused, when she told him one day that it was in fact an evil, wicked word and that he was never, ever, to say it again. So he didn't. But she went on using it. And Hylan says he never minded at all.

Les Vacances

Wɪᴛʜ ᴛʜᴇ ɴᴇᴡ ʀᴇɢɪᴍᴇ ᴀᴛ ʜᴏᴍᴇ, the era of cozy, chaotic, sometimes contentious, holidays *en famille* at La Migoua came to an end, and from 1973 onward my mother and Freddie decided that they would split the long hot summer between them. But who was going to look after little Nick and big Freddie—both equally helpless—when their mother/wife wasn't there? (Apparently Vanessa had decided she couldn't leave her husband and four children for a month to take on the nanny/cook/chauffeur/mistress role at this point—although later on she would.) I'm not sure exactly how my mother found Beatrice, a French student in her late twenties studying law in London, but Mademoiselle Tourot turned out to be remarkably accomplished at every aspect of her new job.

At home in her grandmother's kitchen in the Gironde, Beatrice had been taught at a precocious age how to cook an impeccable *poulet au gratin à la crème Landaise,* she knew that a *salade de L'Île Barbe* required a dressing of lemon juice and *never* vinegar, and from her father she had learned which wines—a Château Pradeaux rouge 1998 and a Château Grenouilles Chablis, respectively—to serve with each of these sublime dishes. She was unfazed by the tortuous roads around La Migoua and equally fearless when it came to dealing with the murderous local drivers. Well brought up, well read, well adjusted, and well dressed, she was also witty and pretty, with curly reddish hair, just the right number of freckles, and had an engaging little gap between her two front teeth. Nick and Freddie were two lucky chaps, and I don't imagine that either of them missed my mother for a single moment.

Nick remembers that Beatrice "made a huge effort to be liked, and succeeded. From the moment we met her, she was permanently in our lives. She could do all the things that Freddie loved—organize dinners, parties, and outings. She was fun and charming and great with children." I suppose it was inevitable that they would become lovers. Freddie was incapable of meeting an attractive woman without wanting to sleep with her, and over the years their relationship—*pace* the other boyfriends Beatrice must surely have had—developed into what? I had no idea. But Beatrice once told me that Freddie had been "l'être le plus significatif de ma vie." My stepfather had always been the ultimate juggler when it came to the ladies who inhabited his life, so for him this was a familiar pattern.

"Pourquoi pas?" was his attitude, although he did admit in a letter he wrote to Heather Kiernan (yet another of his lucky ladies) when he was seventy-three, "You might think that as I get older I would learn how to manage my affairs better but the reverse seems to be true."

Never mind about *managing* his affairs. What was far more amazing, and I think admirable, was that he went on *having* them, pretty well up until the day he died. One particular conversation comes to mind, which must have taken place only a year or so before his death in 1989. Freddie had been staying with me in New York and was having a spot of bother with that perfidious male gland, the prostate. Clearly something was up, and—far more worried about his future chances of *getting* it up than by any fears about his mortality—he had decided to return to London for the dreaded operation. I was full of sympathy and said all the usual useless rubbish about how I was sure everything would be fine, and not to worry, and that I would call him soon to see how it had all gone. But he beat me to it.

Freddie's relationship with the telephone was not an easy one—he preferred letters—and he was especially mistrustful of transatlantic calls, all those complicated codes, all that unnecessary expense. So I was stunned when he telephoned me a couple of weeks later, and even more surprised to hear him sounding so cheerful and chatty. Yes, the operation had been a huge success; all his friends had come to see him; the surgeon had been at Oxford and had asked Freddie to sign his copy of *Language, Truth and Logic;* Nick had brought him smoked salmon and Vouvray; the pretty young nurses had brought him *The Times* every morning—it all sounded more like a hotel than a hospital. And even more like a hotel when Freddie revealed the high point of his visit to this delightful establishment. The surgeon was not just an admirer of Freddie's philosophy, he was clearly a genius with the scalpel, too, or maybe it was the patient whose own powers knew no bounds. Whichever way, the end result was the same—and more than satisfactory. In fact the reason for this amazing transatlantic call was so that I could be the first to know just *how* satisfactory. It was unclear which of his lady visitors had won the jackpot, but apparently almost as soon as she had arrived, with a couple of well-chosen books from Hatchards and a nice fruit basket from Fortnum's next door, she had been bundled into the alluring hospital bathroom, where they had feasted, not upon nectarines or figs but upon each other. I could hear Freddie smiling down the telephone with pleasure as he told me the story, and I hoped he could hear me smiling back when I said how incredibly happy I was too.

NOW THAT MY MOTHER was going to La Migoua with Hylan, the house became a place they could escape to, sometimes alone in the spring, and in the summer with Nick and Alex. It was transformed from a crowded barracks ruled over by an unpredictable sergeant major into a charming love nest. Who knows what our neighbors Monsieur and Madame Tricon made of this abrupt shift in Monsieur and Madame Ayer's arrangements, but I imagine they just poured themselves another glass of *vin d'orange* and sighed, concluding not for the first time that *"Les Anglais sont complètement fous. Mais assez gentils, quand même."* And it wasn't just the atmosphere of the house that was transformed.

Hylan soon found himself on the roof replacing tiles, on a ladder painting shutters, and most ambitious of all, putting up a new ceiling of slatted bamboo in the top-floor rooms. The bamboo looked pretty enough, but how was poor Hylan to know that in creating this bijou effect he was actually building a well-appointed apartment complex for several generations of *loirs*? It took a while for these creatures, which look like obese dormice with fluffy foxy tails, to discover their new home, but over the years they settled down very comfortably in the spacious gap between the bamboo and the roof. Without access to either birth control or toilets, they scuttled around up there, multiplying at an alarming Malthusian rate, and quite soon their shit started to stream down through the slats. The last time I went to the house, the first few days were spent scraping it off the bedcovers, scrubbing the walls, picking it out of the rush matting on the floor, and attempting, none too successfully, to winkle this semi-fossilized crap—I used a knife-teaspoon combo—out of the drain in the shower. But the bamboo still looks lovely.

In 1973 my mother's holiday in France was cut short because the BBC had asked her

to go 15 rounds with that dreadful right-wing Catholic American pig, William Buckley. It is supposed to be recorded on August 22nd. I would imagine he'll wipe the floor with me—he even ties Gore Vidal into furious little snarling knots, and I haven't nearly the smooth patience of Gore. Also I don't *know* anything—and he, alas, though nasty is extremely well informed.

Her misgivings seem to have been justified, and she wrote in a letter to Freddie:

I did my television thing yesterday, but I'm afraid I wasn't very good. He filled me so full of paralyzed despair that I just couldn't work up the energy to fight him. Even the one time I had him cornered, I couldn't find the necessary oomph to deliver the coup de grace. Frightfully depressing it all was, not just being face to face with such a lunatic, but to discover I had lost the will to kill. "Why bother?" was all I felt, and that is, in such situations, the downhill road to nowhere. What an *awful* man. A loony. And though pretty, not nearly as pretty as John Lindsay.

The ill-fated debate between the pig and the sergeant major was also aired in the United States, and soon after, my mother received a postcard from an old friend: "We just finished watching you try to make conversation with William Buckley and I thought we should tell you how lovely you looked and how well you talked. You were extremely pretty on color TV and intelligent, and perhaps best of all, civil to Mr. Buckley." She quoted this message in her letter to Freddie and added:

So I think it is v. kind of them but I much fear that when people start telling you (me, especially) how *pretty* you looked then it perhaps says all there is to say about the quality of the discussion. However I have stopped chewing my bottom lip over it as there is nothing I could do about it at the time, and even less now, so piss to it.

ONCE VANESSA had gotten up the courage to explain to her husband that she would be spending the summer at La Migoua with her lover from now on, there was an awkward day when the two couples overlapped at the house. My mother always called it Checkpoint Charlie. The first time Vanessa came it was Hylan's job to teach her the driving situation (she was, after all, Freddie's chauffeur), and they set off together in the car so he could show her how to get to the beach, the Bandol dump, and where to shop, leaving my parents sitting under the lime tree, chatting away as if nothing had changed. (One of the things that certainly hadn't altered at all was my mother's venom toward her rival, which despite Hylan remained as poisonous as ever. I remember being at the house when she discovered a particularly fetching apron—incredibly short with flirtatious girly ruffles, like something from a bad French farce—in the kitchen cupboard. Clearly bought by Vanessa, who was utterly, irredeemably feminine and had a tiny waist, the offensive piece of fabric was instantly converted into a rag for cleaning the floor, and as I recall, the lavatories too.)

With the summer divided up between his parents, Nick's life at La Migoua took on a more serene aspect. His mother's unpredictable moods had been tempered by love, and she and Hylan tended to leave him alone to do what he wanted. Which sometimes was drugs. "Neglect" is just another word for freedom in a fourteen-year-old's mind, and Nick had plenty of both. One summer he had been lucky enough to find a stash of grass, hidden away in some secret place, so secret that Hylan had forgotten where he had put it, and ever the generous host, Nick was able to treat his friends to several satisfying joints up in his sweltering room under the shit-covered bamboo ceiling.

However, at this point I have to admit that firsthand knowledge of what my curious, fractured family got up to at La Migoua for the next few years is kind of sketchy. Reports would reach me from the various players in the drama—complaints from Nick about Vanessa: "Her arms are so skinny she can't even carry the shopping bags, so I have to. I wish Beatrice was here." Or from my mother, delirious descriptions of Hylan's prowess behind the wheel/grouting tiles/making mint juleps for the Tricons with Jack Daniel's they'd brought from London. All the things Freddie had never done: "Jesus, it's like being on a real vacation." Well, not so much for Nick and Alex. While Hylan was busy slaving away at his various domestic duties and my mother was lounging in the hammock, an ashtray and a stack of English newspapers by her side, they waited sullenly, and in vain, to be taken to the beach.

I was so happy not to be there.

ONE NIGHT during my last year at Oxford I met a man at a party and was surprised to wake up the next morning in an unfamiliar bedroom overlooking the High Street. I've heard it said, usually by people far better behaved than I am, that something that starts this way will never lead anywhere, but who knows how the mysterious affairs of the heart and body work—or don't? All I know is that Tom—for that turned out to be my unfamiliar companion's name—and I have been entwined, in some funny fashion or another, ever since.

Half Spanish and wholly Catholic, he felt doubly foreign to me. Having lived a sheltered life inside my family's atheist anti-Franco cocoon, I'm not sure that I actually knew anybody who believed in God, and I had certainly never been anywhere near Spain—which only fueled my fascination with both these forbidden subjects. The day after my final exam I flew to Madrid.

Tom was staying at his grandmother's apartment, an enormous, gloomy maze of a place on the Paseo de la Castellana, where an endless crusade against the sun was fought daily. Heavily armed with shutters, blinds, lace curtains, and swathes of thick brocade, the servants battled away at those twin scourges, heat and light, and despite the odd setback—I did once see a shaft of sunlight break through the defenses and illuminate a strip of dusty parquet—mostly won. Señora Marañón, who must have been about ninety at the time, inhabited an armchair in a corner of one of the smaller salons, and when I was introduced to her, she smiled and slowly turned her fragile tortoise head up toward me as I leaned down to kiss her withered cheeks. "Encantada," she whispered and reached over to clutch my arm, hanging on tightly, as if she wanted to confide some secret, but then, thinking better of it, eventually allowed me to go. Above her on the faded green velvet wall hung a crucifix; its doll-like Christ, carved in ivory, slim and elongated as an El Greco, slumped against his mahogany cross.

At night Madrid was as dark as Señora Marañón's apartment in the daytime. It felt almost Edwardian compared with the only other cities I knew—London, Paris, and New York—no dazzling neon, no lit-up shopwindows, no sodium yellow glare, just the cozy glow of bars and restaurants and old-fashioned streetlamps that emitted ineffectual pools of flickering light. The restaurant where we had dinner that first night lurked at the end of a cobbled cul-de-sac somewhere behind the Plaza Mayor. Not a single thing did I recognize on the menu, so after a few *copitas* of chilled manzanilla, and a couple of appetizers—fried blood sausage (*morcilla*) and some grotesque barnacles, long black appendages dangling obscenely from their shells (*percebes*)—Tom offered to order for me. Whether he chose the dishes to jolt me out of my effete Francophile ways, or whether they represented the ne plus ultra of Spanish cuisine, or whether he quite genuinely wanted to eat them I will never know. But here's what we had after our rat's penis and coagulated blood *amuse-gueules* at the bar.

Tom and the owner of the establishment were old friends—apparently he used to go there with his grandfather when he was a little boy—and greeted each other with hugs and cries of "Hombre!" After which there was naturally no need to consult a menu, because Tom would be having his usual, and I would be having the roast suckling pig. Suckling. It wouldn't have been quite so awful if the entire newborn baby hadn't arrived at the table on a silver tray with an apple shoved in her mouth—couldn't she have been dismembered in the kitchen first? But no, we had to admire her, and then she was whisked away by her nurse/waiter and returned soon after to her parents, in the form of tender chunks of milk-fed meat beneath a deeply tanned layer of the crispiest and most irresistible skin I have ever tasted.

Tom's usual turned out to be even more frightening. Take a lamb's head, split it open, sprinkle with sea salt, grill, and serve. Simplicity itself. The sightless milky eyeballs gave his face a resigned, dispirited air, as if he had known all along that this would be his fate, and it was quite obvious that he'd never thought to visit an American dentist. Misshapen and stained, his teeth betrayed a lifetime's addiction to unfiltered Ducados and way too many flagons of *vino tonto*. Tom dug into his brains, I took another bite of my roasted baby, and the beaming owner reappeared to check that everything was to our liking. "Perfecto. Delicioso," we replied, quite truthfully.

After dinner we wandered back through the shadowy colonnades of the Plaza Mayor, and I listened as my tutor explained how, in 1589, Philip II had commissioned Juan de Herrera to design him a modern plaza in the fashionable Renaissance style for his brand-new capital. A multi-purpose complex, it was perfect for all kinds of entertainments; everything from bullfights—you could still see faded bloodstains on some of the walls—to executions, and, during the Inquisition, autos-da-fé. So began my first tutorial in Spanish history. We would start on politics later that night at the Café Gijón.

Gregorio Marañón, Tom's grandfather, had been one of the great Spanish intellectuals of the twentieth century. And the Café Gijón on the Paseo de la Castellana, a few blocks from the dark mazy apartment where his widow still lived, was where he used to hang out, and where we went for a drink later that night. A physician, scientist, historian, and philosopher, Doctor Marañón had been liberal in his politics and omnivorous in his interests, and I kept wishing that he and Freddie could have been sitting there with us on the red leather banquette, just so I could have listened to them talking together. But instead we were joined by some of Tom's friends, whose conversation inevitably—because that was all anybody in Spain in the early seventies talked about—turned to Franco and what would happen after the old murderer was finally dumped in his Speer-like mausoleum in the Valle de los Caídos. Surely he couldn't last much longer (he hung on another four years), but nobody knew what his heir, Prince Juan Carlos, would do when he came to the throne.

The Prince with the Pubic Hair on his Head, as he was affectionately known on account of his tightly coiled locks, had been educated in Spain (away from the influence of his exiled family in Rome) under Franco's vigilant eye, and had sworn a public oath of loyalty to El Jefe. So maybe he had been brainwashed and would follow in his soi-disant godfather's jackbooted footsteps. But then again he was rumored to be in touch with his far more liberal father, Don Juan, and with opposition politicians, so maybe he would lead Spain into the promised land of democracy. An enigma wrapped up in the rigid embrace of a dictator, the prince floated in regal ambiguity way beyond the grasp of Tom or any of his friends. And I floated off to unambiguously common sleep, curled up on the banquette, my head in my tutor's lap.

Doctor Marañón's house just outside Toledo had been a monastery in the sixteenth century—the chapel was still intact, and one of the monks' cells had been turned into the doctor's study, seemingly untouched since his death. If you stood by the sundial near the front door, and looked back across the valley, the view—the Alcázar, the cathedral, the steep hills, the bridge, and the swirling clouds—could have been, and was, painted by El Greco. Naively, ignorantly, absurdly, I gazed at Toledo and imagined I was seeing it through his eyes, failing to understand that nobody has *ever* been able to see what El Greco saw. Down some steps on the lower terrace our lunch—bread, wine, and a still-warm tortilla—had been set out on a stone table in the dusty shade of a grape-heavy pergola. Lizards bustled about in the ivy, cicadas thrummed away with no apparent sense of rhythm in the cypress trees, and way off in the distance I could hear the desolate clumsy clanging of church bells.

Later that afternoon Tom said he would take me to see a synagogue that looked like a mosque, improbably called Santa María la Blanca—its Jewish name obliterated during a series of savage pogroms in the fourteenth century. This would be my first lesson in the religious bouillabaisse that had existed in Spain before Ferdinand and Isabella, *los Reyes Católicos*, decided that on the whole they preferred their soup to be composed of a single Christian theme. Heat weakened and dizzy with wine, I listened as best I could to the story of an enterprising rabbi named Solomon ha-Levi, who had somehow or other transformed himself into the archbishop of Burgos, but my thoughts kept sliding back to the claw-footed tub I had glimpsed earlier on in a cool, grottolike bathroom upstairs. Maybe we should continue our discussion of *la Reconquista* up there?

A trickle of rust-tinged water dribbled into the enormous bath, pipes shuddering, as I lay back, eyes closed, and waited patiently for my body to be submerged. I could hear Tom talking to the cook and her husband in the kitchen downstairs, and after that total silence until he appeared at the door about half an hour later—"I've brought you some presents." First he arranged a Leaning Tower of Books on the floor, then he balanced a couple of glasses and an ashtray on top of the laundry basket, and after that he settled into a rickety armchair and began to feed me warm figs, cold wine, and the occasional fiery drag of his cigarette while reading out loud from Gregorio Marañón's book *El Greco y Toledo.*

"But do you know who wrote about El Greco better than anybody? Even better than my grandfather."

I did not.

"He was a German art historian who came to Spain in 1908 to study Velázquez, but he fell in love with El Greco instead. His name was Julius Meier-Graefe."

Who had been married to Busch, our friend in France with the filthy sex-crazed dog. Not much interested in hearing about Meier-Graefe's widow or her revolting new consort, Tom found the book somewhere near the top of the listing tower: "This is what he says. 'All the generations that follow after El Greco live in his realm. There is a greater difference between him and Titian, his master, than between him and Renoir or Cézanne.' And that is the whole point! Which is why he only ever got two commissions out of Philip II, who could not begin to understand his vision. So, deprived of royal patronage, he moved to Toledo where he could paint what he wanted. You'll understand what Meier-Graefe is talking about when we go see *The Burial of Count of Orgaz.*"

No doubt I would, but in the meantime, maybe he could pass me a towel? It was dusk when I woke up in an unfamiliar bedroom overlooking a garden in Spain.

"Too late for the synagogue and the count?"

"Oh yes," he whispered. "Much too late."

HERE WAS OUR PLAN: After Toledo we would drive south through Andalucía, staying in a series of monasteries and castles that had been converted into *paradores,* so I could continue my education in Spanish art and history, partly by osmosis and partly with the help of my traveling tutor. The *Grand Tour à l'espagnol.* I like to think that I made some progress along the way, and by the time we arrived at Tom's family's house on the coast, I was already familiar with the vague contours of Mudejar architecture, knew that when Philip II had the Escorial designed, he took his inspiration from the grisly grid on which Saint Laurence had been barbecued, and I'd learned that a glass of fino must *always* be held by the stem, *never* the bowl. I even made a bit of headway with the language, helped along by a publication called *¡Hola!*, which Tom told me was read only by idiotic shopgirls and even more half-witted cleaning ladies.

Admittedly its editorial focus was narrow, but no less affecting for being so. How could one resist being swept up into the joys, tears, sorrows, and heartbreaks of the assorted royals (reigning and deposed), bullfighters, and soap opera stars who inhabited its colorful pages week after week? Even though I could just about stumble through a story about the tragic death of the Duchess of Ávila's teenage son in a car crash, my spoken Spanish never progressed beyond six words—*hola, adiós, gracias, por favor,* and *cama matrimonial.* The last two being the most crucial. Every time we checked into a hotel, if I didn't kick my tutor hard in the shins and hiss *cama matrimonial* into his ear, the sad, repressed, acne-stricken clerk behind the front desk would invariably show us into a room with two sad, repressed, and extremely narrow single beds.

Eager to please my new boyfriend's parents, I was on my best behavior at their house, and flattered myself that things were going even better than I'd dared to hope. No more swearing—I was particularly careful to avoid any reference to Jesus H. Christ—I listened with genuine interest to his father's musings on Saint John of the Cross, to his mother's memories of life as an exile in Paris after the civil war, and appeared at breakfast, smiling and on time, each morning. Except that after three or four breakfasts we were asked, extremely politely, to leave. How could this be? Apparently the problem was related to the *cama matrimonial* business. When we arrived my suitcase had been firmly deposited in his father's dressing room, conveniently located next door to the parental boudoir, while Tom was to share a room with his brother at the other end of the house. An odd arrangement, but ever the gracious guest, I was more than happy to follow the peculiar customs of these peculiar people in this peculiar country.

And yet, perhaps there was something to be said for their strange, antiquated ways. Forbidden pleasure. Illicit sex. Christianity clearly had its uses. Why had sex in our house never been associated with guilt? Why had there never been any rules to break? Well, I'd done my best and taken up with a Catholic and gone to fascist Spain, but my parents didn't care and were actually extremely fond of Tom. His parents, on the other hand, cared a great deal about their son's nocturnal ramblings, which is how we found ourselves waving *adiós* to them rather sooner than planned, and heading off to Extremadura.

Now, could it be a coincidence that in the very same year, 1492, that Ferdinand and Isabella had finally declared victory over the Jews and Moors, Columbus had sailed the ocean blue and discovered a whole new world full of infidels in need of persecution? Probably. But my kindly tutor at least pretended to take my facile aperçu seriously.

"Well, actually you're quite right, there *are* some historians who see the *Reconquista* as a kind of dress rehearsal for the conquistadores, but I've always thought they got the hell out of Extremadura because it was—and is—the harshest, most miserable, and poverty-stricken region in the entire country."

Not a great deal appeared to have changed in the five hundred years since Cortés, Pizarro, and their henchmen had abandoned their homeland in search of gold and glory. It was the emptiness that struck me first. We drove for hours and hours across a landscape drained of life—no people, no animals, hardly another car on the road, until we arrived at an equally desolate village. Its inhabitants had barricaded themselves away behind shutters to escape the heat; a sad, skeletal dog slept in a doorway; and in the dusty plaza only the church and a bar—the twin opiates—were open for business.

BEHIND THE PALACIO DE PIZARRO, at the top of a steep hill, Tom told me there was a convent where the nuns made the best *yemas* he had ever tasted, and since it was only about three in the afternoon, God knows we had plenty of time to kill before lunch. *Yemas?*

"You'll love them. They're incredibly sweet and sticky, just egg yolks and sugar."

Unconvinced, I nevertheless trudged up the hill toward the convent's stone facade, punctuated by windows barred with Saint Laurence–style grilles and two massive doors tattooed with metal studs. The nuns belonged to a closed order, and from the day they betrothed themselves to Jesus H. Christ to the day they died, they would never again have any contact with the world outside. Imagine. Quite apart from the horror of being buried alive in this prison, I wondered, on a more practical level, how they managed to conduct their *yemas* transactions without ever setting eyes on their eager customers.

"Like this," and my tutor pulled a rusty chain beside a contraption with a small revolving door, waited until it creaked slowly around, put the money inside, waited for it to creak around again, and there was a box of *yemas*, neatly wrapped in brown paper and string.

"Until quite recently they used the same system for abandoned babies, except of course they traveled in the opposite direction."

Oh no, poor little babies. Imagine being brought up by those faceless nuns in that fortress. If I hadn't been quite so hungry I would have worked myself up into a tearful state about them, but instead I followed Tom down the hill and into a dimly lit restaurant hidden away behind Pizarro's palace.

"Today we're going to have an extremely simple lunch. Bread, ham, and wine. That's it. The bread I don't know about, but the ham and the wine will be *más delicioso* than anything you have ever tasted in your entire life. The pigs, who have pretty little black hooves—*pata negra*—snuffle around under the oak trees here in Extremadura eating acorns, until the happy day arrives when they are transformed into *jamón ibérico*."

Tom picked up a slice of ham—rosy, almost translucent with a creamy flutter of fat along the edge—and handed it to me, with a glass of Vega Sicilia wine. With nothing to do, nowhere to go, nobody to meet, surely it made far more sense to linger a little longer at our table by the window, in which case we were in need of *más vino y más jamón, por favor*.

Only rarely, in my experience, and usually for only the briefest of moments, does life—quite capriciously—take it into its head to suddenly give you everything you could possibly desire all at once. And this was one of those mysterious ineffable moments. Which was why I couldn't stop my thoughts from climbing back up that hill, slipping through the barred windows, and creeping along the shadowy flagstoned passages to spy on those ghostly nuns as they stirred their bubbling copper cauldrons full of egg yolks and sugar. Imagine.

"Tom, now we're going to play a game that I made up as a little girl in France many years ago. It's called 'Which Would You Rather?' Imagine we had a daughter"—he smiled, apparently happy with this idea—"and on her eighteenth birthday you have a very, very difficult choice."

He took another sip of Vega Sicilia, and his face assumed an appropriately concerned expression.

"Would you rather she became a nun in a closed order making *yemas* for the rest of her life, or would you prefer her to be a lesbian?"

An impossible dilemma, exquisitely balanced, carefully calculated just to torture my poor tutor. I knew he'd go nuts agonizing over these two equally distressing choices and maybe it might even lead to an interesting discussion about the Catholic Church's attitude toward homosexuality. But no, I had gotten it all wrong. Tom just looked at me as if I were completely mad, and without agonizing for a split *momentito*, replied, "A nun, of course."

Of course.

Le Meule de Foin

WHENEVER THINGS AT HOME got a bit too exciting and my mother's natural exuberance went a bit too far, Freddie would retreat to his study, nervously twiddling his silver chain and muttering, "That dreadful woman, that dreadful woman"; Nick would hide in his room and smoke; and I would run around the corner to the Haystack. The exterior of Colin and Anna Haycraft's house—a grimy brick facade, its details highlighted in olive green, blackened windows, the front door hidden behind an Amazonian jungle of vines—was, I'll admit, a bit alarming. Years before, a cabdriver shook his head incredulously when he dropped me off at 22 Gloucester Crescent, "Blimey, it's the bleedin' 'Ouse of Usher. You'd better be careful in there, Miss." And he drove off cackling at his own witticism.

Inside, however, the House of Usher was anything but sinister, and put you more in mind of that capacious and chaotic shoe inhabited by the old lady in the nursery rhyme, who had so many children that she hadn't the slightest idea what to do. Except that this lady wasn't old at all, and knew precisely what she wanted to do, which was to have lots of babies (there would be seven in all) and write lots of books (about a dozen) while entertaining anybody who felt like dropping in (the front door was never locked). Anna rarely left her kitchen and didn't care for other people's houses. So if you wanted to see her—and everybody did—you never waited for an invitation, or bothered to call ahead, or rang the doorbell; you just hacked your way through the vines, barged through the door, kicked the toys out of the way, pushed aside the curtain of damp laundry hanging on a swaying rack suspended from the ceiling, and shouted, "You there?!"

"Darling, you're just in time. I'm *desperate* for beer and fags." Immobilized by a sturdy child with matted black hair, in boots and corduroy trousers, whose head was buried in her bosom—"Don't bite or kick, you naughty boy!"—Anna handed me an earthenware jug, a crumpled pound note, and I headed off to the Good Mixer, a pub of unmitigated squalor around the corner on Inverness Street. On the way out I narrowly missed tripping over some baskets on the floor; one contained a sleeping baby, the other a pile of potatoes. Anna gently pushed the baby one to safety under the kitchen table with her foot, and went on feeding her booted appendage.

"Good God, I'm not drinking any of that swill." Colin had arrived home from work and needed a real drink. "Beer may be good enough for women and children and servants, but a man needs a stiff whiskey or better still, a champagne cocktail. In fact several champagne cocktails, after the bloody awful day I've had."

Colin's publishing company, Duckworth, occupied an old piano factory at the top of Gloucester Crescent, where he ruled over his empire from a windowless office, not much bigger than a closet, that was embedded like a hubcap at the center of the huge circular building. Some days were indeed bloody awful. "How the hell can a man be expected to make any money in the book business when all people want to read is rubbish and more rubbish? I'm not fucking George Weidenfeld, you know."

Certainly not. Absolutely no danger of confusing those two.

George was a smooth operator who wore perfectly tailored double-breasted suits, smoked cigars that smelled of money, knew everyone worth knowing in the world, had had the good sense to marry two satisfyingly rich wives, lived in a palazzo in Chelsea, and published books that people apparently wanted to buy. Colin, on the other hand, looked like a scarecrow, had a penniless wife, wore whatever he could find dangling from the ceiling in the laundry room (complemented by a bow tie covered in ducks), screamed with laughter, drank too much, lived in a shoe in Camden Town, and published whatever he damn well pleased.

That particular evening, while George was entertaining the prime minister of Israel along with Saul Bellow, Edna O'Brien, Jimmy Goldsmith, and the foreign secretary (I knew because I worked for him), Colin was standing in his saggy underpants (his soup-encrusted trousers had been thrown on the floor for Anna to deal with later) in the pantry, hunting for sugar cubes, Angostura bitters, and a bottle of brandy he knew he'd hidden in the bread bin. Oh no, don't think that George was the only publisher in London who had important authors to wine and dine that night. In Colin's case the wining always played a rather more central role than the dining.

"Oh Christ, I suppose these buggers are going to expect something to eat."

"And which particular buggers would they be, my darling?"

Colin did this all the time. You might have thought it would have driven Anna to madness or murder, but instead it just amused her. Not much interested in eating herself, she couldn't imagine why hostesses fretted and fussed and flapped about what to feed their guests. As long as the people sitting around her table weren't boring (they rarely were) and there was plenty to drink (there always was), she didn't care who showed up, how long they stayed, or what they said or did. A wry observer of the human race and its foibles, endlessly sympathetic to the Sturm und Drang of other people's lives, Anna was oddly immune to these psychic dramas and messes herself. Wise and funny, she took a detached, quizzical view of the world, refusing to be sucked into its lunacy, and was quite content to watch its strange ways, and to comfort its troubled occupants, from the sanctuary of her murky kitchen.

Professor Screech was the first of Colin's guests to arrive. An energetic beetle of a man with darting eyes and a delicate flurry of dandruff decorating his collar, he was a fellow of All Souls and widely regarded as the world's foremost Montaigne scholar. His new book was the sparkling star at the epicenter of Duckworth's spring list and, carried away by its brilliance, and quite possibly by his fourth champagne cocktail, Colin announced to the author that the print run was going to be increased to an astonishing five hundred copies. Before the professor could respond to this surprising but entirely welcome news, a naked child, still slippery from its bath, raced into the room, grabbed a bowl of peanuts and a bottle of tonic water, and disappeared behind the sofa, shrieking in triumph. Professor Screech looked appalled, Colin shouted at the child to get the hell out, then beat it about the head with a pillow, and having failed to drive the terrified creature out of its lair, roared up the stairs, "*Alfie!*"

Alfie had joined the Haycraft ménage after Colin and Anna had come home one night to find an undernourished teenager wandering around upstairs, looking for something to steal. You couldn't say Alfie had broken into the house, since the door had been unlocked as usual, and you couldn't say he was a burglar, since there was nothing he could be bothered to take. He didn't want any of Colin's five thousand books, he didn't want a stuffed alligator, he didn't want Anna's painting of her children, he didn't want the ceremonial sword presented to Colin's father in India, shortly before he had been murdered by a deranged soldier in his regiment, he didn't want a picture of a peacock composed of appliquéd feathers—in fact there was not a single thing in the entire Haystack that he wanted. But what he did want was to escape from his large family who lived in an unappealing house in what he quite aptly called Kuntish Town. Sometimes he worked in the Duckworth office, sometimes he did the Good Mixer beer-and-fags run, sometimes he looked after the children (he was godfather to the one in the basket on the floor), but mostly he told us astonishing stories about his far-from-sane relatives that made us cry with laughter and beg for more.

Alfie had removed the squealing creature, and Colin was now wrestling with the "placement" for his dinner. Not that there was any food in sight. I glanced at the paper in his hand—the alarming words FINAL NOTICE, printed in red at the top, still left plenty of space for a crude diagram of the crowded table below—and recognized my name.

"You, young lady, are in for a rare treat tonight. I'm putting you beside Professor Kenneth Dover. He's written the definitive book on buggery and pederasty in ancient Greece, and has actually come up with a completely new word, 'intercrural,' from the Latin *crus, cruris*—'leg,' to describe what they got up to. Consummation apparently took the form of the lover inserting his penis between the boy's thighs, so I suppose technically it wasn't buggery at all. But it was certainly pederasty."

Colin exploded into messy laughter, champagne and spittle flying, and I said I'd be sure to take this interesting point up with the professor just as soon as we sat down.

My host, who had gotten a first in classics at Oxford, had never lost his enthusiasm for the ancient world—which was why Anna called him Horace, and why the Duckworth list was studded with priceless gems like Professor Dover's opus, cleverly set off against slim but perfectly proportioned novels by Anna and her close friend Beryl Bainbridge. "No point in long novels. Nobody wants to read them, they cost too much to produce, and far more to the point, you can charge just as much for something that's only one hundred pages long."

Plus your wife and her friend could crank them out quicker. Anna (who wrote under the name of Alice Thomas Ellis) and Beryl were so successful that other publishers were constantly trying to steal them away from Colin, but whether out of loyalty or laziness, they both seemed to prefer the bully they knew. I once walked into the kitchen and heard him shouting on the telephone at Tom Maschler, the head of Jonathan Cape, who was apparently trying to persuade Colin to sell him his wife: "Now look here, Tom. You don't think I've spent all these years cultivating this wretched oyster just so you could come along and steal the pearls she's finally producing, do you? So *fuck off!*" And then he slammed down the receiver so hard that he had a coughing fit, and I had to bring him a glass of water.

During the school holidays Anna would gather up her children and decamp to their cottage in Wales. (Colin didn't see the point of the country and stayed in London, where he could finally have "some bloody peace and quiet.") "Cottage" is probably a bit of a misnomer in that it suggests snapdragons and rambling roses, freshly laundered gingham curtains fluttering in the breeze, and bread baking in a cozy wood-beamed kitchen. The Welsh Haystack was not like that at all. Not remotely. Not in any shape or form. In fact it far more resembled a Lawrencian miner's two-up-and-two-down that had somehow been uprooted from a back alley in Sunderland and dumped down beside a babbling brook, halfway up a mountain in Gwynedd.

Anna had been brought up in a place called Penmaenmawr and always thought of herself as Welsh, which for her was an entirely different, and wholly superior, proposition to being English. Many years after we first met she wrote a book about Wales and in it confessed, "I have never felt truly at ease or at home anywhere but in Wales. I fell in love with the land, as I believe people are supposed to fall in love with other people. I wanted to be one flesh with it." Wales was indeed her lover, and as time went by and the children got older, she contrived to spend more and more of her life there, often blissfully alone with the object of her desire. Luckily Colin was not the jealous type.

~

WORKING FOR GEORGE WEIDENFELD allowed me to indulge in three of my favorite activities—gorging on books, going to parties, and yacking with some of the most interesting people around—while getting paid, admittedly not terribly well, for these undeniable pleasures. Coincidentally these were some of the same things that George loved to do, and did with extraordinary finesse. Long ago, before independent publishing houses had been gobbled up by corporations, publishers' lists used to be a reflection of the taste, character, and foibles of the boss. Colin had his crazy classicists as well as Beryl's and Anna's novels, while George's interests veered off in disparate and altogether more worldly directions. His magpie mind flitted about in search of the shiniest and most alluring people and manuscripts he could find to enliven his publishing house and his drawing room. The list fed the parties, the parties fed the list, and both fed George.

Bona fide intellectuals (John Berger), heavyweight historians (Hugh Trevor-Roper), delightful historians (Antonia Fraser), controversial historians (David Irving), and true literary geniuses (Nabokov and Bellow) found themselves in the company of politicians (Harold Wilson, Golda Meir, Charles de Gaulle) and assorted elderly social butterflies of the *ancien régime* like the Duke of Verdura and Prince Clary. George also had a touching faith in the literary talents of just about any beautiful, well-connected, and preferably titled woman who could spell her own name. These ravishing creatures, who added so much to the merriment of his parties, were always assumed to have a book lurking somewhere in their fragrant bosoms, just waiting to be coaxed out by one of his hardworking editors. I recall one particular Italian contessa (flashing eyes and emeralds, glossy hair and sable, all enveloped in an impenetrable fog of Mitsouko) who was put to "work" "writing" a "book" called *The Private Gardens of Italy,* most of which, rather serendipitously, seemed to belong to her relatives. But to be fair to George, that spring he published another, altogether more serious "Italian gardening book," the first English edition of Giorgio Bassani's masterpiece *The Garden of the Finzi-Continis.* In the same manner the supreme frivolity of Cecil Beaton's diaries, a poisonous cocktail of snobbery and maliciousness, was balanced by the supreme

humanity of Victor Klemperer's, which bore dignified witness to the dep-
redations and destruction endured by the Jews of Nazi Dresden.

AS AN AUSTRIAN JEW who had escaped from Vienna after the
Anschluss in 1938, had spent the war in London working for the BBC, and
then had gone to Israel as Chaim Weizmann's chef de cabinet in 1949,
George never could resist the twin sirens of Nazism and Zionism. (And
he wasn't crazy, because there cannot be two more fascinating subjects
in the entire twentieth century. Well, I suppose there is the "rumble and
the rethink"—as Martin Amis used to call it—in Russia in 1917, and
then there's China, but we can't get into that now.) George *had* to publish Albert Speer, he *had* to acquire Joachim Fest's biography of Hitler at
the Frankfurt Book Fair, but it was Israel that remained his true weakness. However, whereas the Nazis could always be relied upon to shift a
respectable—and occasionally spectacular—number of books, the same,
alas, could not be said of the Israelis. When George set off on his annual
pilgrimage/shopping spree to Jerusalem, the managing director, who had
the unenviable task of trying to keep his boss's spending under some kind
of control, would get especially nervous. He knew perfectly well what a
week in the presidential suite at the King David cost, because God knows
he'd been signing that bill for years, but what he lived in terror of were the
contracts that were conceived there in wild moments of patriotic passion.
Abba Eban, Ezer Weizman, a few ex-presidents, an ex–prime minister,
a Mossad agent who had foiled a plot to assassinate Golda—these men
were heroes of the state, and was George about to insult them? He was
not. They were certified superstars, and it was only natural that as their
publisher he would wish to give them advances in keeping with their stat-
ure, and it was equally natural that when they arrived in London for the
publication of their eagerly awaited memoirs, they would expect lengthy
interviews on BBC television and in *The Times*. Which was where my
nightmare began.

Soon after I started working for George, one of these glittering stars
in the Israeli firmament came to town and was given an especially festive dinner at his publisher's apartment in Chelsea. Sinuous, elegantly
pornographic Schieles adorned the front hall, one of Bacon's screaming

popes (after Velázquez) dominated the library, and an eighteenth-century French tapestry hung above a tobacco-colored suede sofa in the drawing room where the grizzled hero (tieless in Gaza—the collar of his crisp blue shirt arranged *outside* the jacket lapels, in the Israeli style) was being feted by *le tout Londres*. Politicians were eager to discuss the long-range implications of taking the Golan Heights, while silken ladies in backless dresses leaned closer to his rugged features to hear what it *really* felt like to command an army of tanks as they rumbled across the Sinai. Unfazed and implacable, the hero made light of his desert romp, the ladies shivered and melted (what *is* it with girls and soldiers?), while I was left to fret about how the hell I was going to persuade the producer of the *BBC Today* show to interview some Israeli he'd probably never heard of. Another glass of champagne was needed to concentrate my mind on this conundrum, and when that didn't work, I found myself indulging in a bit of light flirtation with the hero's handsome bodyguard (what *is* it with girls and guns?) just to cheer myself up and calm myself down.

Despite—or quite possibly because of—the delightful extravagance of George's apartment and private life, the Weidenfeld office was refreshingly modest. A ramshackle arrangement of drafty corridors and boxy rooms, approached by a staircase as long and steep as Jacob's proverbial ladder, it crouched above a dilapidated movie theater across from the railway station in Clapham Junction. Not a part of London that most visiting publishers or authors were familiar with, so George usually contrived to meet his grander foreign friends in the library at home. But occasionally I would run into a snappily dressed New York editor wheezing unsteadily at the top of the stairs, clearly wondering what he, and indeed George, was doing in such an unlikely part of town.

One sunny day, although it was hard to tell since the window was tinted with years of Clapham grime, I was sitting quietly at my desk minding my own business, as distinct from Weidenfeld business, when I was called into George's office. Christ—not another one of those bloody Israelis expecting to go on national television. Oh, but it was. Apparently this one had written a book about Jews killing Nazis, which I had to admit was an entirely welcome reversal of roles, and might even help a bit, since the jaded hacks I was forced to deal were constantly in search of something fresh and unexpected.

"Brilliant. Absolutely brilliant," George was sitting behind his desk puffing excitedly on a Montecristo.

"It's been at the top of the best-seller list in Israel for six months. Taken the country by storm. Snapped up by Random House, the movie rights are already sold, and I am confident it is going to have an even bigger success here."

Oh *please* don't say that. George was bouncing around in his chair, unable to contain his enthusiasm for this astounding book, but then quite suddenly he bounced right out of it and, heading for the door, turned to the beaming author. "David, how I wish I could stay, but alas I am already late for a terribly dull lunch. So I leave you with Gully, who will be masterminding your publicity campaign."

What else could I do but invite David to a terribly dull lunch to discuss the publicity blitzkrieg that would shortly be coming his way? Where we went I don't recall, but I do remember thinking that he reminded me of a somewhat younger (he must have been in his late thirties) version of the grizzled hero (David too had been part of that busy crossing of the Sinai), and that he bore a quite alarming physical resemblance to the fascist hairdresser who had relieved me of my troublesome virginity (except that as a Labor member of the Knesset, his politics were more acceptable and his wife, as far as I could gather, wasn't pregnant). By the time I finally got back to the office dusk was settling in, and it seemed that we had agreed to meet for dinner the next day. As commander in chief of the blitzkrieg, I was well aware that there were many more details of this complicated campaign to be finalized before he returned to Tel Aviv. In fact it was so complicated that it became necessary for us to continue our discussions over dinner on the following night as well.

All of a sudden, upheavals in the Israeli cabinet, Yitzhak Rabin's Interim Agreement with Egypt, and the withdrawal from the Sinai all became fascinating topics I couldn't get enough of. And yet how could I possibly begin to understand present-day politics if I didn't have a clearer picture of the past? Luckily right there in the office were the extensive Weidenfeld library and backlist, just waiting to help me out. The stack of books beside my bed started to lean toward subjects like Chaim Weizmann's pivotal role in the Balfour Declaration, Theodor Herzl and the creation of the Zionist movement, Ze'ev Jabotinsky's fractious relationship with the British Mandate in Palestine, while still leaving a bit of space for Aha-ron Appelfeld, Amos Oz, and Primo Levi. Enthralled as I was with my studies, all too frequently my mind would simply refuse to concentrate on a story in the paper about the collapse of some ill-advised jerry-built coalition (why *did* those Israelis have to have quite so many political par-ties?) and instead would obsess over that impossible and eternal question: When will I see you again? Amazingly the answer turned out to be in a few weeks, when he flew back to London for no good reason except that he said he missed me.

Around about this time I called Tom in Madrid. It must have been at least a week since I'd heard from him. Or maybe even longer. How odd. (Oh dear, had I learned nothing? If your boyfriend doesn't call, it's quite simple. He doesn't want to talk to you. Or see you. And he hasn't the slightest idea how to tell you, which is why he hasn't called.)

"¡Hola! Por favor y muchas gracias, ¿donde es Tom?"

Yes, where *was* Tom? I had telephoned his grandmother's apartment where he lived, and her voluble maid was obviously eager to discuss this puzzling situation with me because she erupted into a high-speed ava-lanche of words, not a single one of which could I understand. (Oh dear, why in five years had I failed to learn any Spanish at all?) Still, a mes-sage of some sort must have been relayed—"La señorita tonta Inglés teléfono"—or something along those lines, because the next day he did indeed call back. It was not a happy conversation. Apparently he had met a sane Spanish señorita (my imagination immediately equipped her with a dusky mustache, unusually short legs, and a Frida monobrow) whom he had decided to marry. Yes, *marry.* Surprisingly no amount of tears or shouting—and there was plenty—could change his mind. Ah, but what if I caught the next flight to Madrid?

"Are you *mad?* Have you forgotten what happened when you took that train ride and surprised Martin at his dad's house?"

I was sitting in Anna's kitchen drinking a tumbler of whiskey, weep-ing, but not loudly enough to wake the baby, who, drunk on milk, greasy eyelids flickering, had just dozed off in his basket next to the potatoes on the floor.

"Anyway, Tom was always asking you to marry him, but you didn't want to, so you really can't blame the poor man."

Oh yes I could.

"Well, you shouldn't. And I do seem to recall you were swooning over some gentleman from Israel only last week."

"Yes, but he's married and lives in Tel Aviv."

"And Tom is about to be married and lives in Madrid. What you need is a nice unencumbered Englishman who lives in London, and I know just the one. He's an incredibly good-looking defrocked priest, who quite sensibly decided he couldn't take another moment of that Vatican II lunacy, and now he's writing a book for Colin about Bernard of Clairvaux and twelfth-century Cistercian monasticism. And best of all, he's coming to dinner this evening, so you *must* stay and meet him."

At least I managed to laugh.

L'Israélien

In my midtwenties, on account of a combination of poverty and laziness, I was still living at home. Except that I wasn't really. What estate agents like to call a "well-appointed, self-contained garden flat" had been created on the ground floor of our house in Regent's Park Terrace, and there I lived quite happily, without ever having to confront anything so disagreeable and adult as a mortgage or an electricity bill. I had my own front door, a pretty bedroom with French windows that opened onto the dogs' bucolic toilet, a tiny kitchen and bathroom, and a large drawing room, but the one thing the flat didn't have was a well-appointed, self-contained telephone. How could I possibly have let go of a number (485-4855/Gul-Gull) that so conveniently spelled out my name? The only drawback to this arrangement was that the switchboard operator upstairs (Freddie and Nick never bothered to answer the telephone) was a bit more au courant with my life than a daughter might have wished her mother to be. Still, since the operator also ran a free intermittently reliable answering service on the side—"Some fag called from your office. Didn't catch his name." "Half-witted sounding debutante called. Fiona Fartface or something. Jesus, I didn't know they still made them like that." "That goddamn Israeli called. Again."—I really couldn't complain.

Sometimes the goddamn Israeli and I would see each other in London, where he liked to stay at the Playboy Club. Once we spent a weekend in a "Fawlty Towers" establishment near Brighton, so he could interview Ben-Gurion's mistress—an old lady with fluffy white dandelion hair, whose memories of her David turned out to be rather more discreet than my David had hoped—but usually we met in Paris. The city I had fallen in love with as a *triste* teenager, staying in Monsieur Bretiane's *triste* apartment on the rue de Rennes. David was a modern man who favored modern hotels of the "Towering Inferno" variety. The infernos tended to be skyscrapers with grotesque chandeliers in the lobby, terrifying elevators that raced up and down the sides of an interior atrium, and rooms where the beds were too big and the plate-glass windows didn't open, but so what? I was much too happy to say anything.

"*Chérie!* I knew you must be here because I saw your friend on television this morning. *Comme il est beau*, but I must tell you that I do not agree with what he says *au sujet des Palestiniens*."

Well no, I didn't suppose that Francette, who lurched ever farther to the left as she got older, and had been a militant supporter of the students against de Gaulle in '68, would have agreed with David on the subject of the Palestinians, but that certainly didn't prevent her from insisting that we come for a drink later that evening.

Francette opened a bottle of Domaine Tempier *cuvée* La Migoua, to remind us both of home, and, tactfully leaving the Palestinians to their own murderous/courageous devices, depending on your point of view, asked how my mother and Freddie were. "Tout va bien avec Vanessa et Hylan?" Having established that all was well in my parents' curious marriage, she turned her attention to David, and quite soon they became entangled in the minutiae of some French political scandal involving the iniquity/brilliance of Valéry Giscard d'Estaing, again depending on your point of view. Since I neither knew nor cared what they were talking about, I sank into the soft velvet folds of the sofa, lit a cigarette, and gazed out the window at Notre-Dame's billowing backside, lost in an inane miasma of contentment. It felt like being in my bed in La Migoua, listening to the grown-ups chattering away below on the terrace after dinner, knowing that nothing could go wrong so long as they kept on laughing and talking.

At one point their voices became more animated, and I heard Francette say, "Mais non, c'est pas la vérité." Oh Christ, they couldn't have moved from Giscard to Arafat, could they? I quickly glanced at David's face— he was smiling, and our hostess was busy filling his glass, but clearly he wasn't about to back down. Backing down was not something he did. Not his style. Would not have crossed his mind. Ever. David's character fascinated me. Never before had I met a man with quite such devastating confidence in himself. (Nor have I met one since.) What could it possibly feel like to be so wonderfully unencumbered by self-doubt, to be so unfamiliar with the concept of self-deprecation, to march across life so sure of receiving the world's admiration and respect? How on *earth* did one become like that? Was it nature or nurture? (Many years later, when I had children, I used to wonder how I could feed them just a fraction of this magic potion.) Maybe there'd been a bit of a muddle with his testosterone dosage in utero? Perhaps it came from a mother who had always had total blinding faith in him? Who the hell knew? But it was certainly most peculiar. And utterly seductive.

WHEN I WAS ABOUT FIFTEEN I fell in love with the Romans. My parents were thrilled—so much more suitable than some greasy lout on a motorbike—and, egged on by them, we used to make regular pilgrimages to the Pont du Gard, the amphitheater in Arles, the Maison Carrée in Nîmes, and the ruins of Glanum, just outside Saint-Rémy. Freddie's classical education illuminated the larger picture—he could, and did, quote great chunks of Gibbon, and would, without any encouragement, recite the dates of every single emperor—but my mother and I were much more interested in poking around the ruined villas, trying to imagine what life must have been like for their inhabitants. A shallow stone basin with a drain in the middle stood in what must have been the kitchen, vestiges of a black-and-white Escher-like mosaic still covered part of an atrium floor, and a gently rounded alcove was the perfect size for a vase full of spring flowers. After a morning spent scrabbling around in the sun-scorched rubble we would all, quite naturally, be in need of a little refreshment.

"I seem to recall there's rather a nice restaurant in the place du Forum in Arles, where I dined during the war on my way north after we had liberated Saint-Tropez."

My mother rolled her cynical American eyes. "And you honestly think it's still there?" But Europe holds on tight to its past, and Freddie was right; the Hôtel Nord-Pinus was still there, and they were still serving lunch outside, under the plane trees in the *place* that had been constructed on the site of the old Roman forum.

"Jesus. Will you get a load of this!" My mother had leaped up from her chair and was pointing up at the corner of the hotel, where two gigantic

Corinthian pillars supported the broken edge of an equally colossal pediment and were embedded, like some ancient parasite, in the stucco of this unremarkable nineteenth-century building. Grotesquely out of scale, they reached way up to the roof and were all that remained of the Roman temple that had dominated the forum two thousand years ago. Clearly a hotel I was going to have to come back to someday.

ROOM NUMBER 10 was where the famous bullfighters stayed—its wrought-iron balcony, overlooking the place du Forum, came in handy for greeting your adoring fans—but if it wasn't reserved for one of these superstars, ordinary people were allowed to have it. Decorated with all the flashy flair of a bullfighter's suit of lights—plenty of gilt and brocade and fringed silk lampshades—it was also the room where Helmut Newton photographed Charlotte Rampling sitting naked on the same table where I had just put down my handbag.

"Come here. I want to show you something."

I led David out onto the balcony and pointed at the *place*.

"That's where I sat and hatched my plan to bring you here before I knew you existed, and this"—I made him close his eyes and ran his fingers across the rough, pitted stone of the Corinthian column—"is our own private piece of Rome."

His hand slowly slid from Rome to my left cheek, and by the time I opened my eyes it was already dark.

David frowned at the menu, studying it with such conviction that it might as well have been a military map of the Sinai—turn right for the Suez Canal—which allowed me to watch his face—the black eyelashes, the hawkish nose—for a long time without his noticing. Why looking at the object of one's desire, unobserved, should be quite so pleasurable is something I have never been able to figure out. It just is. The waiter was hovering, David looked up, and I quickly opened the menu. Oh boy, somebody was having fun in this kitchen, because there, among all the predictable touristy things like *tomates Provençales, daurade grillée,* and *moules marinières* were regional surprises that must have been slipped in to delight the more demanding locals. *Tellines,* tiny clams no bigger than a toddler's thumbnail, from the nearby Camargue; *anguilles de Martigues,* baby eels sautéed in olive oil and parsley; *suppions à l'encre,* squid stewed in its own ink; and *bourride,* a smoother, creamier version of bouillabaisse—I was swimming in fish heaven.

"Alors. Moi je prend la bourride, et pour ma femme, les tellines."

The waiter scribbled away. He must have heard these words a million times, but I hadn't.

"Ta femme?'

"Oui, ma femme." And he smiled at me.

WHENEVER PICASSO'S HUNGER for Spain became more than he could bear, he would gather up his current mistress and a gang of friends and check into the Nord-Pinus. As the supreme superstar, he took precedence over the bullfighters and would always be given room number 10. After lunch, surrounded by his entourage, he would lead a raucous procession through the streets of Arles to the Roman amphitheater, where for a few hours he could forget his self-imposed exile and lose himself in the atavistic drama of the *corrida.* In the evening, refreshed by their siestas, Picasso and his friends would set off to the only restaurant in Arles that served a real *Gardiane,* the Camargue version of a *boeuf en daube,* made from bulls who had met their deaths not in a common abattoir but rather fighting gloriously in the blood-soaked ring. After which it would be time for a late-night *copita* back in the bar of the Nord-Pinus.

As soon as we walked into the dimly lit room it was as though I had returned to Spain. Above the bar a bull's head stared back at me with eyes as dark and implacable as Picasso's, and in the corner I could just make out one of those candlelit altars, dedicated to the Virgin, that bullfighters carry with them, to invoke her tender mercy before they stride out into the arena. And there, behind David, mounted in a glass cabinet on the wall, was the suit of lights—pale green silk, encrusted with rubies, sequins, and pearls, so tightly fitted that it must have been as hot and constricting as a corset—that the great Spanish bullfighter Dominguín had worn when he had fought in the Arles arena in the 1950s. Didn't Ava Gardner fall madly, badly, dangerously in love with him? Hadn't Hemingway written some book about the summer of 1959, and his rivalry with Ordóñez? Yes, it was all coming back to me. Not just Dominguín, but everything I had left behind in Spain. How strange that I should be sitting quietly, happily, with David in a bar in France, while part of my mind had escaped across the Pyrenees and was wandering obsessively, like some lost soul, all over a country I had loved, and thought I would never see again.

The dawn air in Provence, even at the height of the summer, is surprisingly cool, and standing on the front steps of the hotel the next morning in a thin cotton dress, I started shivering. David draped his jacket over my shoulders, and I remember thinking that if I refused to give it up, he wouldn't be able to get to the airport and fly away from me. Just a crazy passing thought. He needed to go home to Tel Aviv, to his wife and his life—I understood that—but still I hung on to him for as long as I could, until he said, very gently, that he was about to miss his plane.

BEATRICE WAS THERE to meet me at the train station and on the drive back to the house filled me in on the scene at La Migoua. Freddie was scribbling away at the marble table under the lime tree, Monsieur Maurice's hunchback and snobbery were more pronounced than ever, the Tricons had constructed a triple-tiered fountain, like a wedding cake, on their terrace, Nick had one of the Haystack boys staying, and Francette's disagreeable new dog Éloi seemed to have moved into our kitchen. Reassuringly, nothing seemed to have changed.

"Ah, there you are."

Freddie looked up from his writing, and greeted me as if I'd just arrived back from a quick shopping trip to the village, where I had presumably gone in search of delicacies to serve him for dinner that night. I leaned over and kissed him on the head, and followed Beatrice through the clackety wooden beads into the kitchen. The sexy kitten-heeled sandals were abandoned at the door (along with my mistress-in-room-10 persona), and barefoot, I slipped into an old apron and back into the familiar fussy homosexual/bustling French housewife role of my teenage years. *Oh là là* it was already six o'clock, and there was so much to do! Not that Beatrice was any slouch. Something delicious was simmering away in a pot on the stove, roasted yellow and red peppers sat on a platter, waiting to be peeled, and a huge triangle of Brie was drooling over the edge of the marble slab we used as a cheese board. And there in the middle of the table, instead of flowers, she had arranged a bouquet of fresh basil, yellow fennel blossoms, and wild mint in that jug my mother and I had bought from the one-armed bandit in Toulon.

"Christ, what the hell is this?"

I had lifted up the lid of the pot and lurking beneath a seething sea of scum was something that resembled a giant's dismembered cock.

"That, my dear, is *une langue de boeuf aux champignons*. Except that I have not yet added the mushrooms to the tongue. It's my father's favorite dish, and I thought Freddie would enjoy it too," and she giggled. "Well, they are about the same age, you know."

Privately I doubted the wisdom of serving old geezers anything that might remind them of just how enormous a cock could be, especially in comparison to a *mushroom*. I told Beatrice that it sounded delicious and I couldn't wait to put it in my mouth.

"You, Mademoiselle, are completely *dégueulasse*, your mind is like a sewer, and *en plus* you don't understand the recipe at all."

No, I certainly did not. But Beatrice was going to teach me. First you simmer the cock in a nice broth composed of an onion, a bay leaf, one celery stalk, salt, peppercorns, and water for about five hours. Then you heave it out, rip off the skin, slice it, and after that you whip up a brown roux with butter, flour, and a little cock juice from the pot, stir in some mustard, the sautéed mushrooms, chopped gherkins, pour the sauce over the sliced member, and return it to the oven in a casserole for ten to fifteen minutes. You can also add white wine or cider and a touch of cream, which will make it even more irresistible.

As Beatrice had predicted, the poached penis was an enormous success, and we even managed to persuade Nick and Ollie Haycraft to taste it by telling them that it was very special chicken.

"Darling, I completely forgot, you've been in Arles looking at those wonderful Roman ruins. I don't imagine they have changed much, have they?"

Before Freddie could launch into quoting Gibbon, which I knew he was about to, I quickly said, "No, not a lot. But, guess what, we stayed at that hotel, le Nord-Pinus, on the place du Forum, and from our balcony you could reach out and actually *touch* the remains of that huge temple. Can you imagine?"

Imagining things he hadn't actually experienced himself was not Freddie's forte, and he looked puzzled. It was unclear whether he even remembered the hotel, and he certainly registered no interest whatsoever in the pronouns "we" and "our." Maybe he was being tactful. But I doubted it. His curiosity about the lives of others had always been minimal to nonexistent, which in this particular case suited me fine. David was my secret, and we inhabited a world of our own. We had no friends in common (Francette was the sole exception, but she was hardly his friend, since they had only met a couple of times, and anyway, what about those pesky Palestinians?), we never went to parties together, I'd never seen his house, nor had he been to mine. The comforting, dreary quotidian aspects of life never intruded on our little adulterous universe; no supermarkets, no bills to be paid (at least not by me), no leaky roof or blocked toilet, no cooking or washing up.

The cooking was the only part that I missed.

ABOUT TWO WEEKS LATER we were all sitting on the terrace at drinks time, when Freddie suddenly said to nobody in particular, "One thing I don't understand is why Francette finds it necessary to keep shouting through the window, '*C'est l'Israélien.*' Has she gone mad?"

"Probably. Would you like another pastis?"

Freddie seemed perfectly satisfied with my answer, and I took his glass and went inside to the kitchen. But of course it was quite simple. Since we had no telephone, and Francette did, when David called she was far too lazy to walk around the corner and get me, so she shouted through Freddie's window instead. From the beginning Francette had been very strict about her telephone: We were allowed to use it only in cases of dire emergency. But if a call from David wasn't an emergency, I didn't know what was. Luckily she agreed.

"And Freddie, since we're talking about Francette's madness, have you ever been to Israel?"

"Darling, I did once go to a philosophical conference in Jerusalem, and I don't mind telling you that I'd be quite happy if I never went back. It was frightfully hot and noisy, and Israelis have the most appalling manners. I do hope you're not thinking of going there, because I doubt you'll like it any more than I did. Of course, for atavistic reasons, I've always supported Israel in its conflicts with the Arabs, and I do think that the creation of a Jewish homeland was important."

He stopped for a moment, took a sip of pastis, and continued: "But Isaiah has always felt much more strongly about Israel than I do. Maybe because he wasn't born in England as I was, possibly because both his parents were Jewish, unlike mine. I'm not sure what the reason is. But I suspect that for him Zionism is as much an emotional as it is an intellectual concept. Not a view that I share."

Oh yes, Freddie, it's those emotions that will get you every time.

While we were having breakfast the next morning, a newly energized and discreet Francette came into the kitchen, closely followed by her repulsive dog, and whispered in my ear, "C'est le bel Israélien."

I leaped up and ran out the door, leaving her in charge of making Freddie a fresh pot of tea and his second piece of toast.

Le Mari

You MIGHT HAVE THOUGHT that with love, fortune, fame, a devoted nest of friends, and a couple of occasionally charming children that my mother would have been content, even happy. But there you would be mistaken. She was as funny and outrageous as ever, she went to parties, she gave parties, she appeared on television, she had written a best seller, and for the first time in her life she could buy just about anything she pleased for anybody who pleased her. Freddie knew his place, caused no trouble, and slept without complaint on his collapsed mattress (the legs had fallen off his bed long ago, transforming it into an impromptu futon) downstairs. She had the house in France, where she could be alone with Hylan whenever she felt like it. She was a success, and she had a man who loved her. What more could a girl possibly want?

A naïve question, I know, and one posed not by me but in a letter from an old boyfriend called Archie Albright, who lived in New York and had just read *Jane:*

> You play games with me when you reject the suggestion that it is remotely autobiographical . . . but it *is* a very good book, and literary critic though I'm not, I have always regarded you as one of the most articulate people I have ever known. You use words, even little ones, so incredibly well. Anyway, I am enormously pleased for you. Do you *feel* any different—do you feel happier—to be rich and "successful" at the same time?

Even when my mother's life was going better than she could ever have dreamed it would, the furies were still there. Her volatility and bouts of depression were merely signs that they were getting bored and restless, and felt like a bit of an outing in the nice fresh air aboveground. Of course not everybody was allowed to meet them. They restricted their social visits to my mother's immediate family, and to a tiny handful of fortunate friends.

Much as Hylan loved my mother—and he truly did—he was sometimes stunned by her behavior.

"The fearlessness and wit could instantly morph into a nasty remark which would be amazingly mindless in terms of collateral damage."

My mother, quite naturally, was better acquainted with the furies than anybody else, and had tried over the years, with the help of shrinks, to evict these troublesome guests from her house. When I was about fifteen she once said that she had never found a shrink as smart as she was. So what was the point?

At eighteen my mother had written a long letter to her closest friend, Bunny Lang, who was one of the very few people who had ever been allowed behind the fortifications. In it she described her family and childhood.

Darling, you hit your head square on numerous nails in your analysis of me—however what I add up to is, and always has been very clear to me. I was a very unhappy, sensitive little girl—I was gawky for years and was continually overshadowed by my brother whom everyone adored and who deserved all the good things he got—that I wanted. My father and mother hated each other for as long as I can remember; my father drank heavily and my mother has never been completely well, and recently has been getting worse rapidly. [She must have meant her mental, not physical health. Ox-strong, my grandmother died at ninety-eight.]

My brother had—call it character—enough to study, never waste time etc and of course has made a success of it—I didn't. We didn't have much money and it was a struggle to keep him in college, so I gave up and laughed my way through high school—literally never brought a book home—and decided I would get the love and security I longed for in my own way.

Once years ago my mother told me she despised me . . . and it did something to an eleven year old that could never be repaired. After the life my mother and father have had together I don't have much faith in love. I don't have much faith in anything. I am a very discouraged, bewildered person who seems doomed to be unhappy.

I know I am an awful listener but I don't mean to be rude. And I admit that I don't like to be told things—the usual way of people who realize they are not the hot shots that they try desperately to believe they are. Stanislavsky again—"If you believe it, the audience will."

So even at eighteen she knew she had to be an actress. A glittering carapace was constructed to impress and entertain the world, and if other people fell for it, which they did, maybe she could trick herself into believing in it as well. But not really. She was not deluded, and I think that as she got older and life got tougher, it became harder and harder to keep the mask in place. The furies would go walkabout more frequently, and the strain of trying to contain them must have been exhausting.

From an early age I remember being told by my mother that my grandmother was crazy (my aunt and uncles believed this too) and not just insane but nasty, bitter, destructive, and foul-tempered as well. She screamed at her sweet, harmless husband (no wonder the poor man consoled himself with cocktails) and withheld from her children the love and encouragement they craved. Apparently her own mother had also been "unbalanced," and had treated her family in much the same way. Could this delightful duo's behavior be attributed in part to their shared genes? A terrifying thought that surely must have crossed my mother's mind and was probably instantly suppressed. Oscar Wilde (so clever, so funny, so tragic) had always been one of her special heroes, and she loved to quote his awful prophecy about mothers and daughters, making me squeal, right on cue, in mock horror. But when I quoted it back to her, she didn't laugh.

Like that maddening little girl with the curl in the middle of her forehead, my mother could skip from one extreme to the other—leapfrogging right over that dull bit in between—with greater agility and conviction than anybody I've ever known. Good Mummy rescued a penniless young friend from a dismal summer in London by sending him a plane ticket so he could come and stay with us in France for as long as he liked. She visited an old friend in the hospital, bringing some of her own homemade leek-and-potato soup—as well as a china bowl, a linen napkin, and an elegant Georgian silver spoon to eat it with. (The spoon was left behind as a birthday present.) Wildly generous, when she went shopping for herself—whether for shoes at Charles Jourdan, cashmere sweaters at Harrods, or a painting at Bonham's auction house—she never could resist getting something for her sister and me, as well as various friends along the way. Checks were sent off to any organization that helped animals, cash was surreptitiously concealed inside an innocent container (once she painted a walnut shell gold, hung it on the tree with all the other ornaments, and when I opened it there was a hundred-pound note), and at Christmas no lonely soul was safe from her absolute insistence that they come and spend the day with us.

Even though she was an actress, the kindness and generosity were not acts. She knew what it felt like to be unhappy, insecure, and to have no money, and she had a visceral empathy for, and a desire to help, anybody who found themselves inhabiting the despairing underbelly of life. Her acting talents were confined to dazzling the world with her wit and brilliance. And since she was a natural writer, her letters were employed to this end. Some people, like my father, stuck them in leather-bound albums; some read hilarious extracts out loud to their families; while others kept them tied up in ribbons in old shoeboxes, and after her death many of them were returned to me, where they now live in a basket at the back of my closet. Years ago I remember running into one of her friends at a party in New York, who couldn't stop talking about all the wonderful letters my mother had written her, which were carefully preserved in a special drawer in her desk.

"You are so lucky, you must have many more of them than I do!"

But no, I don't. Curiously I have none at all, and neither does my brother or my aunt. The letters were part of the glittering carapace, so what would have been the point in sending them to people who had seen through it long ago?

LOOKING BACK, I had no understanding at the time of the depth of my mother's discontent (Hylan was probably the only person who did), and with all the insouciant, and I hope forgivable, selfishness of youth I was far more concerned with what was going on in my own life. Being George Weidenfeld's publicity director may have been fun—the books, the parties, the fascinating writers—but it was starting to bore me.

Maybe I should look for a new job? A friend, Jerry Kiehl, whom I had met in Paris while staying with the *triste* Monsieur Bretiane, was one of the producers of a huge, ambitious documentary project called *The World at War*. Whenever we had lunch in some Italian dive in Soho, I would listen jealously as he told me all about his research at the British Library, the interview he had done with Albert Speer, and his discovery, in the bowels of the Imperial War Museum, of some never-before-seen footage of Hitler stomping around Paris with his favorite architect. Yes, this is what I should be doing. Instead of hustling television producers to interview argumentative Israeli generals, I would switch sides and become a producer myself.

The host of the only program on television that took a serious interest in the arts, he also somehow found time to write searing, sensitive books, in the manner of D. H. Lawrence, set somewhere in the north of England—not that I had bothered to read any of them. He was about six feet tall, with eyes every bit as sensitive as his novels, and hair as thick and dark, but far more lustrous, than any pit pony's mane. Just the man I was looking for. He may not have known it yet, but he was destined to be the magic key that would open up my new career in television. Armed with a glass of warm white wine and a laughable amount of misplaced confidence, never stopping to think whether the gentleman in question had the slightest interest in meeting me, I barged through the crowded party and introduced myself. Sadly, our conversation never did get around to what job on his program might best suit my talents, because he made a lightning escape, leaving me alone with the man he'd been standing with.

From that moment until the end of the evening we never stopped talking. It was that absolutely fatal combination of cleverness and funniness, but in its most extreme form. Lunch the next day turned into lunch once, sometimes twice a week, and still we never shut up. We always went to the same restaurant, Bianchi's on Frith Street, we always sat at the same corner table upstairs where nobody could see us (known as the adulterers' table, except we weren't), and I always had the same dish (brains *au beurre noir*—why waste time with the menu, when we could be talking and laughing instead?). Peter worked at the BBC, where he made documentaries, apparently about anything that caught his fancy. How about a series on the alternative press around the world? We'll get Harry Evans to front it, and I'll go to San Francisco and New York to do *Rolling Stone*,

then I'll need at least ten days in Paris for *Le Canard Enchaîné,* after that
I fly direct to Mexico City for *Proceso,* and from there I'll come back to
London to do *Private Eye?*

"What a brilliant idea! Off you go, you clever chap, and don't worry
about how long it takes or what it costs. Nothing but the best for the
BBC."

That seemed to be how it worked.

Our innocent lunches went on for several months until one day something changed. The fateful turning point came after a particularly lengthy
session, involving too much wine, the usual brains (his and the poor dead
calf's one on my plate), and a meandering conversation encompassing
Freud, Peter's father's childhood in Vienna, his halcyon days at Harvard
studying with Noam Chomsky, and his mother's relationship with Oskar
Kokoschka, who had painted her portrait. Christ, it was after four, time
to get back to the Weidenfeld office above the clapped-out movie theater
in Clapham Junction.

Rather gallantly he offered to drive me in his brand-new claret-colored
MG (affectionately called the "Jew's canoe" by my dear friend Emma
Soames, which only reinforced Peter's theory about the amiable, happy-
go-lucky anti-Semitism of the English upper classes. Still, he did laugh.).
The "Jew's canoe" weaved its way toward the South Bank via Parliament
Square, where it stopped obediently at a red light beside the sober, gray
walls of the Treasury building. Then, quite suddenly, its driver leaped
out, leaving the door wide open and the engine running. What the hell
was he doing? I couldn't drive, the light was about to change, and the cars
behind us had already started honking.

A quick pee—that was all it took to make me fall in love. The chutzpah, the recklessness, he'd taken a chance—it was exactly what my
mother would have done if only she'd been a man.

"Ooh, he's got ever such a nice voice, that fellow who keeps calling for
you. I've always been partial to a man's voice; tells you everything you
need to know about them. I think you should marry him."

Maureen, the kindly and, as it turned out, prescient lady at the office
switchboard, spoke the truth. Peter had the most seductive voice on earth,
and she hadn't even heard what he could do with it beyond, "Please may I
speak to Gully?" And she hadn't seen his hands, as beautiful as a Michel-
angelo drawing, or his almond-shaped green eyes, or his smile. She didn't

know that when I was with him I felt as though I'd finally come home to where I belonged.

OH, TO BE YOUNG, in love, and in Paris—and I was. No more "Towering Infernos," but rather an old town house (now a hotel) just off the rue Jacob that had been divided up somewhat haphazardly into a warren of rooms, wallpapered in faded toile de Jouy, with uncertain plumbing and a cagelike elevator that cranked its way up to the top floor, where we collapsed in a daze of happiness on our sagging bed. Once again Peter had come up with an idea for a documentary that the BBC could not resist. Sitting around one afternoon, with an inspiring bottle of Glenlivet between them on the desk, he had told the head of his department about a book called *Montaillou,* by the French historian Emmanuel Le Roy Ladurie that he had just finished reading.

The title referred to a village in Languedoc where, during the early fourteenth century, Jacques Fournier, the bishop of Pamiers (later Pope Benedict XII), had led the Church's inquisition into the inhabitants' obstinate dedication to the Cathar heresy. While snuffling around in the Vatican archives, Le Roy Ladurie had found the bishop's astonishingly detailed notes on the case, which illuminated every aspect of these poor, deluded, and doomed peasants' lives—what they ate, whom they slept with, how many sheep they had, all their innermost desires and beliefs—and from this had fashioned his brilliant book. Peter was going to take Ladurie back to Montaillou, where they would shoot some footage of sheep and goats wandering about the hills, and talk at great length to the descendants of these brave heretics, most of whom still spoke the ancient local language (*La langue d'Oc*) and bore the same names as their ancestors.

Now, if that didn't keep the viewers glued to their television screens, Peter didn't know what would.

"Sounds splendid! We're bloody well not going to be dragged down to the level of those ghastly commercial channels. We need to maintain our standards. Nothing but the best for the BBC [etc.]."

Peter could not have agreed more.

∼

MONSIEUR LE PROFESSEUR was everything a distinguished historian should be. Silver-haired, sexy in an elderly Frenchman way—tweed
jacket, suede patches at the elbow, mouse-colored corduroy trousers, an
old Hermès tie—supremely erudite, never boring, and delighted to take
us to his local bistro for dinner. *Bien sûr,* he knew my Oxford tutor Theodore Zeldin, and yes, of course Claude Lévi-Strauss was an old friend,
who had inspired him to set forth on his particular path, uncovering the
hidden lives of forgotten ordinary people who had been unjustly neglected
by old-fashioned historians' obsession with the nefarious doings of kings,
queens, and emperors. *Oui, s'il vous plaît,* a silver platter of oysters (rest-
ing on their green mattress of popping seaweed), a bottle of Sauvignon
Blanc, and then we will look at the menu again. Would Mademoiselle
prefer the *civet de lièvre* or the *canard aux navets,* or maybe she was more
in the mood for a simple coq au vin? Mademoiselle was lost in love, for
Peter, for the Professor, for the two sad ladies at the next table, for the
fussy old waiter, for the drooping tulips in a jug at the end of the bar, for
Paris, for the entire world, and could not have cared less what she ate
next—or if she ate anything else ever again.

Sometime later that night we decided to get married.

LIKE ANY AMBITIOUS Bostonian matron in the Gilded Age who had
dragged her daughter to London for the season, my mother assumed I
would "marry well." She had given me all the things she'd never had as
a child—pretty clothes, deep love, an education, stability, and an easy
entrée into the sunny uplands of London social life. And what did I do? I
went to Paris with some man she had never met and came back and told
her I was going to marry him.

"Is he rich?"

A very good question. I'd forgotten to ask. But I had to admit (but not
to her) that it seemed unlikely. The BBC was definitely a bad sign, and
so were the émigré parents, who had left Vienna just before the *Anschluss*
to make a new life in London. Can't pack a castle in a suitcase, always
assuming you had one to pack. In fact Peter's mother came from what I
suppose you'd call the landed gentry, and before the war there had been
lots of servants, a brick factory, and a hunting lodge on a small estate
in northern Germany, but by the time Mr. Hitler had finished with his

shenanigans, everything had disappeared. Peter's father's story was even worse. A penniless Viennese Jew (he had been even more of a hit with his wife's mother than Peter was with mine) who through his not inconsiderable wits had turned himself into a publisher. Not an easy journey and, alas, not necessarily a wildly profitable one either. It was not a pretty picture.

But what about the house in Hampstead? Apparently it was so big that Peter had divided it into two flats, and kindly allowed his elderly, and presumably hard-up, parents to live in the spacious ground-floor one, which opened onto a lovely garden full of apple trees. Sometimes we would spend the night there, and as I nodded off to sleep, I would think of those nice people in their cozy flat downstairs, and marvel that they had managed to produce a son with such a huge heart, overflowing with so much parental love. What a good father he would be to our children. (The situation, oddly enough, turned out to be quite the reverse. In fact, it belonged to his kind parents who allowed Peter to live in the upstairs flat, but when they died, we inherited the house, so what was a mere slip of the tongue?)

However, the fact remained that Peter was not a half black socialist duke who had set up a foundation to save Africa's entire population of dogs from disease and starvation and had recently been awarded the Nobel Prize for Literature.

And for that my mother never forgave him.

THE WIND RUSTLED in the willows, boxing-glove clouds scudded by, baby ducks bobbed about in the river, and a beet-faced man in a boat called *Fancy That* chugged by and turned to wave at the wedding party lined up on the dock. The bride was leaning over to adjust the sash on the little girl's dress, so she didn't see him, but the tall older gentleman with a sunny wide-open smile—must be her dad—waved back, and so did all the others, except for that lady in the sunglasses, who didn't look too pleased with the proceedings and kept her arms folded in front of her. The man in the boat thought back to his own wedding day, and felt a twinge of masculine sympathy for the nice-looking young man with the flower in his buttonhole—must be the groom—who had no bloody idea what he had just let himself in for.

Somewhat surprisingly lunch moved along smoothly from champagne on the terrace, with something or other to eat in the dining room in between, and then on to more champagne with dessert. The two publishers—Peter's father and Colin Haycraft—talked books, my mother-in-law charmed Freddie, and Nick, an assiduous scholar of all things punk, kept some sort of conversation going with my Wells brother, Christopher, an international relations major at Columbia. And there were my mother and father laughing away together—she even had her hand on his arm—the thing that every child of divorced parents always longs to see. Peter was chatting with my beautiful stepmother, and I gazed around the table, lost in some inane reverie about the miraculous melding together of all the members of my funny family.

Wreathed in yellow rosebuds, pale green leaves trailing prettily across its snowy icing, the wedding cake rose up in sedate tiers, a silver knife sitting by its side. My father got to his feet, tapped the side of his glass, and I heard my mother mutter, "Oh Christ, he's going to make a speech." Yes, that did seem to be his boring, conventional, sentimental idea. The father of the bride had come flying across the Atlantic for his only daughter's wedding, and he'd quite like to say a few words on this happy occasion, if that was okay with his ex-wife.

A few months later Peter persuaded the BBC that he would be just the man to run their office in New York.

"What a good idea! There's quite a nice house in Greenwich Village that comes with the job; don't stint on the entertaining, frightfully important to show the BBC flag in America. I'm sure your wife will be a splendid hostess. Off you both go. Bon voyage!"

New York

Do ALL SANE—OR EVEN SEMI-SANE—children know they need to run away from home? I think so. Hardly bothering to wave good-bye, indifferent to our parents' feelings, unable to imagine that they might miss us, thinking only of our own desires—and self-preservation—we flee, and sometimes forget to come back. And then if we're lucky, and haven't made a total mess of our own children, they do the same thing to us. Many years ago Anna Haycraft explained to me how the world works. She said it was really quite simple: Men love women, women love children, and children love hamsters. That's just the way it is, and there is absolutely nothing to be done about it. Not being a mother at the time, and crazily in love—as usual—with some man or another, I couldn't begin to understand what she was talking about. But now I know precisely what she meant. Men love women—that's obvious, and quite right too—then the women have babies, and become totally besotted with them—that's natural, but not so much fun for the fathers—and then the children fall for a furry animal, and the next time you turn around they're off. Peter and I just upped and left, never stopping to think that my mother, Freddie, and both his parents would all grow old and die in London while we were gone.

At first I was mystified by my happiness. Was it just the thrill of starting a new life with a new husband in a new city, or the scent of the wisteria blossoms that floated up to our bedroom from the terrace outside, or being in New York, where I couldn't ride in a cab without hanging my head out the window like some mad panting dog so I could see every single building all the way to the top? No, something else was going on:

I had escaped, I was independent, I had my own house, my own telephone number (really grown-up, that bit), and my mother wasn't stomping around upstairs.

> I arrived at Bank Street eight o'clock sharp, in the very last of the light.
> Overhead the sky still scintillated, but there was a film of green up there
> among the pinks and blues, an avocado tinge of beautifying city sick-
> ness. . . . Bank Street looked like a chunk of sentimental London, black
> railings and pale blossoms girding the bashful brownstones, even a cau-
> tious whiff of twig and leaf in the night-scented air.

Not my words but Martin Amis's description in *Money* of the street
where we lived. The house had been thrown in with the BBC job, and
Martin was right, it was "a chunk of sentimental London," which must
have been why I felt so at home there. The stairs were crooked, the windows didn't fit, the roof occasionally leaked, the bathrooms and kitchen
had been put in before the war, but what did any of that matter as you
drifted off to sleep to the sound of owls hooting from the trees in the garden below? In the hot jungly New York summer nights there were even
mosquitoes—and if that isn't the ultimate urban luxury, then I don't know
what is.

Before we had children the house on Bank Street operated as a hotel
for our friends. Some stayed for a night or two, others for a few weeks,
and one—Christopher Hitchens—lived with us for six months when he
first arrived in New York. The previous December, Peter and I had fled
Christmas in London—when the entire place packs up, forcing you back
into the familial bosom for perhaps longer than you might wish—and
had borrowed a creaky old apartment in Greenwich Village, where we
happily ignored the whole wretched business. Christopher must have
had the same clever idea, because soon after we arrived we ran into him
with Anna Wintour in Mortimer's, a restaurant on the Upper East Side
owned by a poisonous, snobby old queen who placed his favored customers up front where they could be seen but allowed riffraff like us to
lurk at the back. Carried away by the glamour (could that be Jacqueline
Onassis walking by on her way to the ladies' room?) and the energy (you
could actually get a cab on Christmas Day!) of the city, the three of us

(Anna was already living in New York) decided this was clearly the place to be. And so the "pact of Mortimer's" was sealed. Peter got the BBC to deliver, and Christopher persuaded Victor Navasky, the kindly editor of *The Nation*, that his publication would sparkle even more brightly with the addition of the Hitch.

Christopher was the ideal guest: hardly ever there, didn't eat, bought his own whiskey and cigarettes, spent no time in the bathroom, and— this was easily the best part—he made us laugh. The room he occupied was called Smike's parlor, in honor of the pathetic stunted Smike, who is rescued from Dotheboys Hall by Nicholas Nickleby, and whose sad end allows Dickens to wallow in yet another of his long-winded, mawkish deathbed scenes. The longer Christopher stayed, the more Smike-like his parlor became, with cigarette butts floating in old mugs of tea, clothes draped over the radiators, the desk piled high with papers, until the cleaning lady decided it might be simpler for everyone if she bypassed the room entirely.

In those days before cell phones, part of my role as hostess was to act as an answering service, and nobody got more calls than Christopher. Usually his friends were perfectly polite, but there was one especially pushy lady, a real ratbag who looked like a snake and masqueraded as a writer (her first novel had been snapped up by a publishing house owned by her hapless husband) and never stopped calling. I suppose she must have had designs on Smike's undernourished body. Whatever her motives, the old—she was well past forty—hellhag rang one morning and was not best pleased to be told that the object of her desire was in the shower.

"Okay. Just say it's Patsy. I'll hold on until you get him out."

I made a gargoyle face into the receiver and said I'd be sure to trot along and fetch him immediately. The bathroom door was ajar, so I pushed it open and there, protruding from the shower curtain, was Smike's paw holding a cigarette, with a neat little pile of ash on the tiled floor below. Oh Smike, *must* you?

As a guest Martin was no more trouble than Christopher and just as much fun. If the two of them happened to be in New York at the same time, they liked to meet for a late hangover-haunted lunch at some Italian place in the Village, and then they would while away the afternoon at the Show World Center in Times Square where—boys will be boys—the entertainment consisted of watching naked girls dancing. Naively I envisaged a stage with prancing showgirls in sequined G-strings and stilettos, silk tassels glued to their nipples; but it wasn't like that at all. Apparently the management thoughtfully provided each member of the audience with his own cozy little cubicle, furnished quite simply with a chair (upholstered in plastic), a box of Kleenex, and a window whose shutter was somehow connected to a ravenous machine that had to be fed a constant diet of tokens if you wanted to experience Sheri in all her glory.

Whoever came to stay with us was always included in our social life, as we were in theirs. Sometimes we had dinner with old friends like Anna— Hitch had accompanied her to our wedding and used to call her the "foal" on account of her ludicrously long, slim legs and the thick chestnut bangs that almost, but not quite, covered her eyes—sometimes we went to an awful pinball parlor on University Place where Martin could indulge his addiction to video games, played on clanging, fridge-size precursors to Xbox, and sometimes we went to parties. One memorable evening Martin's date decided she had something better to do with her time than see him, so instead of a solitary return visit to the pinball parlor, he decided to come out with us.

The apartment occupied the top floor of a building somewhere in Chelsea. Its hallway, illuminated by a fizzing fluorescent light, was painted a dispiriting pea green, and, just to add to its charms, the architect had forgotten to put in an elevator. Martin manfully took the lead and started the trudge up, stopping for a reviving wheeze on each landing, until we finally heard the distant beckoning sound of too many people crammed into too small a space, trying to have too good a time. Standing by the open door was our hostess, dressed in an off-the-shoulder ruffled chiffon number, a necklace of shells, beads, and seedpods draped across her freckly décolletage, and a bloodred hibiscus flower tucked optimistically behind one ear.

"Hello, I'm Martin Amis."

Not necessarily the words she wanted to hear. Not the ideal greeting from the man you had slept with just a few days before.

Still, you could see how the poor fellow might have become confused: "The thing is she had her hair up, and it was rather dark at the top of those stairs."

~

SOON AFTER we settled into our apartment on Bank Street with the bumblebees and owls and mosquitoes, I received a truly alarming letter from my mother. At first I didn't quite understand what it was about, so I read it again slowly. It seemed that she had finally had enough. She was done with snobby old England, she was done with that old fart Freddie, she had sold our nice old house, she was getting divorced, and she and Hylan were about to board an ocean liner to start a new life in the New World. My job was to find them a sublet where they could live while they looked for a permanent home.

I settled on the Chelsea Hotel, an Edwardian pile on West Twenty-third Street, ten blocks from Bank Street. It was just their kind of place, and I knew they would be happy there. Diego Rivera had lived at the Chelsea in the thirties while he was painting his mural *Man at the Crossroads* for Rockefeller Center, which featured Lenin's heroic visage and had caused such a furor that it was soon taken down; Sid Vicious died there; Dylan Thomas had had his very own "Smike's parlor" there—but had chosen to die at the White Horse Tavern instead; Andy Warhol made his movie *Chelsea Girls* there, and Charles James, the great American couturier—this would surely appeal to Hylan—had also been a longtime resident. The ceilings were high, the rooms dark (perfect for my mother), it was cheap, and best of all, El Quijote, a lugubrious establishment on the ground floor, served lobsters for only six dollars a pound. My mother adored lobster.

Still, the question remained: What had possessed these two middle-aged people to abandon their lives—and children—in London and set out on this insane—at least in retrospect—enterprise? My mother had always been an adventuress, so maybe she felt she needed to reinvent herself one last time before it was too late; then again it may have been some nostalgic impulse that made her want to come home to the country she had left when she'd bought that one-way ticket to Paris in 1947. Many years later I talked to Hylan about it. "It was crazy, almost incomprehensible. We had conjured up this 'other America'—it was pure fantasy. An escape from our slightly false, slightly ill-fitting Englishness that was so attractive, but was not really us."

Whatever their motives and whatever I felt about my mother's becoming my neighbor once again doesn't really matter, because there were two other people—Nick and Alex—whose lives were turned upside down and inside out by their parents' decision. Sixteen and seventeen, respectively, they had both been left behind in London. Nick told me later that he has no memory of talking to our mother about the move, and that he just arrived home one day to find that the house had been sold, although he does admit that it's entirely possible that she *had* told him, and that he had subconsciously blocked out this unwelcome news. Either way it was a bit of a shock for a teenager whose difficulties with both school and drugs continued, and who now found himself homeless. Freddie had gone off to live with Vanessa in Fulham, and since his son had not been invited to join the lovebirds in their new nest, Nick went to stay with a series of friends. Some had managed to hang on to their parents and were still begrudgingly at home; others had had quite enough of the old codgers, and had taken over an abandoned building, where they lived as squatters. Alex's situation wasn't a whole lot better. At least she had Hylan's flat—her own mother, being something of a free spirit, was living in a caravan in Holland at the time—and at least she had a nice boyfriend, Ronnie (now her husband), who moved in, helped with the bills, and gave her life some kind of stability.

AT THIS POINT you may be wondering what had happened to my brilliant career. Or at least what the hell I did all day long while Peter was running the BBC's American empire from his office in Rockefeller Center. The truth is that I had only one interest in life: to have a baby. Ever since little Nick had been placed in my arms when I was twelve, ever since I had held an unending stream of leaky Haystack babies on my lap, ever since I had fallen in love with Peter, actually ever since I had picked up my first doll, I had wanted to be a mother. The pills were flushed down the toilet in a sea green marble bathroom in Barbados on our honeymoon— but nothing happened.

Doctors were consulted, tests were conducted, sex was scheduled for a few purposeful nights each month, purple dye was injected into my tubes, poor Peter was dragged up to Columbia-Presbyterian on One Hundred Sixty-eighth Street, where he was locked in a Show World

Center—type cubicle—with a copy of *Playboy*, rather than a gyrating Sheri in split-crotch fun panties, for company—and still nothing happened. If Peter was too busy for the three-hour hospital trek, I would make a mercy dash up to the hospital with a glass jar nestled in my armpit (to keep the temperamental creatures warm) where they would be spun around in some contraption and then let loose inside me to swim about. This depressing routine went on for more than three years, driving me and my patient loving husband to the point of madness, until one day in the bathroom of the Cadogan Hotel in London, my pee turned a pregnancy-test strip the most beautiful shade of Tiepolo blue I have ever seen. (Twenty-six years later it remains my favorite color, and the room where I am typing these words now is painted that same magical blue.)

Barefoot, pregnant, and in the kitchen—I had finally been allowed into heaven. All I did was waddle around with no shoes on, cook strange new dishes that I would never have attempted before, lie on the sofa reading Proust, trying to remember what Theodore Zeldin had taught me, and make regular sorties uptown to visit the saintly Dr. Scher. As the months passed, my experiments in the kitchen took off in ever-more-fanciful directions—"Darling, that pig's ear was delicious, but I just can't eat any more" (a dimly recalled crunchy snack in a bar in Barcelona had been my inspiration)—the duchesse de Guermantes remained as elegantly elusive as ever, and even Dr. Scher, indulgent though he was, wondered, out loud and frequently, just how much more weight I could possibly pack on. One hundred and ten pounds on day one, I had without any difficulty at all gotten myself up to 165 by the time Peter carted me off, nine months later, shrieking—poor driver—in a cab to Mount Sinai.

When I woke up, Dr. Scher gently explained the situation. Nothing serious, he said holding my hand, but I had an infection, he had prescribed antibiotics, and just as a precaution, the pediatrician was going to put our daughter in an incubator. They were being extra cautious, the cleaners had been on strike for several weeks, the hospital had become a gigantic, bubbling petri dish of bacteria, and several babies had become sick. There was no question of feeding her my milk, on account of the infection, so I needed to pump every few hours to stop my breasts from exploding and get them used to their strange new role in life. There was absolutely nothing to worry about, your daughter is healthy, perfect in every way, and you need to rest. For the next week I shared a room with three other ladies who fed their snuffling babies while Rebecca lay, resplendent in her transparent incubator—like a gigantic doll in a plastic gift box from FAO Schwarz—up in some distant wing of the hospital, and I watched my milk trickle down the drain. Not precisely what I'd had in mind, and sometimes I slid into a self-pitying wallow, but mostly I hung on tight to Dr. Scher's words and reminded myself that it was only a few more days before we would be back home together, sitting under the wisteria with those lazy, drunken, corpulent bumblebees buzzing around us.

"Hey, we're here to spring you out of jail. Quick, grab the kid and let's make a run for it!" My mother was standing at the foot of the bed, smiling; Rebecca was all wrapped up; the papers were signed; my bag was packed, and we could get a cab on Fifth Avenue and be way downtown before they even noticed we'd gone. The taxi skidded and bumped along the potholes, its driver clearly had no notion of the exquisite treasure he had in his backseat—oh, please slow down, we'll triple the tip!—until we got to Bank Street, where my mother, true to my promise, gave him three crisp twenty-dollar bills.

She helped me up the steps and then went around to the deli to get us BLTs, lightly toasted white bread, lots of mayo, an extra pickle for me, please, and two Cokes. We sat down together on the terrace and ate our sandwiches, and as she took the plates into the kitchen, she asked if I needed anything else? Not a single thing, thank you. I had everything I had ever wished for. Except for *The New York Times*, which she brought up to me in bed. "I'll call tomorrow to make sure you and the critter are okay." Peter was coming back from Boston that evening, but for the next few hours Rebecca and I were all alone together for the first time in both our lives.

L'Été Infernal

Despite all her protestations about never having liked babies and her insistence that she would never, ever answer to "Granny," my mother couldn't fool me—she had fallen in love with the critter. In France that summer, when money had been especially tight, she wrote to Hylan, "I just bought the prettiest little dress for Gully's little chimp . . . a ridiculous thing I know, but irresistible. And only 70 francs at the big Flea Market in Le Beausset."

One of my mother's more incomprehensible prejudices was her preference for girls over boys. It was totally irrational and she never attempted to explain it, but then again she was never big on explanations when it came to her behavior. *Qui s'explique, s'accuse*—"Whoever explains himself, accuses himself"—was her motto, and luckily Rebecca and I had had the good sense to be born female. Nick and my son, Alexander, had been less prescient. At any rate there was no keeping her away from this baby girl. Rebecca was dressed up like a pretty dolly in her *broderie anglaise* christening dress—without any thought of her actually entering a church—toys and more practical garments would be dropped off regularly, and if I needed any shopping done, she would rush off to Balducci's, returning with wicked indulgences like blinis, red caviar, and sour cream, and we would sit around the kitchen table, sipping ice-cold vodka, pretending we were on a red leather banquette at the Russian Tea Room.

A couple of months after Rebecca's birth, Peter's mother, Katherine, whom I had fallen for shortly after I fell for her son, arrived from London to meet her new granddaughter. The two grannies could not have been less alike. My mother-in-law was no pushover, but she certainly didn't believe in rocking boats until they capsized. She preferred gentle persuasion to confrontation. Dignified, discreet, a listener rather than a talker, she was without a single malicious bone in her tall elegant body. A great beauty, a wife, hostess, and mother who had abandoned her hopes of becoming an actress when she had left Vienna in 1937, to move to London, she had never worked a day in her life. Still, they did have a few traits in common: extreme generosity, intelligence, a natural gift for captivating men, and their love for Rebecca. What more admirable qualities could you wish for in any grandmother?

By the time Katherine returned to London, it had been decided. My mother had offered us the house in France for ten days the following summer so Peter could take a well-deserved vacation there with the ladies in his life—his mother, his wife, and his daughter.

"Are you absolutely *sure* she won't be there?"

"Don't be silly. Weren't you listening? She didn't invite us to *stay*—she's generously *lending* us her house. There's a big difference."

"Damn right. There's a *huge* difference, which is why I think you should check up on her understanding of that word 'lend.' "

"Oh do shut up, you're being ridiculous."

"Okay. But you will check, won't you?"

"Yes, yes, I'll check."

And he actually believed I was going to call her and make sure that La Migoua would be delivered to us without its sitting tenant? Of course I wasn't. There was no way I could have done that. Much too terrifying, and rather impolite when you came to think of it, so in my desire to please—and placate—both my husband and my mother, I did nothing. We had all heard her say "lend" quite clearly, so that must be what she was going to do.

Peter was not being churlish. From the beginning, he had always been unfailingly polite and friendly to my mother, but sadly, since he had yet to turn himself into a mulatto Rothschild, the ground still had not been broken on that multimillion-dollar complex for stray cats, and the Nobel committee's invitation must have got lost in the mail, his mother-in-law remained immune to his charms. Not overtly hostile (although one Christmas she did call him a prick, to which he replied, rather wittily I thought, "Surely, you mean a brick?") but he got the message, and quite naturally, she never changed her mind. I tried to console Peter by pointing out that her brother-in-law, John, was given the same treatment—"Christ, that fucking fool is building a *boat* in his backyard, can you believe it?"—but it still hurt. Dear sweet John had the distinction of holding the world record for the number of times (twice) he had been thrown out of La Migoua Other less tolerant guests tended not to return after their first hasty departure. The boat, by the way, was a thing of great beauty, created entirely with his own hands, that grew bigger and bigger, blocking all light from the living room, until one day it was all grown up and ready to leave home. The problem, which I am sure John had taken into account when he started on this ambitious project, was that the garden was entirely surrounded by a solid wall of extremely tall brick houses. The only solution was to summon a gigantic crane—so heavy that it destroyed the underground sewage pipes running along the street outside—which heaved the boat up over the roof, drove it off to Southampton, where it slipped into the icy water, and repaid its creator with many years of innocent pleasure.

JUST BECAUSE MY MOTHER had decided she'd had quite enough of Freddie certainly didn't mean that I had. He was as much a part of my life as my real father, and not only did we love each other, but we truly enjoyed each other's company, to the point that she would sometimes say, in mock exasperation, "You two are just the same. Identical cool, nitpicky, logical minds, both Scorpios—all you ever think about is sex and death."

Which wasn't entirely true because neither of us had much interest in the second topic. Still, she was right; we were alike in many ways and the divorce didn't change a thing. In some odd way it may even have brought us closer together, since Freddie felt that I was one of the few people who could begin to understand what had gone on in their marriage.

Both nonstop talkers, with similar interests and intellects, Freddie and Peter took to each other instantly, and I loved listening to them yacking away, happy that at least part of my family appreciated the man I had married. Drawn together by me, they also had another lady in common, and as poor Freddie became more and more distressed about my mother's behavior over the divorce, he confided in Peter, knowing they were both up against the same frightening force of nature: "I don't mind telling you, Peter, that she doesn't much like me, and she doesn't like you at all."

True enough, but at least Peter didn't have to worry about my mother's letting her lawyers loose on him.

Just as it is impossible to know what really goes on inside other people's marriages, so it is probably a mistake to get involved in the minutiae of their divorces, especially when they are your parents. So what follows is Freddie's story. My mother never talked to me about it in any detail.

In early 1982 Peter received a letter from Freddie that began "I am sorry to foist my troubles on you and I leave it to your discretion how far you involve Gully, but Dee's behavior is reducing me to despair. . . . She is employing a sharp lawyer who will obtain a settlement which will be ruinous to me. . . . In the meantime she wants no further communication between us."

You have to wonder why Freddie didn't go shopping for an even sharper lawyer for himself, but he wasn't an American. He was a man of habit who would never have thought of leaving good old Gerard Shuffle, who had been at Christ Church with him, had shuffled his first divorce through the courts, and was a fellow member of the Garrick Club.

He then moves on to his real concern, his son, Nick, about whom he wrote at the end of his autobiography, "My love for this child has been the dominating factor in my life." Freddie adored Nick, far more than any of his other children, and I think the certainty of his father's love gave Nick a bit of extra strength when it came to coping with his more mercurial mother.

"My immediate worry is Nick. There is little doubt that Dee will try to turn him against me and I should be wretched if she succeeded."

Well, he needn't have worried. Our mother didn't try to turn her son against him, and Nick's loyalty to his father never faltered. He looked after Freddie toward the end of his life, he slept in his room in the hospital, and was there holding his hand when he died. My brother—who looks like Kafka's sexier and far more handsome younger brother—was lucky enough to inherit his father's gentleness and his mother's wit, which, combined with both his parents' mental acuity and their effortless ability to charm the opposite sex, has kept him supplied with a succession of dazzling ladies over the years. An enviable quality that always made his dear old Dad beam with parental pride and admiration.

In the next part of the letter Freddie turns to the vexed subject of Hylan. "I should never have accepted the humiliating conditions under which I lived in Regents Park Terrace. . . . I was allowed into my own house only for short periods on sufferance." (It's quite true that Hylan moved into the house every Tuesday the minute he set off for Oxford, and was still there, on one or two unfortunate occasions, when Freddie returned on Friday.)

"And I should never have allowed her to walk off with so much spoil — but there comes a point at which the worm turns." (Apparently my mother was claiming more than half the sale of the house in London, La Migoua, and whatever furniture and pictures she chose to take to New York. He had also agreed to pay her three hundred pounds per month.)

Which brings us to the subject of money. Actually money and Hylan combined, which was twice as vexing. At this point Freddie's brilliant analytical mind seems to have deserted him completely, and he came up with this ludicrous non sequitur as the only possible explanation for his wife's desire to bring about his financial downfall: "*Either* Hylan is a pauper, *or* he proposes to leave her."

Sadly, in the end, both propositions turned out to be true. So much for Freddie's logic.

BY THE TIME WE SET OFF with Peter's mother for our family holiday at La Migoua, Freddie had married Vanessa and they were living in a house just off Baker Street, where I visited them on the way to France. Immediately I sensed something was horribly wrong. Vanessa was upstairs in bed, Freddie was visibly agitated, swinging his silver chain around, and although he didn't quite say so, I knew she must be dangerously sick. The curtains were drawn, and Vanessa lay motionless in bed, her face as pale as the sheet covering her body, scarcely whispering as I leaned over to kiss her cheek. I recognized the perfume she had worn that day fifteen years before, when I'd seen her by the porter's lodge in New College, looking like Nefertiti in a little girl's party dress, and had directed her toward Freddie's rooms: Fidji by Guy Laroche. What useless, inconsequential rubbish clutters up one's head, even at life's most awful moments; but it was *her* scent, she never wore anything else, and there beside the bed was a child's drawing of the bottle, with "You are my Fidji Mummy" written across the top in uncertain capital letters. She was only forty-eight.

I somehow knew my mother would be standing by the front door, underneath the lime tree, ready to welcome her guests into her cool kitchen, where a jug of homemade lemonade stood on the marble table, surrounded by mismatched glasses from the flea market in Le Beausset. Oh God, why hadn't I screwed up my courage and had the conversation that I lied to Peter about, every time he'd asked me if I was quite sure she understood the meaning of the word "lend"? His calm smiling mother was cradling Rebecca in her arms and, looking across the table, I had this feeling—idiot that I was—that the two of them would make everything come right in the end.

"But you *promised* me that we would be alone."

Peter wasn't so much angry—that would come later—as aggrieved that things had turned out exactly as he had predicted. After working like a dog all year in New York, he just wanted a peaceful, relaxing week in Provence—was that too much to ask? Maybe if he calmed down it might be more likely to happen. Maybe I could persuade my mother to stay with some friends for a few days. Maybe we could all just get along and pretend everything was fine. Maybe Vanessa wasn't dying.

That evening Freddie called our neighbor Francette (we still didn't have a telephone) and told her Vanessa had been diagnosed with liver cancer; she was in the hospital and the doctors said it would move very quickly now.

Rebecca lay asleep in her basket beside my chair, the warm night breeze rustled the leaves in the lime tree, a flickering candle shone through the bottle of rosé on the table turning it into pink stained glass, the platter of grilled mackerel (the same fish I was cooking the night I had discovered the love letter she had written Freddie lying on top of the garbage) was passed around the table.

I wish I could say things calmed down, but they didn't. In fact they got much worse. Peter was still upset, and my mother was even more upset after I suggested she might like to stay with her friend Sylvia for a couple of nights; I slapped Nick on the face when he made it clear he wasn't grief stricken over Vanessa (admittedly she had never been particularly nice to him, but she was *dying*); Katherine wasn't feeling well (she too would be dead from cancer before the end of the year); and I was mostly in tears. Rebecca was the only one of us who laughed and burped and giggled her way through that nightmare summer.

The day after Peter drove his mother back to London, Freddie called again. It was over. The woman who had stolen her husband and destroyed her marriage was dead. Did that make my mother the victor? I wonder if that's how it works. She was left standing on the battlefield, or rather stomping around her kitchen shouting at Francette's dog, while her opponent was being carried off in preparation for her burial—surely that must count for something? And yet, if the battle had been about possessing Freddie's heart and mind—which presumably it had—then Vanessa had triumphed long ago, and her victory over my mother was total and irrevocable.

"Tired and emotional" is an English euphemism—made up by *Private Eye*—for being drunk, but my mother and I started arguing at breakfast, so how could those nice, innocent bottles lined up on the sideboard have been to blame? Emotional I certainly was, and after the week that had just passed, utterly exhausted too. How it began hardly matters, but what fueled it was my dismay at her reaction to Vanessa's death—the same hysterical impulse that had made me slap Nick. The absence of feeling, the refusal to even fake some empathy, the inability to utter the customary soothing platitudes—and I was demanding *that* from a person who had spent a lifetime scorning, and attacking anything she judged to be dull, hypocritical, predictable, and worst of all, conventional? Shows you how far gone I was.

I suddenly needed my daddy. The gentle, happy, smiling man who had stood up—"Oh Jesus, he's going to make a speech"—and said all the usual cheerful boring things that a father should say at his daughter's wedding. It had always been my plan to take Rebecca to see him that summer, and after lunch I went down to the travel agent in the village and booked us onto the night train from Toulon to Geneva, leaving at eleven that evening.

WHEN THEY HAD DECIDED to get married in Paris in 1949, my mother and father both secretly knew they had not made the wisest choice of partner, and as their friends had predicted, they were divorced within five years. The next time around their judgment had improved dramatically, and a few years later they both presented me with a perfectly chosen set of extra parents. Freddie was easy—we were already old friends by the time my mother married him—but what about this hussy in Washington, who had come out of nowhere to seduce my father away from me? I felt rather the same way about her as my mother had felt about Vanessa. A spoiled only child, I was not accustomed to sharing my toys.

The hussy was called Melissa. Tall, blond, and beautiful, she possessed some special witchy magic that, over one summer in Georgetown, transformed a disagreeable and extremely jealous nine-year-old into an adoring stepdaughter. She gave me a baby alligator, no bigger than a lizard, who liked to lounge around in the sun being fed steak tartare; she curled my eyelashes, put up my hair, painted a new face on top of my old one, hung pearls from my ears, dressed me up like a grand duchess, and took a picture that I still have. She picked leaves from the fig tree that the two Eves wore instead of bikinis as they sunbathed in the backyard, and she took me to a silly movie that we both agreed my father would hate, so we left him behind at home. I trusted her completely.

Twenty-five years later Melissa was working for the UN in Geneva, and my father was slowly restoring the old stone manor house they lived in at the edge of a village just over the border in France. She had become an ambassador, and while she was at the office my father went around banging nails into things, Rebecca splashed about naked in an old stone trough in the courtyard, and every day at one o'clock sharp he would put down his tools, which was the signal for us to get into the car and go out to lunch. We always went to the same place. Grass grew down the middle of the dirt road, oak trees joined together overhead, creating a cool green tunnel that we drove through, up and up, ears popping, until we reached the top, where a vast sunlit meadow suddenly opened up ahead of us.

A few wooden tables were set up under the apple trees—no chairs, just wobbly benches, and no kitchen—just a tiny cuckoo-clock chalet where apple-cheeked Madame stood in front of her stove, melting butter in a frying pan until it bubbled and frothed—*omelette aux fines herbes* was the only dish on the menu. Behind her, homemade fruit pies—apricot, cherry, plum—were lined up, cooling complacently on the shelf. Outside, Rebecca took a twirl on the swing, watched over by her handsome grandfather, while a ridiculously appealing puppy tumbled around in the daisy-strewn grass. "À table, à table," I called out, clapping my hands. An earthenware jug full of wildflowers stood in the middle of the table along with a bottle of red wine, a platter of *saucissons, cornichons,* and a loaf of *pain de campagne.* Madame's glistening omelette, scattered with fresh herbs, and a bowl of mesclun followed and after that we shared one of the complacent fruit pies. The whole thing was too good to be true—a cliché out of some ad campaign dreamed up by the local tourist board.

It was past three when we gathered ourselves together, said *Merci beaucoup* and *Au revoir* and *À demain* to Madame, and started back to the car. I turned around for one last look, and there at the edge of the woods, two sleek girls on two sleek horses were cantering across the meadow, hoping they were not too late for Madame's famous *omelette aux fines herbes*.

Le Voyageur

How it happened I do not know. But in 1979 I had sailed off to start a new life in America, leaving my family safely behind me in London, and then one way or another they all ended up in New York. The gloom and lobsters of the Chelsea Hotel had pleased my mother so much—or maybe she was just lazy—that she looked no farther and bought an apartment in a brownstone one block away on Twenty-second Street. And there two Americans who had finally come home set up house together, not in the New York of their imagination but in a harsh, expensive, ugly, and indifferent city where, instead of being feted by *le tout Londres* nobody paid much attention to them at all. Hylan wrote me a letter describing what a punishing adjustment it had been:

> America was meant to be some kind of rebirth with little reference to the social reality. And the realities were so much more than we had imagined. Our little English souls were tried. Gone was the exceptionalism and in its place a sordid squalor that permeated everything we even vaguely understood. Holing up in the Chelsea Hotel with its shabby glamour, we struggled through our separate terrains, wandering New York like ghosts looking for a lost time. Dee was still funny through it all with that pilgrim's resilience shielding, somewhat, a state of disbelief. . . .

The awful irony was that their "little English souls" were far more disturbed in New York than their big American souls had ever been in London. Playing the brash outsider while married to Freddie, whose fame had turned the lonely little boy at Eton with the funny name and looks into the consummate insider, was easy. As Lady Ayer (acquired when Freddie was knighted in 1970) she could piss all over anything and anybody she wanted from inside the tent—to borrow LBJ's inimitable metaphor—but with Professor Sir Alfred Ayer removed from the construct, Dee Wells found herself entangled in a mess of soggy canvas and frayed ropes, in a strange campsite that she didn't care for at all.

ALTHOUGH HIS GYPSY WANDERINGS around London, squatting with various friends, had come to an end when he moved in with Freddie and Vanessa, Nick was still having trouble staying in school and staying off drugs. He had dropped out of City and East College, then he had dropped back in, and by the time he left he had pulled off a major coup by failing to pass a single solitary exam. The drugs business was much more serious. If Nick didn't break out of that world soon, he knew he would get sucked in deeper and deeper, until Christ-knows-what happened. Just about the only thing his parents agreed upon, as their divorce cranked its venomous way through the English legal system, was that their son needed to get out of London and make a fresh start in—where else?—New York.

Professionally Nick was willing to give anything a whirl. He started out with Larry's Italian Ices, sold from a street cart, with Larry taking most of the profits, moved on to a similar arrangement with the Great Dane Pastry Company, which always made me think of those gigantic dogs but was actually a silly pun. Nick soon tired of being outside in the healthy fresh air all day long, and his next venture involved a vintage clothing store called Trash and Vaudeville on St. Mark's Place, followed by a short spell at a rival establishment, Andy's Chee-Pees, located on the same busy street. But maybe Nick wasn't cut out for the *schmatte* business after all; perhaps home furnishings would be a better bet? And so it turned out to be. Having started as a stock boy at ABC Carpets, by the time he left he was the manager of the new furniture department.

Still, Nick knew that his picaresque adventures in the ice-cream, carpet, pastry, distressed-jeans, and sofa business couldn't go on forever, so on a visit with his dad to Bard College, where Freddie was being given an honorary degree, a deal was made: If he could pass his SATs (which he did with no trouble at all) he could start at Bard in the fall of 1984.

For an extremely bright kid whose education—through no fault of his own—had been a total dog's dinner, Bard was just the answer. Apart from stuffing Nick's head full of possibly useful, or at least interesting, notions and knowledge, it had the added advantage of getting him out of Twenty-second Street and two hundred miles away from his mother.

That first Christmas after Vanessa died, Freddie came to stay with us in New York. Deeply wounded, almost unable to function, he'd had a true *coup de vieux* and was suddenly a vulnerable old man in need of looking after. At home with baby Rebecca, my life floated by in a milky miasma watching my daughter lurch about the playground, cooking soothing nursery food, and teaching her to put bits of it in her mouth. When Freddie arrived in Bank Street, I just set another place at the table, and we all had shepherd's pie and rice pudding together, served on Peter Rabbit plates. Without the strength to do much of anything beyond reading, and writing a bit, he would sit slumped on the sofa, an unopened book by his side, and stare despairingly out the window. How, alone in his midseventies, could he ever hope to rebuild a life for himself?

ONE DAY when Rebecca was well over two years old, Peter and Harry Evans had lunch, and as they parted on the sidewalk outside the Century Club on Forty-third Street, Harry asked him what I was up to. Not a lot, bugger all. She has sunk into a bottomless milky pit, lost her mind, and fallen in love with somebody else: "Actually, we've just [*sic*] had a baby, but I know she is really eager to get back to work."

"Ask her to call me, please. I'm starting a new magazine."

Until Harry came along, travel magazines published yawn-inducing rubbish cobbled together by sycophantic hacks who roamed the world, courtesy of the airlines and hotels they wrote about. But what if you did things in a completely different way? What if *Condé Nast Traveler* were to send writers incognito, pay its own way, tell it like it is, and run stories that sometimes scared advertisers away?

"You mean, Harry, I can call up any writer I like and send them any-where in the world?"

Oh, this was going to be *way* more fun than dealing with those argu-mentative Israeli generals at Weidenfeld & Nicolson. Edna O'Brien got tangled up in the romance of Dublin; V. S. Pritchett explored his private

London; Peter Matthiessen trekked through the Himalayas; Norman Lewis, at age eighty, returned to the Ronda; Christopher Hitchens profiled the incomparable Patrick Leigh Fermor; Jan/James Morris described what it was like to travel both as a man and as a woman, as only she/he could have done; Christopher Buckley cruised the Amazon with Malcolm Forbes; Gregor von Rezzori went back in time to his childhood home in the Danube Delta—and so it went on. On a trip to London I discovered a book by Wilfred Thesiger, documenting his travels among the Marsh Arabs in the thirties (a half century later the marshes and their inhabitants would be decimated by Saddam Hussein) that became a twelve-page feature, illustrated with Thesiger's own photographs. Reading *Granta* in the bath one day, I came across an extract from a book by Martha Gellhorn, who had famously reported on the Spanish civil war (she'd met Hemingway, her future husband, while they were both being shelled by the Nationalists), and after a long epistolary courtship, persuaded her to write a piece for me.

I don't recall how Harry and I came up with the idea, such as it was, but I remember we both thought it was rather inspired at the time. Martha Gellhorn lived in Wales, Lord Snowdon had a Welsh title; why don't we send them off to wander around this country so dear to both their hearts, and see what happens? At first Ms. Gellhorn quite sensibly resisted our scheme, but after an evening spent getting drunk together on vodka and orange juice, served in tooth mugs, in her hotel room in New York (for some reason she'd refused to go to the bar), we agreed that she *might* think about it again. Her next letter began "Dear Gully, I think boozing in a hotel room justifies first names, don't you?" But she was still holding out on the earl. And after I'd given up hope of ever getting her to do it, I suddenly received this: "Dear Gully, I may be loopy and you may have found another writer, but I've changed my mind. Suddenly it seems funny to me, Snowdon and me, really the Odd Couple. We have in common being branded for life by our first mistaken marriages. Only I am much worse off than he is."

However, Martha was an extremely busy lady, and it was impossible to pin her down on dates. She was revising two books, starting a new one, making a television documentary in Finland, looking after her roses, and if that wasn't enough, she had just been visited by a plague of Welsh locusts:

A hamsin was blowing yesterday and there is an invisible and inaudible insect, called the harvest bug because it appears in the spring, lasts all summer and disappears invisibly at harvest time. It attacks only under clothes and preferably in the erogenous zones. Its bite beats anything I have met in jungles, tropics, or anywhere on earth, size of a really strong hive, burns for days.

She ended the letter with "Are you well and pretty and still short-skirted? When I see new fashion pictures I think of you." I was touched and ridiculously flattered.

But back to the earl:

I think I've made a five star mistake in thinking it would be fun/funny to travel with the Earl . . . the telephone rang, a young female voice said, "Is Martha there?" I tried to think who it was, always frightened of forgetting and hurting feelings. Then she said, "I have Lord Snowdon for you," and I sat holding the telephone, waiting. I've read of this, but never experienced it. . . . I think my mad habit of trying out any new experience may have led me into a minor horror journey. . . . I was warned by chums in London, but paid no heed.

The trip turned out to be less awful than she'd feared: "Dear Gully, It is over and I am exhausted. He wasn't so bad, the Earl, and I reckon he'd say the same of me."

So that was good. I eagerly awaited the piece, congratulating myself on having pulled off this editorial coup. Her next letter was addressed not to me but to Harry, who had taken the liberty of rearranging one or two of her paragraphs: "Dear Mr. Evans, I am appalled by the treatment of my Wales article. Would 'shambolic' be too strong . . . I am told that you think it would be a good idea to move the goal posts; now a touch of Tony-and-Marty-in Wales is needed. . . . In fact the trip was cold, wet, unbelievably uncomfortable and boring. . . ."

In the end I managed to broker some kind of peace, and the article was published alongside the earl's moody (as she had informed Harry, the weather had been rainy, cold, and cloudy, just for a change) photographs. Somewhat surprisingly she forgave us both, and a few months later wrote telling me about a new trip she was anxious to embark on as soon as possible: "I have to get myself to Diksmuide in Belgium, the last Sunday in

June, where if you can believe it, Neo-Nazis from all over Europe meet to honor the Nazi dead in WW2, in Nazi uniforms etc." Possibly not quite the thing for the *Traveler*, but if we didn't want that, how about sending her scuba diving in the Maldives? She was eighty at the time.

What's with all the geriatrics? What had possessed me to collect a stable of writers whose combined ages approached the millennial mark? Apart from the fact that they wrote superbly—which would be the main point—they were living witnesses to a now-vanished era of travel. Long before tourism became the world's biggest industry—which it is today, extending its tentacles to every back of beyond on the planet, engulfing us all in a flood of sweaty fellow travelers—they had ventured to foreign places when they really were *foreign*.

But perhaps I could write, too. Hadn't I spent every summer since the age of eleven in that house in France? Surely in all those years I must have learned *something* about Provence. Of course I had. How about a story on Haute-Provence, where an enterprising Parisian architect had just opened a hotel in a remote Saracen village called Crillon-le-Brave? It worked. Now why hadn't I thought of that before?

Next, I took on the Romans who had given Provence its name (Provincia was their Miami, the place where retired generals and legionnaires settled to enjoy their hard-earned sunset years) and returned to Arles, Nîmes, the Pont du Gard—and of course, the Hôtel Nord-Pinus. After that it was Avignon, the Palais des Papes and a hotel of laughable perfection where I slept in a room wallpapered with delicately painted pagodas, peacocks, and chattering monkeys swinging through a forest of bamboo. French windows opened onto a terrace, which in turn led down to the garden, where the air buzzed with the sound of bees, drunk on sticky oleander-flower cocktails.

Still, I really couldn't expect the magazine to keep gobbling up course after course of delicacies from this one small corner of the world. What other dishes could I tempt them with? Not yet confident enough to write about a place I didn't know (that would come later, with pieces on Russia, Jamaica, Brazil, China, Mexico, Estonia, Sicily, and God knows where else), there was only one other option: Spain. During the five years we had explored the country together, Tom had taught me well, and I was rather proud to have graduated top of the class in my college of one. According to my tutor I was unusually gifted at art and history, my grasp of current affairs was less assured, and as for my language skills—the sorry results spoke for themselves. Which was more than I could do.

The editors loved the idea of Madrid—the rebirth of a democratic Spain, the excitement of *la Movida,* King Juan Carlos's relationship with the Cortes—but now I was in a total panic. Could I write the story all by myself? Probably. But could I produce a piece with real insight, quotes from interesting politicians, an overview of the revolution that had taken place in Spain since Franco's death? You must be kidding. It had been fifteen years since I had set foot in Spain, fifteen years since Tom had called me in London to announce he was getting married, fifteen years since we had last spoken. But what were old friends for, if not to help you out in an emergency?

We met at the Café Gijón on the Paseo de la Castellana, the same place his grandfather used to go before the civil war—oh, if only the old man had lived long enough to see Franco entombed in the Valle de los Caídos, and his country's triumphant return to democracy.

"Una manzanilla La Gitana para la Señora, por favor."

What else would I drink in Madrid?

"Y dos raciones de chipirones en su tinta."

And two portions of squid in black ink.

Tom smiled and leaned across the table. "As I was saying yesterday. . . ."

"Ah, Miguel, how could I forget?"

Miguel de Unamuno, a friend of Dr. Marañón's, and one of the great Spanish intellectuals of that generation, had been the rector of the University of Salamanca during the dictatorship of Primo de Rivera. Famous for his liberal views, he had been thrown out in 1924 and sent into exile on Fuerteventura, in the Canary Islands. After Rivera's fall in 1930, Unamuno returned to the university and began his first lecture with the immortal words, "As I was saying yesterday. . . ." As if no time had passed at all.

As we were saying fifteen years ago . . . as if no time had passed at all. The tutorials resumed, and over the next week Tom introduced me to journalists, politicians, writers, the man who ran the Prado, the woman who ran the mayor of Madrid—people I could never have met or interviewed if we hadn't had lunch at El Gijón.

"Hey, you remember that place we went to the first time I ever came to Madrid, off the Plaza Mayor, where we had coagulated blood and rat's penis to start, and the poor little calf's head with the milky eyeballs, and the dismembered baby pig? Do you think it's still there?'"

"Of course it's still there. It opened the year before Cervantes lost his arm in the Battle of Lepanto. Why one earth wouldn't it be?"

"Okay. Since you have been the fixer from *al cielo*, I propose we go there tomorrow night before I fly back to New York in the morning."

The Madrid piece ran a few months later, and I was thrilled to get a letter from a Spanish reader complimenting me on how well I had captured his hometown. It was forwarded, with love and gratitude, to my tutor.

SOMETIMES I DIDN'T EVEN have to dream up an idea for a story to get on a plane. Every year the magazine gave a big party at the ASTA (American Society of Travel Agents) convention, wherever it happened to be—Rio, Hong Kong, Budapest, Lisbon, Sydney. The agents lived for their work, and didn't mind how many thousands of miles they had to travel (first class) to be feted at various extravaganzas laid on by the titans of their industry.

In 1993 the convention was to take place in Cairo, and Tom Wallace, who was now the editor (restless Harry had left to become head of Random House), asked me if I would go with him. The climax of this dazzling evening would be the presentation of awards—the Oscars of the travel business—to whatever airline, resort, hotel, spa, car rental agency, and city the discerning readers of *Condé Nast Traveler* had voted best in the world. It seemed that my role was to play Vanna White to Tom's Pat Sajak.

However, not all the recipients were glossy advertisers. Vladimir Chernousenko, a Russian physicist, had gone into Chernobyl as leader of the team that had the grim job of trying to clean up and contain the disaster. He was rewarded for his bravery with the loss of his job, after he had spoken out publicly about the situation, the Condé Nast Traveler Environmental Award, a trip to Cairo, a check—and cancer. Vladimir was staying at our hotel, and some days he was so weak he couldn't leave his room, but that night was different. His eyes shone as he gazed out at the Pyramids—"You know, when I was a small child I used to dream of them"—he enjoyed his wine as only a Russian can, flirted energetically with every lady in sight, and when the band started to play the first bars of "Strangers in the Night"—"Ah, my favorite song!"—he asked me to dance.

Okay, it was a cliché. Sinatra, champagne, candles, camels outlined against the Pyramids, but a transcendental, unforgettable cliché because of the heroic dying man I was dancing with.

NO MORE THAN six or seven, younger than Rebecca, wearing shorts, flip-flops, and a torn T-shirt, the boy darted through the rush-hour traffic, almost getting hit by a bus, garlands of tiny white flowers dangling from one skinny brown arm. The lights turned red, he ran toward the car holding one of his fragile jasmine necklaces out to me, smiling, and I gave him whatever money I had in my bag. It must have been quite a lot because he seemed momentarily stunned and pushed the rest of his flowers through the window, trying to make me take them. "No, no, you must keep them. But please, please get out of the traffic." I waved frantically toward the sidewalk, pleading with him. Laughing, he made it back just as the lights changed. I slipped the jasmine necklace over my head.

Yes, it was the same scent that had infused the magical tent. No, the obscene tent. How much had that ridiculous circus cost, anyway? How much food had been thrown out last night? (Or had the staff taken every last bit? I hoped so.) Oh, do shut up. If you *really* cared, you wouldn't be weeping in the back of an air-conditioned car, you wouldn't be telling Park Avenue orthodontists where to go on vacation, you wouldn't be prancing around in Chanel. Go get a job at Oxfam, why don't you? Work for the UNRWA in a Palestinian refugee camp, or how about joining the Peace Corps? But of course you could never leave your family, could you? So find something in New York; plenty of kids in the South Bronx who need help. With no snappy comeback, I reverted to my usual faute-de-mieux reply and told my conscience to fuck off.

No, after careful consideration, I thought I'd just continue with my own peculiar, erratic, impetuous, highly emotional, disorganized response to poverty. Go on giving Vinnie—who hangs out on the corner of Sixth Avenue and West Tenth, entertaining passersby with strange whistling noises—coffee, cigarettes, and sandwiches, and in the winter enough money for the shelter. When in St. Petersburg, give your complimentary fruit basket, with additions of brandy, a chocolate bar, and a pack of

Marlboros from the minibar to the old man with one arm, selling pencils on Nevsky Prospekt. Always hand out rubles to roaming bands of raucous street kids, ignoring the advice of Russian friends who will tell you: "You mustn't do that. It just makes them wilder, and we'll never get rid of them." Olga was right. It did, and we didn't.

"They're just *sharamigas;* pay no attention to them."

"And what the hell are *sharamigas?* "

So she explained. During the retreat from Moscow, Napoleon fled back to Paris in his sable-lined sleigh, while his poor starving frozen soldiers were reduced to begging, "Cher ami, cher ami—aidez-moi s'il vous plaît."

Never, ever haggle. Why would you want to cheat somebody with so much less than you? Why not go on handing out beer and a bag of pretzels to anybody who looks as though they could use a drink? Jesus, don't we all need a stiff cocktail when the going gets rough? And I might just hit the next person who, when I stuff a couple of bucks into a *sharamiga*'s empty paper cup, says, "Oh, you mustn't give him anything. He'll just go straight out and spend it on drugs or alcohol."

Well, perhaps I won't actually hit them. Instead I'll tell the truth: "Oh, but I must. You see, it's entirely selfish. If you're a member of the Good Luck Sperm Club, you have to do *something* to stop yourself going completely mad."

La Bouillabaisse

ONE SUMMER WHEN I WAS ABOUT SIXTEEN, after reading a few too many books by Elizabeth David, I became obsessed with the idea of cooking bouillabaisse. My poor mother was bullied into getting up at dawn and driving to the market in Toulon down by the old port, where we immediately headed for the bellowing harridans who inhabit the fish stands—overflowing with a mélange of grotesque sea creatures straight out of Hieronymus Bosch's fevered imagination. Spiky black *rascasses;* terrifying moray eels; weavers, their hideous eyes bulging out of the top of their heads; combers, known as *serans écritures* on account of the blue-and-purple scribbles carelessly dashed across their red scales; Saint-Pierres, shiny black *moules,* multicolored *girelles,* and tiny green *favouilles* (crabs) were wrapped in newspaper and piled into our baskets. Still alive, some of the more adventurous *favouilles* decided to make a break for freedom in the car on the way home. The next morning I found one of them scuttling around on the backseat, so of course he had to accompany us, in a plastic bowl filled with water and two teaspoons of sea salt, to Bikini Beach, where he disappeared into the sand.

For some reason, probably nerves at the thought of embarking on this tricky enterprise with only my mother as sous-chef, I had decided to invite our two neighbors, Francette and Jeannine Tricon, gifted cooks both, to come and help me transform my Quasimodo creatures into this sublime Provençal dish. Naively I had failed to take into account the explosive, proprietorial emotions that could be ignited when it came to the composition of *une bouillabaisse véritable*. Some purists (usually people who come from Toulon or Marseille) will tell you that the real deal can be found only in their hometown and in a few places along the coast between these culinary lodestars. (Other less fanatical aficionados will allow that the permissible area extends as far as Monaco but not a single kilometer beyond.) So at least we had the geography right. The trouble began when Francette spotted the basket of small, round potatoes, soil still clinging to their rosy skins, that Madame Tricon had smuggled into my kitchen.

"Les pommes de terre, *je pense pas!*" she hissed in my ear while our neighbor was washing her offerings in the sink. "Jamais les pommes de terre!" Long practiced in the delicate art of conciliation, and perhaps misguidedly convinced of the beneficial properties of alcohol when it came to smoothing over disagreements, I ignored her and instead offered them each a double dose of rosé de Bandol while we set to work cutting up the fish. First the tiniest ones, freshly netted rockfish, were put in the pot along with the less-than-lively crabs, who had survived a night in the fridge (the cold must have sapped their fighting spirit), along with some fennel, leek, celery, olive oil, salt, and the bleeding guillotined heads of the bigger fish. Francette, a cigarette dangling from the side of her mouth, poured in water (traditionally the fishermen who cooked this on the beach over driftwood fires added seawater in lieu of salt), and the broth was put on the stove to boil (the *bouille* part), after which she lowered (the *baisse* bit) the flame and it was set at a steady simmer. At this point I saw the ashy tip of her cigarette disappear into the soup—oh, what the hell.

"Oh lá lá, j'ai jamais vu ça!" Madame Tricon exclaimed with entirely false bonhomie. Christ, what now? Francette had produced a bagful of *cigales de mer,* a type of lobster that she was seriously proposing to add to this controversial witches' brew. "Perhaps this is something they do in Paris?" she asked her neighbor brightly. "Non, pas du tout, Jeannine, it is something I learned from my friend who is the chef at Chez Fonfon in Marseille." Time for more wine. I have absolutely no memory of the rest of the evening, or what the bouillabaisse tasted like, but I swore then that I would never, ever get into cooking it again.

What changed my mind was a book called *Lulu's Provençal Table* that landed on my desk in New York twenty-something years later. Lulu Peyraud lived in Le Plan du Castellet, and her family owned the rightly famous Domaine Tempier that produced some of the—if not *the*—best wine in the area. I had been introduced to her by Nick and his girlfriend, Jemima, who were friends of Madame Peyraud's daughter, Catherine.

Feeling inexplicably flush one day, Nick and I had driven over to their house for an informal wine tasting and had returned home with a case of—what else—*cuvée* La Migoua. The memory of that brief visit never left me. Surrounded by vineyards, the old farmhouse—its dusty blue shutters closed to keep out the ferocious summer heat—was approached by an *allée* of plane trees, its terrace shaded by a huge, slightly lopsided umbrella pine and a vine-covered pergola. The air was thick with the thrumming of cicadas and the scent of rosemary, flowering fennel, and wild thyme. Madame Peyraud's great-grandmother Léonie had been given the property as part of her dowry in the mid-nineteenth century, and I remember thinking that if she had decided to return that day, she would surely have been happy to see that nothing had changed at all.

Sitting in my office in Manhattan, I opened the book and started reading. Alice Waters, who wrote the introduction, had met the Peyrauds in the seventies and credits "the Peyraud family's example with helping us find our balance at Chez Panisse." She remembers

> one evening when Lulu had not expected us for supper but neverthe-
> less insisted on cooking us a little something. She had a basket of wild
> mushrooms that she proceeded to quickly brush off and then sauté with
> garlic and lots of herbs. Although she seemed to be cooking them almost
> unconsciously, chatting away with us over a welcoming glass of rosé,
> they were probably the most flavorful wild mushrooms I have ever eaten.

A few days later I picked up the telephone and asked Madame Peyraud if I might come see her when I arrived in La Migoua later in the summer. Perhaps we could cook bouillabaisse together? "Absolument. Je serais ravie."

No, it wasn't exactly dawn, but it can't have been too long after when I arrived at the Domaine Tempier to accompany Madame Peyraud to Ban-dol so that we could meet the fishing boats as they came into the port with the night's catch. How else could one possibly be sure not only of the freshest fish but also of finding some of the more elusive creatures who might otherwise be stolen from under one's nose by other sharp-eyed and -elbowed shoppers? I hopped into her car, and as we drove along the still-cool back roads down toward the coast, Lulu, who bears more than a passing resemblance to Simone Signoret, with her wide-set dark eyes and short blond hair, started to talk bouillabaisse.

To start with there is no "correct" recipe. The fishermen on the beach had just used whatever they couldn't sell, and to this day, the list of ingredients is somewhat elastic, but not entirely. *Baudroie* (anglerfish) for instance is vital. Its head, the cartilaginous central bone, chopped small, and other trimmings go into the broth, while its pinkish beige liver, as smooth and delicious as foie gras, is an essential ingredient in the *rouille*. Those frolicsome *favouille* crabs lend a necessary peppery flavor to the broth, which should also include a generous slice of conger eel, an entire head of garlic, a couple of pounds of the tiny rockfish, as well as onion, tomatoes, leek, celery, carrots, and a bouquet of the fennel that happens to grow outside Lulu's kitchen door. Francette's cigarette ash is entirely optional.

"Whenever I cook fish, I always add lots of herbs, but for bouillabaisse I leave out the thyme and bay leaf, and concentrate on fennel." We were back in Lulu's kitchen with our baskets of fish, and out came the knives. The cut-up pieces of fish were set to marinate in a mix of ground fennel seed, saffron, crushed garlic, and olive oil on a platter, while we got to work on the broth. Raised up off the ground and almost big enough to stand up in, an enormous fireplace—just like the one in our house—dominated the room and would have been built as much for cooking as *chauffage*. Regrettable electrical intrusions like the refrigerator and dishwasher were concealed behind antique wooden doors, and marble mortars, wooden pestles, and spoons, metal whisks, ancient metal grills, copper cooking pots, sharp knives—all things her great-grandmother might have used—constituted her entire *batterie de cuisine*. (Perhaps the shiny new Cuisinart, blenders, electric knife sharpeners, and other equally regrettable modern innovations were hidden away in a cupboard—but somehow I doubted it, and certainly didn't dare ask.)

"Alors, maintenant on fait la rouille!" Without which there can be no bouillabaisse. Cayenne peppers were attacked in a big marble mortar, coarse salt and garlic added, the sublime anglerfish foie gras was pounded until we had a smooth paste, then an egg yolk and a mix of bread crumbs and saffron, moistened with fish stock, and after that I dribbled in a steady stream of olive oil. This celestial, garlicky, fish-infused mayonnaise is spread as thickly as you dare on garlic bread crusts at the bottom of each soup plate, the rest being passed around at the table, just in case you feel that you might have been shortchanged on your daily garlic ration. And what of Madame Tricon's problematical potatoes? "Mais oui, toujours les pommes de terres!" Lulu added them to the broth, with the tomatoes, *more* garlic, *more* saffron, fennel, followed by the mussels and marinated fish. And what of Francette's controversial *cigales de mer*? "Oui, absolument. But I couldn't find any this morning. Sometimes I add octopus as well."

Ever the sly diplomat, when I got back home I made sure to tell Francette and Madame Tricon (separately, of course) that the great Lulu Peyraud had decreed that they had been completely right. Unsurprised at being vindicated, they both shrugged and said I told you so, whatever that is in French. And—having experienced perfection—I never cooked bouillabaisse again.

THAT SUMMER Peter had stayed behind in New York while Rebecca and I made our annual pilgrimage to La Migoua. The truth is that after the horror show of our last visit with Peter hissing in my ear, "But you *said* she wouldn't be here," the thought of them together for several weeks in the same house was more than I could take. If I hadn't married somebody quite so much like her everything would have been easier, or so I thought. But as it was I had fallen for a man who was every bit as smart as she was, who made me laugh just as much as she did, who did outrageous things like stopping his car in traffic to have a pee in the middle of Parliament Square, who had yet to master the useful art of suffering fools, who couldn't help showing off his considerable intelligence, and whose love I have never doubted. Just as I never doubted hers.

Of course they had their differences. Peter wasn't much use as a snob, never having seen the point of posh people per se, his tongue lacked that fine stiletto edge, and with all the expensive education his parents had given him—and hers had failed to give her—he could win any argument that depended on real knowledge as opposed to my mother's preferred, but highly effective, weapon of wit and wild chutzpah. Sadly his swearing never approached the masterful pitch of hers and his desire to shock the world into submission was minimal, but these were minor, and forgivable, failings.

Like the Jesuits, my mother had gotten hold of me at an impressionable age and had nourished me on such a rich and unpredictable diet that most other people seemed utterly bland in comparison. The terror of boredom—this came from her, whether by nature or nurture I do not know—must have made me crave the kind of emotional and intellectual excitement I had grown accustomed to. And which both she and Peter provided, sometimes in exhausting abundance. No danger of ever being bored with those two roaming around inside your psyche, but plenty of danger of thrilling fireworks with them roaming around inside the same small house. Or at least that's how it seemed to me. So for the sake of my fragile sanity I preferred not to put my theory to the test.

THERE WAS NOTHING Freddie adored more than a party. An extraordinarily good dancer—he taught Rebecca the Charleston when she was four and he was seventy-seven—he liked to flirt, he liked to talk, and I'm afraid he never could resist showing off, which is always lots more fun with an audience. That first fall he was with us, after Vanessa died, I thought it might cheer him up if the two Scorpios—"Jesus, all you two ever think about is sex and death"—had a joint birthday party. We would have lots to drink, get Balducci's to do the food, hire a barman, Freddie would ask all his old—in both senses of the word—friends, Peter and I would round up ours, we'd throw them all together and hope that at least a few people misbehaved. It would be a strange mix—but isn't that the whole point?

Distinguished oldsters like Meyer Schapiro (the brilliant art historian, pushing ninety), Mary McCarthy, Arthur Schlesinger, Jr., and the birthday boy were carefully propped up on the sofas, people who liked to drink (Anthony Haden-Guest, Charles Kuralt, our downstairs neighbor, Christopher Hitchens) stuck close to the bar, the lady (no name) who was up to no good with somebody else's husband (no name) hung out in the shadowy hallway, kindhearted people (Nick, Quentin Crisp) talked to Rebecca, and everybody else just did the best they could in whatever space was left over. I can't say there was any serious misbehavior, unless you count the host going to bed before the last guest had left, and the hostess disappearing to Da Silvano's for spaghetti puttanesca with an old friend (Michael Stone) soon afterward. Jeffrey and Caron Steingarten stepped into our delinquent shoes and ended up cooking Freddie, Ed Epstein, and his date, Susannah Duncan, the best bacon and eggs any of them had ever tasted. La Rochefoucauld was right, hunger is *always* the best sauce.

Ed's date was the highlight of Freddie's evening. A doctor in her late thirties who looked like a dark-haired Grace Kelly, crisp and detached in that cool English way, she had driven the poor man into a terminal tizzy. Battling a ferocious hangover the next morning, I did what I could to calm him down.

"Oh dear, oh dear, I can't possibly call her. Can I?"

"Of course you can. Did she give you her number?"

"Yes, she said it was G-R-A-B-T-R-Y."

The minx.

"That must be a secret code for those very special men she's attracted to. The rest get the numbers."

"Do you really think so?"

"Absolutely."

A few days later, at about four in the afternoon, a beaming only slightly intoxicated Freddie was entertaining Rebecca with a soft-shoe shuffle and a soulful rendition of "Night and Day." After that he moved on to "If You Were the Only Girl in the World."

"How was lunch with Grabtry?"

"Well, now that you ask, I have to say it went *extremely* well."

That night after I had gone to bed, Freddie and Peter sat up, with a bottle of brandy to keep them company, and wrestled with that age-old masculine conundrum: How to figure out if an irresistible, flirtatious minx has the slightest intention of ever sleeping with you.

"One doesn't want to make a total ass of oneself."

"God, no!"

"And yet, if one does nothing, how's one ever to know?"

"Too true, too true!"

Several more lunches followed, but I suspect that Grabtry's honor and Freddie's dignity must have remained intact, because if they hadn't my dear stepfather could never have resisted telling me all about it.

~

THE MANAGEMENT'S POLICY at the Hotel Bank Street was to include our guests in all invitations. Which is how Freddie and Fernando Sánchez, a charismatic designer of ladies' lingerie, came to meet. Introduced at a dinner given by my friend Sarah Giles, they had so charmed one another that Fernando called the next morning and asked us all to a party he and his boyfriend were giving the following week.

For whatever reason Peter and Bob Friend, a BBC colleague, had thought it would be a good idea to arrive chez Sánchez early and drunk. They found their surprised and irritated hosts, dressed in matching silk peignoirs still attending to their hair and makeup. Parked in the drawing room, Peter and Bob helped themselves to a few more drinks, and by the time the other guests started to drift in, Bob Bloke (as Hitch used to call him on account of his total blokishness) was in a fine state. Of course he knew that such people existed, he was a sophisticated man of the world, and he'd met one or two of them in his time, but it was a bit much to find yourself *surrounded* by the buggers.

"I expect you're a homosexual. Everybody else here seems to be."

Freddie looked appalled.

"I most certainly am *not!*"

"Well, thank God for that, is all I can say!"

Apart from us the guests looked as though Fernando had chosen them by flicking impatiently through the pages of model-agency look books, rejecting all the dogs—"Oh dear, can't think *he's* much in demand. Honey, you're wasting your time—take my advice and get back to Kansas!"— and picking out the hundred or so true dazzlers. A perfectionist with an artist's eye, Fernando worshipped at the altar of beauty—whether it was the priapic black ambergris candles (how Robert Mapplethorpe would have loved them!), the gigantic flowering gardenia bushes, the heavy white linen curtains, or the exquisite creatures that filled his apartment.

But he was also a kindhearted host, and when he saw one of his guests standing all alone, he grabbed my arm. "You *must* meet Naomi Campbell, she's just arrived from London and knows no one."

Naomi was ten feet tall, sixteen years old, and unspeakably beautiful.

"Mum and I got here last week. I'm doing a bit of modeling."

"Sounds to me like you have chosen the perfect career."

"Yeah, I hope it's going to work out."

"I don't think you need worry."

Naomi smiled. She didn't look worried at all.

Freddie was just about to get up and pile lots more smoked salmon on to his plate, when Sarah came rushing over to our table. "The most terrible thing is going on upstairs. This poor girl is pinned up against the wall and the man won't let her go."

Who better than a seventy-seven-year-old philosopher to take on an overenthusiastic suitor? Perhaps he could try engaging him in a discussion of ethics.

The scene was just as Sarah had described it. Naomi was squealing, the man had her rammed against the wall, and, distracted by the effort of trying to shove his tongue down her throat, he didn't notice when Freddie tapped him on the shoulder. So Freddie tapped him a bit harder; the man swung round, adjusting his fly, and glared at the old geezer. "And who the fuck are you?"

"I happen to be rather a famous philosopher. My name is Professor Sir Alfred Ayer. And who are you, if I may ask?"

"I'm Mike Tyson—the heavyweight champion of the world."

"Well in *that* case, my dear boy, we are both supreme in our field."

Which settled everything.

Whether Naomi really needed rescuing, I'm not so sure. All I do know is that Freddie was thrilled with his heroic feat that there was no dragging him away from the party. No, he didn't want to come home with us— it was well past midnight—on the whole he'd rather remain just where he was, on a sofa surrounded by admiring ladies eager to hear what had really happened when the two champions had gone mano a mano, or at least come face-to-face.

The next morning something was wrong with Freddie's hearing. He hopped about, shaking his head to one side, then the other, as if he was trying to get water out of his ear. Nothing serious, but he did hope it would get better soon. And what could possibly have caused this? Around two in the morning, when he finally left the party, Freddie had gone down in the elevator with a group of extremely large, high-spirited black men who turned out to be part of Tyson's entourage. Hey, it's that old-timer who stopped Mike having a good time! Playfully, they meant no harm, it was all a joke really—they started boxing him around the ears. Mess with Mike and here's what you get!

The doorman was not amused. He didn't need a gang of hooligans laughing and shouting and jumping about in his hallway at that hour of the night. That little gray-haired man couldn't just let them run wild. "Hey, you their manager? You gotta keep these guys under control. Get them outta here!"

Poor Freddie. First Bob Bloke thought he was queer, and then he had turned into a boxing manager. But at least his hearing came back.

Les Cigarettes

As a child I never thought about smoking. Like getting divorced, it was just something most grown-ups did. My mother and Freddie did it, just about all their friends did it, and I assumed I'd do it when the time came. Newspapers, coffee, and cigarettes were what my mother had for breakfast; Martin followed a similar diet, as did Tom, Anna Haycraft, Peter, his mother, Nick, Emma Soames, Francette—all of them my favored breakfast companions at one time or another. Since I was a bit slow on the uptake, my smoking only really got going in my early twenties, but I was a quick study and soon caught up. Every now and then I would contemplate quitting, until one day a profligate boyfriend gave me a gold Dunhill lighter with GW engraved on the top. Reassuringly heavy, perfectly proportioned, like a miniature Seagram Building, it was an object of great beauty that nestled in my handbag, following me wherever I went. Now you couldn't just abandon a lovely thing like that, could you?

By nature defiant, by choice delinquent, my mother had been a precocious smoker, starting around thirteen. It suited her. It's what bad girls did. Of course she knew it screwed up your health. But since when had she ever played it safe? She despised goody-two-shoes behavior on principle. Regular brisk exercise/plenty of leafy greens/no more than one glass of wine/and forget about anything and everything you might *enjoy* putting in your mouth, which of course would include cigarettes. Imagine actually *living* like that. I couldn't, and neither could she.

Forty years after my mother had shared a cigarette with her brother

Jackie in that drugstore in New Bedford where they used to hang out, she wrote to Hylan. She was frightened:

> Lovely Hylan, I haven't written before now because I am so desperately trying to stop smoking and I can't type without smoking so therefore I can't type. So this is an experiment: can I get all the way through a letter without smoking? I never have. But I'm so truly worried about what the smoking is doing to me that I'd do almost anything to stop . . . yesterday I thought I'd call the miracle acupuncturist in Marseille . . . but then I made up 27 convincing reasons why he wouldn't be there on a Saturday in July, so I didn't call. (*And* now I've just lit the cigarette, I really have. . . . I don't want to die before Nick's about . . . well, 25, in my more bleak moments but to be truthful 45 would suit me better. Now—and how about this for feeble—I'm trying to see how long I can just let it lie in the ashtray without me touching it.)

Late in 1985 Peter's mother, Katherine, lay dying of lung cancer in a London hospital, and one night I went to see her on my way back from dinner. The nurse showed me into her room where she lay in bed, her eyes closed. She had given up on eating, watching television, listening to the radio, or reading—what would have been the point? She had lost her hair, she could barely speak, the chemo made her nauseated, she was so thin her body hardly seemed to exist, but there was still one thing we could do together to distract us from the horror. We could share a cigarette. Too weak to lift her own arm, I held it up to her lips as she inhaled, took a puff myself, and held it up for her again. After that I sat with her while she drifted off to sleep, kissed her good-bye, and tiptoed out of the room. She died later that night.

You might have thought that her son's grief would have inspired him to quit—it certainly had that effect on her daughter-in-law—and Peter did for a few months. After that he smoked in secret, or so he thought. (Cigarettes, like mistresses, never stay hidden for long.) And after that he smoked anywhere he damn well pleased, and his wife stopped nagging him about it. Naturally there was no point in nagging my mother about anything, least of all her smoking. As far as I know she never succeeded in stopping for more than an hour or two, and by the time she had her first heart attack, she must have been at it for fifty years.

It wasn't a drop-dead kind of heart attack, it was more a dizzy feeling that took her to the hospital where they did some tests and by the time I got there, she was sitting up, eating ice cream, and making the nurses laugh. The doctors did an angioplasty, propped her arteries open with stents, gave her blood-thinning drugs, and sent her home a few days later with a list of goody-two-shoes instructions of the brisk exercise/leafy green vegetables/one glass of wine/lose weight variety. And for almost a year she behaved extremely well. Hylan helped her keep on the straight and narrow, watched her diet, made tempting salads, and encouraged her when she started writing again.

But, as she had said in that letter to him—"I can't type without smoking, therefore I can't type"—and it was the writing that did her in. Try following up on a wildly successful first novel—it sold two million copies worldwide—when you know that it wasn't a novel at all. She liked to pretend, disingenuously, that *Jane* was a work of fiction but she understood better than anyone that the heroine—an American journalist in London with an evil sense of humor, three boyfriends, and an outsider's take on the bizarre ways of the English—was her. I imagine—because she never liked to talk about it, at least not to me—that she felt she wasn't a *real* novelist, she didn't know how to make things up, create characters, and place them in situations that she herself had never experienced. So what was she supposed to write about? I tried to persuade her to start a memoir, but I don't think she could face going back to the misery of a childhood that she had spent her entire life trying to escape. And so she sat there alone in the apartment worrying, staring at the blank sheet in the typewriter, until one day she reached for a cigarette.

She worried about not working, she worried about money, she worried about Nick, she worried about growing old, she worried about Hylan (with good reason), she worried about my disastrous choice of husband (unnecessarily—her daughter was happier than she had ever been), and I am sure she was haunted by the realization (if she could bear to face it) that the move to New York seven years before had been a huge irrevocable mistake. It was enough to drive anybody back to the comfort of nicotine.

Hylan was horrified: "When she started smoking again, I knew she had chosen slow suicide. She didn't care. She had given up the fight." Which didn't mean she had given up fighting. Oh no. She was full of

energy and would stomp around in her favorite T-shirt, black, with
"DIE YUPPIE SCUM" printed across the front in big white letters, her
ire usually directed at the idiocy of the people who thought they were
in charge of running the world, but sometimes the gun turret swiveled
around and caught one of us in its sights. Frustrated, angry, frightened,
and depressed—this wasn't how her life was supposed to turn out. She
had gambled and lost, first with New York and now, far more heartbreak-
ingly, with Hylan. That was the terrible truth.

The man she had loved for sixteen years had decided to leave her. That
summer, 1987, she went to the house in France alone, and by the time she
returned in September, he would be gone. They both agreed it would be
less painful that way. So why, I have always wondered, did he have to wait
until the day she came back from JFK to start moving? Nick remembers
turning onto Twenty-second Street and seeing, halfway up the block,
Hylan and his friend going in and out of the house, lugging cardboard
boxes, suitcases, bulging trash bags, and dumping them in the back of a
van. This was a horror show he wanted no part of, so quite sensibly he hid
around the corner until it was all over. Nick wasn't deserting his mother,
he just needed to gather his strength for the night ahead.

The only time she ever saw Hylan again was for a brief drink a few
months later. After which she wrote him a letter:

> What a star-crossed pity it all is. You left here the other evening so
> relieved at having handled the unwelcome and dangerous encounter so
> deftly and with such virtuoso charm and grace. A recklessly extrava-
> gant hour had been squandered on me. . . . I had so hoped that we'd
> at last be able to talk to each other . . . it never seemed possible you'd
> still choose to evade it all and just dart from trivia to banality and back
> again.

But since that's what he had done, she was going to say all the things he
had not hung around long enough to hear:

> See Gully if you must. I would much rather you didn't but Gully is free
> to be friends with whomever she chooses . . . but please make your
> orbit from now on one that does not include Rebecca. She is a trusting,
> delightful generous little creature and I think it would be sad were she
> to grow up believing you to be a family friend . . . now that there's been

such an irreparable rift in the family we once shared, it shouldn't be any more difficult to vanish from her life than it was to vanish from mine.

And then there was Nick. The man who had been his de facto stepfather for sixteen years had vanished from his life, too. Apparently Hylan was going to write to him.

In some way it might be best to leave things as they are, and not send this letter or whatever it is you have not quite yet come up with. It caused him such pain to see the home-core dissolve again (and then seemingly not to have been given another minute's thought by you—which may not have been how it was, but was certainly how it appeared . . . and one can only go by the evidence) that if it has healed over by now, there's no point opening it up again. Except I know it hasn't.

She has one last question for him:

Why was it not possible to give me just time enough to make an exit? Just time to figure out what to do. Where to go. . . . You say I knew it was coming. Must have/should have. I didn't though. . . . Why did I suddenly have to be Carthage? To be some mysterious symbolic obstacle that must be smashed to smithereens and dust and rubble?

It is hard to believe I'm likely never to see or talk to you again. And it seems so sad now that I really had believed we could win in the jungle where pretty nearly everybody loses. Still, I did believe it.

She never did see him again. But she did write to him one more time to apologize for her previous letter:

The letter was the monster child of anger. . . . And if anger can be seen as a horse, this one was descended from Bleak Sorrow . . . Small Hope . . . Dashed Hope . . . and Anguish. On its mother's side anyhow; I can't speak for its sire. In any case, Monster Child was the product. (It will never race again. We took him out in back of the barn and shot him.)

She wonders how she could have been such a fool to believe in what they had together:

Oh so much I believed in it. After truth, compassion, Justice and dogs (as Mrs. Wharton said) it was just about all I did believe in. . . . All I'm trying to say is that I'm sorry and that I apologize for whatever it was I did to you that made me Carthage. . . . But now I feel you have so trivialized me into cheap currency and reduced me to nothing but an annoying, still-rattling skeleton in your closet, that there is nothing left to salvage. It is a star-crossed pity.

REBECCA MISSED HER GRANNY, I missed my mother, and the *Condé Nast Traveler* readers, their appetites no doubt aroused by Peter Mayle's never-ending variations on the theme, had fallen in love with Provence. And thank God and Mr. Mayle for that. (My mother, however, was not the least bit grateful. When he hit the big time with his first Provence book, I remember her banging down a pan on the kitchen counter in La Migoua: "The little fucker, that's the book *I* was supposed to write!" Boiling with indignation, she busied herself instead with composing a poisonous, and incredibly funny, review of *A Year in Provence* for the magazine, which sadly never ran.) Early each spring I would scrabble around inside my head, come up with a few plausible ideas, and then attempt to persuade my long-suffering editor that he couldn't live without just *one* more story from that fabled, pastis-soaked, sun-kissed, lavender-scented, aioli-guzzling country now known as Mayleland. If I was lucky I would leave his office with a commission and a round-trip ticket to Marseille.

One summer the magazine was lucky enough to acquire the exclusive world rights to a rather exciting story on Les Calanques. Take a miniature Norwegian fjord, fill it full of warm Mediterranean water, dump some white sand at the tip, replace the Christmas trees with scrubby oaks and umbrella pines, sprinkle the beach with leathery overtanned topless women and men in embarrassingly small bathing suits—and there you have a rough idea of these inlets along the coast between Marseille and Cassis. My friend Alain, a cabdriver in Le Beausset, who was also a rabid sailor, had told me about Les Calanques years before. Apparently you could reach them only *à pied* or *en bateau*, and never having been much of a walker, I naturally chose the boat. On the drive to La Migoua from the airport, Alain offered to take me in his *bateau*, but it was so *petit* that we would have to wait for that mercurial trickster, Monsieur Mistral, to calm down if we didn't want to end up at the bottom of the sea. He had been blowing for three days, and since he was known to favor odd numbers, we might well be able to set out the day after tomorrow.

About a week later Alain called (yes, we *finally* had a telephone!) and told me to be ready to leave at dawn the following day, since Monsieur Mistral was not a morning person, but you never knew what nonsense he might get up to in the afternoon. The boat was indeed extremely *petit*, and possibly to compensate for its size, Alain treated it like a racing car, driving at terrifying speed across the bay toward the jagged rocks of La Ciotat, before heading straight for Cap de l'Aigle. As soon as we rounded the cape the sea became rougher, and enormous cliffs, contorted by the wind and waves into what looked like the slender pipes of some gigantic church organ, dropped straight down into the sea. Up ahead, at the entrance to Calanque d'en Vau, a stone steeple called *le Doigt de Dieu* pointed an accusatory finger toward heaven, while a man, no bigger than a fly, dangled from a thread as he slowly inched his way up the rock face toward the summit.

The word *calanque* is derived from *calenco,* meaning "steep" in Provençal, and originally these stark white cliffs, as well as the land behind them, were covered in oak forests so dense that François I used to hunt wild boar here in the early sixteenth century. The wood from these same forests had built the ships for the Crusades, but by the time of the Revolution most of the trees had been chopped down, and the few that survived are regularly destroyed in the forest fires that rage across this part of the country every summer.

And it isn't just the topography that has changed. The sea was once so thick with tuna that the *calanques* were used for *la madrague,* the Provençal version of the Sicilian *mattanza*—that ritualistic slaughter of fish that still continues in the southern Mediterranean today. When Louis XIII visited Marseille in the fall of 1622, his host, the marquis d'Ornano, invited him to Morgiou, where the king was presented with a vermeil trident, which he used to murder the hordes of luckless tuna that had been driven deep into the *calanque* for his entertainment. Over the centuries *la madrague* became nothing more than a dim atavistic memory, and probably the only *madrague* that anyone remembers now is the house of the same name in Saint-Tropez, where God—or was it Vadim?—created Bardot.

I didn't like to ask, and anyway couldn't on account of the noise of the engine, but I did wonder about Alain's lunch plans. Ever since we had roared past Cassis, where I'd looked longingly if fleetingly at the restaurants along the port, the coastline had become steadily wilder and more deserted, with nothing more than a few rickety little cabins scattered across the barren hillsides. It got to the point, around two thirty, when I would happily have settled for an ice cream and a bottle of Pschitt, always assuming we could find a shack, like the one on Bikini Beach, at the end of the next calanque.

Suddenly Alain's rocket swerved to the right and headed full speed toward the Calanque de Sormiou, where he slammed on the brakes and pointed, with a big smile on his face, to some tables set up on a terrace beneath a magical sign that spelled out "LE LUNCH" in huge red letters painted on the side of a wall. A French flag snapped in the wind, and I couldn't resist humming under my breath, "Allons enfants de la patrie, l'heure du lunch est arrivée." Alain waved at a man standing at the entrance—"Mon beau-frère, Marius!"—and we waded ashore, looking like the survivors of a shipwreck, and sat down under a parasol, where a bottle of local *blanc de blancs* was waiting for us. Alain laughed—"J'ai telephoné en avance!"—thrilled to have fooled me, while Marius disappeared into the kitchen, returning a few moments later with a plate of grilled sardines and an earthenware dish of baby octopus stewed with tomatoes and wild thyme. After lunch Marius sat down with us to chat—we were his only guests—until Alain glanced up at the increasingly agitated flag and said we should head back before the mistral got any fancy ideas into his head.

When Alain dropped me at home, Rebecca and her grandmother were busy bringing the wasps their evening cocktail: "Poor little things, they get so thirsty in this dreadful hot weather." Rebecca had filled a large shallow bowl with water, carried it carefully, without spilling a drop, placed it on the windowsill, and then stood back waiting for her customers to arrive. Word got around fast, and they soon started to fly in, hovering just above the surface, decorously sipping their sundowners before heading home for dinner. I suppose all children love animals, but in Rebecca's case my mother helped nurture her natural affection for living creatures into something deeper that was as much intellectual as it was emotional. Rebecca eventually studied biology at Oxford, got a graduate degree in environmental science at Imperial College in London, and now works for a splendid organization called Fauna and Flora International in

Cambridge. Impossible to fault her career choice, especially if you happen to work for a glossy magazine, and I have nothing but admiration for what she does, but how about doing it in *New York* is all I can say—and *do* say all too frequently, so now I will shut up.

Francette's arrival for dinner was, as usual, announced by her filthy companion bounding into the kitchen, hungry for his *amuse-bouche* of freshly fricasseed lamb's heart, which he quickly spotted in the cat's dish on the floor. "Fuck off, Éloi! You *know* I didn't make that for you." Age had done Éloi no favors. His halitosis was more pungent than ever, he had put on weight, lost several quite crucial teeth, and his coat was covered in hideous bald patches, but oblivious to his defects, like many old geezers, he suffered from the delusion that people actually enjoyed his company. My mother had always welcomed him into our house with the same warm greeting, "Fuck off, Éloi!" and reassuringly that hadn't changed, so was it any wonder that the fat old fool continued to assume that his fans were as enthusiastic as ever?

I handed Francette a glass of pastis, she lit a cigarette, and before she could even sit down, my mother got going on the *sujet du jour,* which was their shared custody of *la fosse septique.* Fearsome handwritten warnings were Scotch-taped to the wall in both bathrooms in our house—"Do NOT even THINK of EVER putting anything STRANGE down this toilet. No tampons, bleach, sanitary napkins, paper towels, condoms, Kleenex etc. NOTHING can be flushed except the TWO things that come out of your BODY." (Being a pedant, I was never quite sure where that left vomit, but had always assumed it must be included in the TWO.) We lived in constant fear of the septic tank's temperamental nature. Like a fretful baby, it could digest only its TWO favorite foods, and any upset or peculiar addition to its diet might make it regurgitate the contents of its sensitive stomach. Quite naturally neither of the baby's divorced parents was ever willing to admit that the upset might have originated in *their* house.

Alerted by the foul smell that had been drifting up the hill for the past few days, my mother sent Nick down to investigate. Overgrown with ominously luxuriant brambles and bushes, the septic tank was hard to get close to, and I seriously doubted that Nick had bothered to climb over them, but when he returned from his expedition, just as we were about to sit down to dinner, he claimed to have spotted signs of *seepage and oozing* around its edges. Oh come off it, Nick. I knew he had just gone down there, had a fag and, hoping to enliven the rather dull evening ahead, had decided to wind up our mother and Francette.

Our neighbor, believing the best defense to be a vigorous offense, pointed out with impeccable Cartesian logic that our house was much bigger, we were more numerous, we had many guests to stay, *donc* it had to be our fault. Francette presented herself as *une vieille femme* who lived *toute seule* and had long ago forsworn *les garnitures périodiques, donc* she was innocent. Not so fast, lady. Did you or did you not have your god-child, Dominique, to stay only a week ago? And did she not have a baby with her named Nicolas, who several witnesses saw wearing disposable diapers? In addition your daughter, Christine, has been to visit this sum-mer. It was highly unlikely that at the age of forty-three, she had been through the menopause, *donc* she could well have been stuffing tampons down the toilet. The jury was still out when Francette and Éloi got up to leave, a bit earlier than usual, pretending they had an important appoint-ment at *la mairie* first thing in the morning, *donc* they needed to go to bed *tout de suite.*

Disappointed by her failure to secure a guilty verdict in the *fosse septique* case, my mother was casting about for some other entertaining disagree-ment as we moved out to the terrace after dinner. An argument with Nick about the garbage unfortunately didn't go anywhere (he promised to take it out), so she went into the kitchen and consoled herself by putting on a Frank Sinatra cassette and finishing off the rest of the *tarte au citron.*

"Hey, there's a picture of your old boyfriend, Gary Hart, in the *Herald-Trib.* He seems to be losing some of his hair, but he's still pretty enough."

She was leaning out the window, flapping a newspaper about, her mouth full of *tarte.*

"Mum, I have never *met* Gary Hart, so how could he possibly be my boyfriend?"

"Don't be ridiculous. Surely you remember the seventy-six election when we watched the BBC coverage together? Gary Hart and Mayor Lindsay were being interviewed by some English fool who knew piss-all about American politics, and we played 'Who Would You Rather?' And then you met him the next night. You told me all about it. How could you have forgotten?"

"I haven't forgotten, but it was Lindsay I met, not Hart."

"No, it wasn't. It was Hart."

"No, you're wrong, it was Lindsay."

"Well, you *said* it was Hart."

"No, I didn't."

"You did too."

Oh Jesus. You'd think I would have learned by that stage in my life not to contradict my mother, and I had—mostly. Instead of continuing with this edifying conversation, I shouted through the window and asked her to turn up the volume on her tin-and-plastic cassette player, and "Strangers in the Night" came blaring out onto the terrace. Oh, Mr. Sinatra, the perfect song, how did you know?

My mother had gotten the first part of the story right. We *had* been watching television together that night, and *did* get a little overexcited when the two gentlemen in question lit up the screen.

"You know Lindsay roomed with Archie at Yale, but I've never heard of that other one, have you?" (Archie Albright had been her boyfriend when she was seventeen, and they had been friends ever since.) No, I hadn't heard of Gary Hart either, but we both approved of the casting director's choices, and settled down with our drinks, cigarettes, and bags of crisps on Freddie's collapsed bed to enjoy the movie.

The day after the election an American friend who happened to be in London called up and wondered if I was free that night—some friends of his were putting together a small dinner at a restaurant in Chelsea, and perhaps I'd like to join them? Without a boyfriend, with no food in my fridge, and nothing better to do, I graciously accepted.

My memory of the first part of the evening is kind of hazy, but there must have been about eight of us. I was placed between the host and my friend, and the conversation revolved mainly around the election, the makeup of the new Congress, and what kind of a president Jimmy Carter might turn out to be. Laughably handsome, ludicrously charming, unfairly blessed with his insider's knowledge and experience of politics, no wonder every person around the table listened when Mayor Lindsay talked. And no wonder Senator Hart had been the loser in that silly game my mother and I had played the night before.

Somehow or other in the chaotic scramble for taxis after dinner I found myself sharing a ride with three other people who happened to be going in my direction. Two were deposited home along the way, so now, by some miracle of geography and mathematics, Mayor Lindsay and I found ourselves in the cab.

"I don't know what's wrong with the BBC," he said. "I told them I'd be happy to fly to London and do their program, and I asked them to put me in the Connaught, but they said I had to stay in some Hilton in a place I've never heard of called Shepherds Bush. I just can't understand it. It's a truly terrible hotel, but if you'd like to, why don't we have a drink in the bar anyway."

How could I have said no?

The black silk moiré pantsuit—a Saint Laurent take on a man's tuxedo—and the slippery white satin shirt with the sparkly cuff links may have looked quite fetching at night, but I had to admit it wasn't quite the right outfit for lunch the next day at an Italian restaurant in Soho with my future husband. Far too polite to comment on the strange clothes sense of a lady he had only just met, Peter talked instead about the American election and told me all about the BBC coverage. "We flew over John Lindsay, who used to be the mayor of New York, and some senator I've never heard of called Hart; it was actually quite interesting." I could not have agreed more.

After we moved to New York, I saw him a few times across a crowded room at big parties, and once he was sitting at a nearby table at a funny little place around the corner from our house in the Village. Wiping pasta sauce off Rebecca's face, I glanced up and noticed him looking at me with a slightly puzzled expression on his face—perhaps he was wondering what kind of a crazy mother would take a five-year-old out to dinner in a restaurant at that hour of the night.

A few years later, on one of those perfect sunny but cool New York spring days, when the popcorn trees are in full bloom along on the sidewalks, I was getting out of a cab outside the Café des Artistes, feeling stupidly happy, and saw him coming out of the door. Now, why shouldn't I just smile and say, "Isn't this the most beautiful day, Mr. Mayor, and what a pleasure it is to see you again." No, on second thought, the "again" probably wasn't such a great idea. I definitely would *not* say "again." But as I reached out my hand to him, he suddenly grabbed hold of my arm to steady himself, and losing his balance, almost knocked me over. Christ, something was very wrong. He didn't respond when I asked if he was okay, just kept flapping his free arm at some parked limousines, so we shuffled toward them until I eventually found his driver, who helped me get him into the car. Then, with the beautiful mayor slumped in the back-seat, he drove off and disappeared into the rush-hour traffic.

Le Mariage

During the summer of 1987 the house in France became the scene of an improbable—or maybe not so—reconciliation between my mother and Freddie. She was on her very best behavior, and he wrote, possibly somewhat surprised and relieved, to his old girlfriend Jocelyn, "Dee arrived a few days after Nicholas and I did, and has been very easy to get along with."

My mother knew that Hylan would be gone by the time she returned to New York in the fall, and it must have been especially painful to be back in the house where they had once been so happy together. However, she had always been a gifted actress, and put on a cheerful facade for Freddie and Nick, and maybe took some comfort from reverting to her primal role as the wife/mother and undisputed ruler of La Migoua. Without Hylan she knew that New York would be even more desolate, and without his income, her financial arrangements would be even more precarious—the time had come to move back to London. The second siege of Freddie was about to begin.

Freddie hadn't been overeager to marry her thirty years before, and after their poisonous divorce, why would he wish to repeat the experience? Being a gentle, reasonable soul, he certainly wanted to be her friend, but her *husband*—was he *mad?* No, just weak and, sadly, increasingly sick. Cancer had removed Vanessa from the equation, and now emphysema (those goddamn cigarettes, of course) and pneumonia would come to my mother's rescue, and transform her into Lady Ayer once again.

Sitting up in bed in the hospital the following June, recovering quite nicely from yet another bout of pneumonia, Freddie thought he would cheer himself up with a little treat, and reached for the smoked salmon that one of his lady friends had smuggled in that morning. In his haste or greed or hunger, he gobbled a morsel of the delicious oily fish too fast, choked, passed out, his heart stopped, and technically he "died" for four minutes before the doctors managed to revive him. Here's how he described the experience. He had felt himself being pulled toward a blinding red light—"exceedingly bright, and also very painful"—which he understood was responsible for the government of the universe. "Among its ministers were two creatures who had been put in charge of space," but they wanted nothing to do with him, so knowing that the ministers in charge of time were nearby, he tried to get their attention and became "more and more desperate" when they too ignored him.

Beatrice, who was sitting by his hospital bed when he woke up, remembers his talking, in French, about crossing a river—the Styx?—and that he seemed deeply disturbed by what he had just been through. In the first article Freddie wrote about the experience, he admitted that it offered "rather strong evidence that death does not put an end to consciousness," but in a later one he backtracked a bit and said he had meant only that the mind or brain doesn't stop functioning with the heart, that it had all been nothing more than a strange dream, and then proudly declared himself to be "a born-again atheist." The *National Enquirer,* which picked up the story, begged to differ and went with a far more exciting version of his adventures that ran under the headline—"Incredible after-life shocker! Man dies and meets . . . The Masters of the Universe."

An interesting postscript to this puzzling episode surfaced in 2000, eleven years after Freddie's death, when Dr. Jeremy George contacted William Cash, after seeing a play that Cash had written based on the incident. Dr. George had been on duty when Freddie had been admitted to the hospital, and by a strange coincidence had been a student at New College in the 1970s. He immediately recognized his patient, and after Freddie's experience with the smoked salmon and the Masters of the Universe, Dr. George returned to his bedside later that evening.

> I came back to talk to him, and asked what it was like, as a philosopher, to have a near-death experience. He suddenly looked rather sheepish. Then he said, "I saw a Divine Being. I'm afraid I am going to have to revise all my books and opinions." He definitely said "Divine Being,"

and I think he felt slightly embarrassed because it was unsettling for him as an atheist.

Freddie admitted he had seen a Divine Being? How could that possibly be? He certainly never said this to anybody else, but then again, eminent doctors don't usually tell lies.

That summer my mother once again joined Freddie in La Migoua, where, he wrote in a letter, they had gotten on "even better than last year. There has been no further talk of our remarrying. I think we both realize that this would endanger our present good relations." Oh dear, that may well have been what *he* thought. His future bride, however, had no such misgivings, but she wasn't foolish enough to bring up the dreaded subject. Instead, with a little prodding from Nick, his father agreed that maybe they should try living together again. Freddie was too frail to manage on his own, she hated New York—it was the perfect solution to both problems. Once she had sold her apartment she would move into his house in London.

Freddie may have been old and sick (he was back in the hospital again in October), but he had escaped the red light, defied the masters of the universe, returned to the right side of the river, so who could blame him for wishing to celebrate this magical renewal of life with—what else— love? Heather and Freddie had met at a party in Toronto about fifteen years before; the next day they declared—and demonstrated—their passion in the back row of a movie theater, and then embarked on an intermittent affair that had been going on ever since. And now the temptress had suddenly turned up in London. After a couple of delirious weeks together he was telling Heather, and his friends, that he wanted nothing more than to spend the rest of his life with her. Perhaps he felt that with Heather by his side he could trick death—and my mother—into leaving him alone for just a bit longer.

Sadly, it was not to be. Heather lived in the United States and by Christmas, Freddie was back at La Migoua with Nick, our aunt, Beegoonie, and his once and future bride. Despite feverish letters and telephone calls to his "princess" in California, he was having a surprisingly good time with my mother, and after quite a lot more judicious prodding from Nick, Freddie capitulated and decided that on the whole he *did* want to marry her again. What with the warm weather, the dry air, his pride in his son's

prowess at chess, and my mother's talents as a chef/wit/nurse and pro-
curess of the English papers and delicious things to eat, he was feeling
remarkably cheerful, and even had the strength to challenge Monsieur
Tricon to a game of *pétanque*. But the dramas weren't quite over yet.

ON SEPTEMBER 11, 1942, Freddie had been having dinner in New
York with Sheilah Graham, the Hollywood columnist, when Sheilah
suddenly put down her fork and announced that she simply couldn't eat
another bite—her contractions were getting too painful. Taxi! Freddie
rushed her to the hospital, where later that night she gave birth to their
daughter, Wendy. At the time he was married to his first wife, Renée, and
the new mother had celebrated her own whirlwind wedding to Trevor
Westbrook in January of that year. As a little girl, on trips to London with
her mother, Wendy used to come visit us in Regent's Park Terrace, and I
had grown up knowing that she was Freddie's daughter. (Just as I knew
that Julian Ayer was not his son. In that accepting way of children, neither
fact seemed the least bit odd to me.) You had only to look at Wendy's face
to see it was true. She had his bright dark eyes, his hair, the same-shaped
head, and the same expression around her mouth.

In the summer of 1988 Freddie was once again having dinner in New
York, this time with Peter, Christopher Hitchens, and me at a restaurant
in the Village where he always ordered the same thing: *soupe aux poissons,
daurade grillée,* and Domaine Tempier red wine, "to remind me of La
Migoua." Wendy happened to be sitting at a nearby table so she joined
us for coffee, and when the two of us slipped off to the bathroom, Freddie
turned to Hitch and announced—beaming with pride I was later told—
"There go my two daughters!" Indeed.

Just over a year later, in the middle of packing up her apartment in
New York and getting ready to spend Christmas in France with Nick and
Freddie, my mother came to dinner with us in Bank Street. Sheilah had
died a few weeks earlier, so thinking Wendy might need a bit of cheering
up, I invited her to come along as well and seated them next to each other.
In her memoir, *One of the Family,* Wendy describes their conversation.

> Dee's plan was to join them [Nick and Freddie] at their house in France.
> "And we'll probably even get married again," she said, clearly pleased.

She made a passing wry reference to the Oxford widow's pension, but I felt the heart of the matter was something else. "Freddie could have so many beautiful women—even now. And it's *me* he wants," she told me. There was an intensity in this expression of triumph that made me feel I had seen something too intimate—a wound, a desire; I wondered if she knew she had shown it to me.

I don't imagine it was pure coincidence that my mother asked Wendy to drop her home. She must already have decided that with Sheilah dead, and Freddie not likely to last terribly much longer (Trevor Westbrook had died ten years before), it was time to tell Wendy the truth. As my mother got out of the car, she turned to her and said, "Has it never occurred to you that Freddie is your father?"

No, it had never occurred to Wendy, not once.

"How do you know this? Is it from Freddie?"

"Yes," she replied.

As Wendy describes it:

He (Trevor) was a man in whose company I had never been at ease; I had always felt the stress of trying to be his daughter. Freddie was the blithe sparkling hero of my childhood, who had bought me *Tess of the D'Urbervilles,* walked me through the Tate looking at the Turners, introduced me to small French restaurants in Soho and Mayfair. As I got into bed late that night, I allowed Dee's revelation a final moment of unreserved magic. "Freddie Ayer is my father." The sentence reverberated in my head—a question, an exclamation and something close to a prayer.

Finally convinced—after looking at photographs in Freddie's autobiography and discovering that her parents had married in January '42, and *not* in December '41, as Sheilah had always claimed—Wendy was both thrilled and angry. She felt "a great swell of fury at my mother, who . . . had kept this attractive father from me . . . for robbing me of Freddie was in an important way robbing me of myself. The question now was to what extent I could recoup the loss, redress the wrong."

After writing a tactful letter to Freddie, saying she wondered if he *might, just possibly, maybe* be her father (my mother had asked Wendy not to land her in the shit, and to pretend she had worked it out by herself), she got a letter back confirming that this was indeed the case, ending with, "For my part, I am happy and proud to own you as a daughter."

Wendy was "deeply moved" when she read these words. "I felt rescued from my old life and self . . . transfigured by Freddie's acknowledgement into someone new and better—or perhaps someone who had been there all along but unperceived and unappreciated—a person who deserved this father."

Freddie, on the other hand, was the same as ever, and even if he had been younger and healthier, I somehow doubt that he would ever have been able to give Wendy everything she needed and desired. It wasn't just that it was way too late; the problem was also the Aspergian snail side to his character—his lifelong difficulty in connecting with the complicated depths of other people's emotions. But what if she had been told ten years before, after Trevor died (or even before), who knows how things might have developed? Of course Freddie would never have taken the initiative—that's just the way he was—but I honestly believe that if Sheilah had talked to him about telling their daughter the truth, his kindness, his natural sense of justice, and his affection for Wendy would have made him happy—and proud—to welcome her into the insane, capacious bosom of our family. And I still can't think of one good reason why that shouldn't have happened. Which I guess only goes to show that I have never been able to think straight when it comes to children—even grown-up ones.

Freddie's momentous letter led to an invitation to visit him in London that April, which is how Wendy found herself at Marylebone Register Office witnessing her father's wedding to my mother. Iris Murdoch and her husband, John Bayley, were the only other guests. Nick and I had decided to visit the newlyweds on their honeymoon in France that summer. And in any case Freddie would be back at Bard in the fall, and I would be back in Bank Street once again cooking Sunday lunches for him—and his lovely new bride.

I AM NOT QUITE SURE why I didn't fly to London as soon as the shipwreck started in the middle of June. But that's a lie. The reason was a combination of great love and shameful cowardice—the truth is I couldn't bear to see him dying. A terrible admission. Knowing he was surrounded by people who loved him, most of all Nick, who slept in his room toward the end, I hung on desperately, selfishly, guiltily, to my memories, most especially those of our last two years together in New York. We spoke on the telephone once, I called for daily bulletins, and he died on June 27, 1989.

Instead of burning in hell, wicked Londoners who don't believe in God get consumed by flames in a far more depressing place called the Golders Green Crematorium. Evil roses that feed on dead people's ashes fill the flower beds, and a hideous redbrick facsimile of a "Lombardic" campanile—the chimney—fitted out with electronic chiming bells, rises up above a glowering toad of a building that stinks of floor wax and disinfectant. Outside on the terrace dead people's wreaths—stridently colored, cards attached—are propped up against a wall, waiting to be admired by groups of murmuring mourners, while hearses creep silently up and down the dank driveway. If you woke up feeling a bit low on the morning of your loved one's funeral, once you get there you are guaranteed to be dragged down to the slimy, inky bottom of your own private pit of misery.

Some of Freddie's favorite tunes—"Bye, Bye, Blackbird," "Oh, You Beautiful Doll," "I Get a Kick Out of You," cranked out on a desolate organ—were all we had to listen to, and the coffin was all we had to look at, as we sat in—what? An approximation of a dark, wood-paneled chapel in a particularly nasty Edwardian boarding school, minus the cross, pulpit, drooping flowers, and the hearty sermon, was what it felt like. No eulogies (Freddie was very specific about that), and there, off to the side of where the altar should have been, were the ghastly doors that opened up, just as the last chords of "Cheek to Cheek" faded away, allowing the coffin to creak its way along the tracks and be consumed in the fiery furnace.

God must have been cackling away. *"See, I told you so.* This is what you end up with if you doubt me—ugliness, desolation, ashes, and despair. I cornered the market on beauty long ago—the stained glass of La Sainte-Chapelle, Mozart's Requiem, Giotto, *all* of Bach, the gilded reliquaries in the Cathedral of Santiago de Compostela, the King James Bible, that grassy graveyard behind the white clapboard church in Connecticut—they're all *mine.* And I could also have given you redemption and everlasting life—but you've missed out on that too." Cackle,

cackle. Oh piss off, God. We can look at your art, listen to your music, and read your books anytime we damn well please, and by the way, Mr. Know-It-All, only a lunatic would want to live forever. Or believe in you.

The newly widowed Lady Ayer had always known how to give a spectacular party, and this time she was determined to get it absolutely right. The guest list encompassed every aspect of Freddie's life from philosophers like Isaiah Berlin to politicians like Roy Jenkins, poets like Stephen Spender, novelists like Iris Murdoch and Martin Amis, neighbors like Jonathan Miller, V. S. Pritchett, Alan Bennett, Colin and Anna Haycraft, old girlfriends like Beatrice and Jocelyn Rickards, and new ones like Heather, as well as his family—all of us, plus Vanessa's children and his "new" daughter, Wendy. In the end there must have been about four hundred names on her list. There would be speakers—the widow, of course, Jonathan, Roy, a couple of philosophers, Peter Strawson and Ted Honderich—and Peter O'Toole had agreed to read a poem.

Now all she needed to do was to find just the right place for Freddie's memorial service—I mean, meeting. It wasn't so easy, and in the end she settled on a rather dispiriting, garishly lit lecture hall adjoining University College London, with a melancholy cafeteria next door for the reception. My whole life, my entire family, everybody I'd ever known in London, everybody who had ever loved Freddie, swam before my tearful eyes that morning. One of the philosophers described him as "a hussar against nonsense," which he would have loved; Roy Jenkins remembered him as "a fine ally with whom to go into a fight" against the forces of reaction; but it was my mother who gave the performance of her life.

After everybody else had spoken she stood up in the middle of the stage, dressed in high-heeled boots, a coat of many colors, eyes blazing, hair perfectly in place, and let rip with a speech that was part love letter, part paean of admiration, and part a call to arms against some Tory schmuck in Thatcher's government who had dared to criticize Freddie within days of his death. She was at her sarcastic, rabble-rousing best as she laid into the unfortunate minister for education with her whiplash tongue, praising her husband as the tireless champion of the underdog and leaving the schmuck for dead by the time she was done.

After it was all over we—my mother, Nick, Peter, Rebecca, and a few others—walked over to Freddie's favorite restaurant, L'Étoile, on Charlotte Street for lunch. I must have been seven or eight the first time he took me there, guiding me through the French menu, gently suggesting I might like to try something other than *sole meunière;* why didn't I have turbot or the *civet de lièvre* with *gratin dauphinois*? No, thank you, I was a boring little creature of habit, and always had sole, always on the bone, and if it happened to be a lady, carefully separated the fat worm of roe from the rest of the fish and dipped it into the melted butter before gobbling it up. Nothing seemed to have changed in the thirty years since: Most of the dishes on the menu were the same, white-lace-bordered curtains still hung in the windows, and—greedy for the past, clinging to every remembrance of him, hungry for childish comfort—I knew exactly what I was going to order.

Le Bébé

About six weeks after I gave birth to Rebecca, I had gone back to see Dr. Scher for a checkup. With understandable professional pride he examined his neat little incision, pronouncing it to be "healing very nicely. You'll be back in a bikini in no time," and then we moved on to the subject of birth control. *Birth control—was he completely insane?* How could he possibly imagine that, having spent the past four years trying to become pregnant, I would ever want to "control" this all-too-elusive process? Dr. Scher looked a bit taken aback at the vehemence of my response, but he was probably used to dealing with crazy hormonally unbalanced ladies, and said he understood completely and looked forward to delivering my next baby. "But not *too* soon, I hope," he added, smiling.

He needn't have worried. Over the next nine years the whole infertility psychodrama revved up once again, and with each month's evident failure to become pregnant, I was back in the hands of the doctors, clutching glass jars of murky liquid in my armpit and delivering them to Columbia-Presbyterian Hospital. However this time the problem wasn't just the creatures, it was also my aging, sluggish, no-good eggs. Dr. David, who occupied a reassuring, wood-paneled office on Park Avenue, his desk covered in silver-framed photographs of his numerous grinning children, said they needed to be shocked out of their catatonic stupor with some serious drugs.

"Are you sitting down?" I didn't recognize her voice, and yes, I did happen to be sitting at my desk, feeling depressed because none of the drugs had worked, and by the way who was this? "The lab results just came back," Dr. David's assistant said, "and you're pregnant!" I celebrated by bursting into tears, and Rebecca and Peter celebrated by taking their delirious mother/wife out to dinner since she was clearly in no state to cook for them that night.

When my mother heard this shocking news she remarked to a mutual friend—quite accurately—that I was much too old and poor to have another baby. At forty-three I was certainly aged, and of course we had no money, but I refused to see any connection between these two undeniable facts and the exquisite little person growing inside me. On October 22, 1994, Dr. Scher got out his scalpel once more—like his sister, Alexander had refused to enter the world the conventional way—and made another neat incision, out of which he popped, looking, according to his dad, deeply affronted by this uncalled-for disturbance in his peaceful aqueous existence. His grandmother, a lifelong connoisseur of good-looking men, pronounced him "a handsome little bugger," and so he has remained to this day.

Now that my mother was living in London, and Nick was working at an establishment called the Arvon Foundation in Devon, where credulous punters paid good money to be introduced to the mysteries of "creative writing" by people like Will Self and Beryl Bainbridge, our summers in France became the only time we could be together *en famille*. All this bouncing about between New York and London and the calamities of the "real" world made La Migoua—the house that never changed, the one constant in all our lives, the place where we felt settled and indisputably at home—seem all the more comforting. Fathers died, girlfriends went mad, lovers left, husbands shouted, apartments were sold, but this totally undistinguished little house in the middle of nowhere, surrounded by olive trees and vines, had some ineffable quality that slipped down like Valium to calm our jittery souls.

As soon as I walked into the kitchen I recognized the familiar cool musty smell, I saw the one-handled pot that the one-armed Algerian in the junkyard in Toulon had given us thirty years before, the big-bellied grandfather clock stood in the corner, and upstairs, the handsome little bugger would go to sleep in the same curly white wrought-iron crib that my mother had carefully lined in netting—"Can't have the critter getting its head stuck"—when Nick had been a baby. Dressed in a billowing Edwardian gentleman's nightshirt from the market in Le Beausset, her hair now pewter gray, her eyes bluer than ever, my mother came downstairs, happy and amazed that Alain had managed to find us among the huddled masses at Marseille airport and had brought us safely back to where we belonged.

The marble-topped table beneath the lime tree, where Freddie used to work, was still there, but instead of being covered in his papers, it had uncaringly turned itself into a dining table that had already been set for lunch. I glared at it, just as I had glared at poor Isaiah Berlin, who had been sitting quite innocently, near us at L'Étoile, after the memorial meeting, and had the temerity to be *alive*, enjoying his cheese soufflé, while Freddie inhabited a box at the back of the same dark closet where his suits still hung. After lunch Isaiah had come over and said all the right things, so I decided to forgive him, but it would take me a bit longer to come to terms with the table.

Sitting about after we had finished eating, it didn't take my mother long to move on to one of her favorite topics: her daughter's stubborn refusal to acquire a driver's license. "Jesus, when *are* you going to learn to drive? You can't just go on using poor old Alain for the rest of your life, you know." Ah yes, a very good question and one that, year after year, I failed to answer because I honestly had no idea when that miraculous day would come. How it had happened I do not know, but somehow the misguided notion that men had been put on this earth to do things for me, including drive me around, had gotten into my head, and despite plenty of evidence to the contrary, refused to leave.

Maybe it was my father's fault. All those years of being the sole object of his adoring attention, all those trips around Europe, just the two of us, in his little white convertible that smelled of new shoes, all those leather-bound books stuffed full of letters I had written him, my artless drawings, photographs of us together—no wonder I believed that men were naturally disposed to give me an extremely good time. Then again, maybe it was a reaction against my mother's fierce independence and determination to prove that anything they could do, she could do far better herself. Whatever its origins the end result was the same. If I wanted to go anywhere that trains didn't reach, "poor old Alain" had to drive me, an arrangement that, much to my mother's irritation, turned out to suit us both admirably.

Although I've never had much time for the kind of lushly mirrored, damasked, gilded, Limoged, multistarred restaurant that Alain Ducasse

created at Le Louis XV in Monte Carlo, when I heard that he had opened
a simple country inn high up in the hills of Haute-Provence, I thought
that maybe the other Alain and I should go and investigate. "Simple," I
was to discover, in Monsieur Ducasse's vocabulary, is an entirely relative
concept.

It was just after dusk when we arrived at La Bastide de Moustiers. A
single black cypress tree, as elongated as a Giacometti, stood silhouetted
against the wall, the cool night air was full of the scent of rosemary and
roasting *gigot d'agneau*, and the old stones surrounding the front door had
soaked up the sun's rays and were still warm to the touch. In the kitchen,
baskets full of fresh vegetables and fruit were arranged on a long wooden
table: baby courgettes with their butter yellow blossoms still attached—
a lost bumblebee buzzing about above them—orange tomatoes the size
of gooseberries, and a mixture of white currants and *fraises des bois* that
would later be transformed into fruit tartlets. One of the chefs was pouring a dollop of thick green olive oil—the color and consistency of motor
oil—over a pan of miniature aubergines that he shook gently over an
open fire. Dinner would be served in half an hour.

For pampered souls, exhausted by a lifetime of frowning at enormous
tasseled menus, what could be more of a luxury than being handed a single creamy card that describes what the chef has already decided you will
be having for dinner that night? So charming, so simple, so easy—it was
just like being at home, except that of course it wasn't at all. Neither my
mother nor Alain's wife could ever have produced a meal like his. Tomatoes stuffed with some magic combination involving basil and olives;
michon bread, full of all the flavor and strength that ordinary baguettes
lack; a classic Niçoise crêpe made of chickpeas (*pois chiches*); courgette
blossoms (*sans* bee); the *gigot d'agneau* I had seen roasting over the kitchen
fire, flavored with *poivre d'âne*, an herb that grows wild in Provence and
nowhere else. I looked across the table at Alain, and we both smiled. "Pas
mal?" he asked, and I had to agree that it was "pas mal de tout." Nor was
it over yet.

A wooden platter appeared, covered with more varieties of goat cheese
than I knew existed: some smooth and blue with a hard crust, others covered in fresh herbs, tiny pyramids of sharp flavor, logs of creaminess, and
none of them had traveled more than twenty kilometers to arrive at our
table. No other kinds of cheese were permitted. No Brie de Meaux, no

Camembert from the Pays d'Auge, no Saint-Florentin from Burgundy,
no Comté from the Jura, no Bleu de Bresse—all would have violated La
Bastide's fanatical devotion to its own Provençal *terroir*.

These days there are only a few winemakers left who still maintain
the old tradition of cultivating the special peach trees among their vines
that produce the famous *pêches de vignes*. Tiny white peaches that are the
concentrated, perfumed essence of peachiness on account of being left
to ripen slowly on the trees and not ever being watered, they are almost
impossible to find in any market, and I have never actually seen one with
my own eyes. But that night I tasted them, in the form of an oh-so-simple
sorbet, for the first and only time in my life.

When simplicity is raised to this level of perfection it is really most
confusing and can't help but put you in mind of Marie Antoinette, who,
just before the deluge, had discovered that there is nothing more soothing
to a jaded psyche than country living. Exhausted by the stress and strain
of her very public life, tired of the formal rituals and endless banquets, she
chose to escape to her *faux-rustique* toy farm hidden away in the woods
at Versailles. There she could dress in muslin, not satin, drink milk still
warm from her own cows, and live the kind of bucolic existence that no
real peasant could ever dare to dream of. It was a world in which cottages
were covered in fragrant wildflowers, the lambs' fleeces were as white as
snow, the baby vegetables emerged from the *potager* covered in dew, not
dirt, and the pretty young shepherdesses all had rosy complexions, milky
bosoms, and smiling eyes. Instead of sitting down at a damask-covered
table in the Hall of Mirrors and eating off golden plates, the doomed
queen and her entourage would picnic outdoors at a wooden trestle table
in the shade of an old chestnut tree. Which was just what Alain and I had
done that night.

WHILE MARIE ANTOINETTE HAD BEEN frolicking at La Bastide
de Moustiers, all manner of hell had broken out at La Migoua. No, my
mother hadn't had another heart attack, but she had been taken to the
hospital; she would need to have some tests and probably stay there for a
couple of days. It was not a happy scene. Nick was wild-eyed with worry;
Katharine, a large, kindhearted friend of my mother's from New York,
was crashing around the kitchen boiling up a cauldron of artichokes for

nobody in particular; Alexander wanted to go to the beach—my mother was sick and everything was falling apart. Screw the artichokes. What we all needed was to go out to dinner that night, and the place we needed to go was called L'Oursinado.

Lulu Peyraud had told me about this restaurant the summer we had cooked bouillabaisse together. Hidden away on its own rocky spit of land, surrounded by crooked umbrella pines, high above a secret cove, it had an air of passé but still sexy chic, the kind of place that Romy Schneider and Alain Delon might have gone for an adulterous dinner in a sixties movie—or in real life. In homage to its name, we ordered a huge platter of *oursins*—Rebecca was persuaded to take one bite of their strange orange flesh but refused to contemplate a second—and in honor of Madame Peyraud bouillabaisse followed—the children were understandably even more horrified by this dish—and to calm us all down we had a *digestif* of local marc, to settle all the fishy creatures I imagined were still swimming around inside me. Yes, all in all, I told myself complacently, L'Oursinado had indeed been one of my more inspired ideas.

The rest of the evening was considerably less edifying. The first sign of trouble, as Alain was driving me home, was an open suitcase—a bottle of shampoo, bras, the odd shoe, a hairbrush, crumpled clothes scattered about—in the middle of the road up to the house. The second was the sound of sweet gentle Nick screaming, "Get out *now*. You are *not* spending another night in this house. Go find a hotel, just get out!" What fresh hell was this? Katharine was collapsed in a heap on the sofa, Nick was apoplectic, the children were cowering up on the top floor, and Alain drove off just as fast as his trusty taxi could take him down the hill to the relative sanity of his wife in Le Beausset.

I poured Katharine a drink, always the first step in these tricky situations, told her there was no question of her going to any hotel, ran upstairs to reassure the kids, and took poor Nick, who was totally unhinged with worry about our mother in the hospital, outside so he could explain what the fuck was going on.

"What's her bloody suitcase doing back up here? You know I'm only going to kick it down the road again."

Well, all right if you must, but maybe while you're kicking you can tell me what happened? So I stumbled alongside Nick in the dark, and the whole story came out.

"The stupid cow was gossiping on the telephone about us."

Apparently Katharine had said Nick was leading poor innocent little Rebecca down the slippery slope to debauchery—and no doubt drugs— by taking her to a sleazy pool hall after dinner, and that I was clearly having a tempestuous affair with a local cabdriver.

He gave the suitcase another kick. "And she said that this was the most dysfunctional family she had ever seen"—I picked up an armful of clothes—"I couldn't take it any longer so I snatched the receiver from her hand, slammed it down, and told her to get out."

Oh I see. Grateful as I was for Nick's robust but unnecessary defense of my honor, and tactless though Katharine undoubtedly had been, surely we couldn't chuck a lady out into the night. Later on I brokered the best deal I could. Poor old Alain would be summoned in the morning to cart Katharine off to the train station in Toulon, I would help her retrieve her suitcase and its scattered contents, and now could we *please* all just go to bed?

The next day my mother got back from the hospital and started complaining about the state of the kitchen. "Jesus, can't you guys at least do the dishes when I'm not around?" which cheered us all up. And I am happy to report that the rest of our dysfunctional family's summer went by in an entirely peaceful, uneventful blur.

La Jambe

I HAD NEVER HEARD OF Buerger's disease until the day my aunt called me in New York and told me that my mother was in the hospital. Also known as thromboangiitis obliterans, it is a recurring inflammation of the small and medium veins and arteries of the hands and feet. There is no known cure. As the disease progresses, the circulation of blood in the extremities is so restricted that gangrene sets in and amputation is necessary. The disease is strongly associated with smoking.

My mother had already had two heart attacks, the second far more severe than the first, and although she had tried to stop smoking, she never completely succeeded. And even if she had been able to pack it up, how can you erase the damage caused by fifty years of relentless addiction to cigarettes? By the time I arrived in London the doctors were discussing just how much of her right foot, and possibly leg, would have to be amputated.

Brave she had always been. She mocked the hell that came her way, refused to cave in to self-pity; she didn't believe in asking for help or showing weakness. Wit was her weapon of choice against fear—that's how she had behaved all through her life. And now, face-to-face with true horror, why should she have changed? Just before the operation she wrote to her old friend Claus von Bülow:

> They, the ultimate THEY, are coming shortly to do whatever it is they are going to do and so just in case I pull an involuntary Oates on the expedition, I wanted to thank a few—you in particular—for noble and

kind behavior. It was so good of you to make the boring trip [to the hospital] so often, and it was much appreciated. I suspect they're going to go for that particularly skinny easy-chop area just below the knee— I don't think there's a hope of saving my poor little foot that has been with me since I was a baby . . . they haven't *said* any of this, mind you, but they have shifty eyes when they speak and they say guarded things.

Still in the hospital after the amputation, she called another old friend, the art dealer Gene Thaw, in New York, and said, laughing, "Next week I'm getting fitted for a parrot." But the jolly old wooden leg would take much longer to fit, and in the meantime she was sent home in a wheelchair to a house that was nothing but stairs. Nick was living in the basement flat in York Street, and without him I don't know how she could ever have managed at all. Friends rallied—most especially Claus—and her sister, Beegoonie, who had nursed her through her last heart attack, was nearby and ready to help with anything, anytime. But she was still alone. Even in the days when she'd had two legs she hadn't been any good at it, she hated it, it had never been her thing, and now it must have been torture.

Back in New York I called constantly, full of anxiety and guilt at being unable to do anything useful, but she would tell me, as she had so often when I was a child, that there was absolutely nothing to worry about, it was all going to be fine, and not to be such a silly girl. One day she even made me laugh out loud describing her attempt to clean the cat's litter tray while sitting in a wheelchair. Leaning forward, ready with her scooper, she had toppled right over and, arms and leg flailing about, had landed in the shit. "Jesus, can you believe it? I'm still picking bits of that awful gravel out of my hair!"

Of all her friends Claus was the most constant and the only one, in the end, who knew how to lift her up and trick her into forgetting, for a while at least, what had happened to her life. They had met in New York in the early eighties with their mutual friends, Clare and Gene Thaw, at a time when Claus was trapped inside his own living hell. Convicted in 1982 of the attempted murder of his wife, Sunny, he had appealed, but it wasn't until 1985, at his second trial, that he was found not guilty of all charges. Perhaps, at the beginning of their friendship, she had been the one who knew how to make him laugh, lift his spirits, and give him some respite from the nightmare. She had always had sympathy for, and a desire to help, anybody in serious trouble, and, Christ knows, a thirty-year prison sentence must qualify as pretty serious trouble. Thirsty wasps, abandoned dogs, starving birds, and any human being unjustly convicted of a crime were all equally in need of support, sustenance, and love.

Clever, kind, and funny were the qualities that she had always looked for in men, and Claus delivered all three in abundance. He used to write her long letters and silly postcards; he took her to parties even when she pretended she didn't want to go; brought picnics to her house when she was stuck in her wheelchair; and never stopped calling even when she was too depressed to call him back.

In July 1984, when he was in the middle of his appeal and a virtual prisoner in New York, she had written to him from La Migoua. Here's his reply:

> What a lovely letter. First the element of surprise. The envelope, embossed with the impressive logo of the Hotel Francuski U1. Pijarski 13, Krakow, naturally led me to believe that this was just another letter from my fans behind the iron curtain, who sympathize with me as a martyr of the capitalist judicial system.
>
> I am of course all for the imaginative employment of surplus stationery. One lady, I knew, salvaged enough writing paper from one weekend at Blenheim, to carry on an upwardly mobile social career for decades. On my last visit to Istanbul I could not resist replenishing my supply of paper and envelopes from the Kunt Palace Hotel, although I was in fact staying at the Hilton. . . . However, as I am still without a passport you must not expect any sympathy from me regarding the hardships you have encountered abroad.
>
> *Veuillez agréer, chère milady, mes baisers les plus lascifs.*
> Claus

Around about the time my mother left New York and went back to Freddie, Claus too decided to move to London. I imagine that he was fed up with his unwanted celebrity, bored with being constantly stared at, tired of reading about himself in the papers, and most important, he wanted to be close to his daughter, Cosima, who lived in England. My mother was delighted, and even though they were now in the same city and saw each other all the time, the letters flew back and forth between York Street and his flat in Kensington. In 1995 my mother's campaign to persuade the Westminster Council to put up a plaque on her house in commemoration of Freddie had finally succeeded, and she wrote to Claus inviting him to come to its unveiling, inauguration, opening, or whatever it is you do with plaques. She was planning to give a small party.

> It will be a motley lot—but that you must forgive, because there is no one in the world better than you at dealing with a roomful of ill-assorted Vanilla Allsorts. It's outrageous that I lean on you so heavily and ruthlessly but . . . well what the hell, you are Curiously Strong. Like the mints.
>
> Obviously the Internationale always makes me tearful and maudlin but a greater truth is that I love you dearly and count you as a treasured friend, a most treasured friend. Trouble with the truth is that truth sees the light of day so rarely it can't help looking all bleary-eyed, schlurring ish schyllables and sounding drunk. . . . But that dushent make it not the truth.

THE THING ABOUT prosthetic legs is they never fit properly, they are too heavy, they hurt, they cause suppurating blisters that take a long time to heal, and it is impossible to walk normally with them. The thing about amputated legs is that the stump is constantly shrinking, hence the difficult fit, but far, far worse is the excruciating not-in-the-least "phantom" pain that no drug can control. And if you were used to having the kind of legs that men lusted after and other women envied, why not add that to this witches' brew, and let's not forget—how could you—that your suffering was entirely your own fault. Your leg wasn't blown off defeating Hitler on Omaha Beach, nothing as splendid as that, it was destroyed, along with your heart, by a million deeply inhaled cigarettes. But none of this is of the slightest interest to anybody else, in fact it was so dull and depressing that there is absolutely no point in discussing it. Which is why my mother never did.

The little brother whom she had always protected and looked out for in that madhouse they had both grown up in was now a gentleman in his sixties, and it was payback time. Woody loved his older sister, and for the next ten years he and his wife, Mary, would fly in from Boston, pick my mother up in London, and take her to France for the summer. Savagely independent, she found it hard to admit that it was the tough older sister/ mother who needed looking after now, but without Nick, Woody, and Mary she could never have continued going to La Migoua for as long as she did. I could come for only a couple of weeks, her sister was often there, friends dropped in and out, but as her health slid downhill, she couldn't be left alone in the house, not even for a single night.

In addition to the leg and the problems with her heart, my mother's narcolepsy became more serious as she got older. She would fall asleep quite suddenly, not just after dinner and a few glasses of wine, but in the middle of a sentence, or walking down the street. Woody and I worried about her driving; sometimes he would pretend he couldn't find the keys—as if that was going to stop her—and the ghastly day came one summer in France when I refused to allow the children to go in the car with her on some expedition. Cruel and heartless, I know, and of course she was upset, but she must have understood, because after that she never insisted upon driving again. For her to have abdicated so easily was the saddest part of the whole episode. Why hadn't there been more of a fight? What had happened to her wonderful, sometimes terrifying, combative spirit? It was as if her character was slowly, subtly changing. There were fewer outbursts of the Jesus H. Christ variety, she allowed us to take over more of the running of the house, the vulnerability that had been so carefully concealed her entire life was exposed for all to see. I wanted my old mother back.

"He's a good-looking little bugger, I'll give him that" had been her first reaction to Alexander. And not just good-looking, he also shared his grandmother's dedication to anarchy. When he was about six he decided to embellish the admittedly boring pale yellow walls in the living room— "Tinkerbell's piss" was how my mother had described the color—with a daring abstract design executed in a medley of colored crayons. I attacked his artwork with chemical sprays, scrubbed away with Brillo pads and brushes, and having failed to erase it, turned to him in exasperation, "Now, why did you do that?" Surely the explanation was self-evident, his expression suggested: "Iss my essitement." But of course! What a fool I was. Had I forgotten that there is nothing more exciting than behaving badly, taking a risk, breaking the rules, doing something you know you should never have done? His granny understood completely.

～

WHEN I FELL IN LOVE with Peter, he was making a documentary for the BBC about the Cathars, based on a book called *Montaillou*, by the French historian Emmanuel Le Roy Ladurie. Lying in bed in our hotel room in Paris, in preparation for our dinner with the *très charmant et séduisant professeur*, I read the story of this small mountain village in Languedoc and its brave inhabitants who had dared to defy the church, and made Peter promise to take me there one day. Twenty-five years later, the editor of *Condé Nast Traveler* got lucky with the story—thirteenth-century heretics, Crusades, massacres, the smell of flesh roasting at the stake, the readers will love it—and, leaving the children behind at La Migoua, clutching a copy of *Montaillou* and both *Michelin*s, red and green, we headed due west toward Albi.

Accustomed to the stupefying beauty of cathedrals like Chartres and Rouen, with their jewel-tinted rose windows, gargoyles, and doorways carved with such elegant precision that they seemed more like lace than stone, I was affronted by the sheer brutality of this building. Buttresses that looked like the cylinders of a loaded gun punctuated the monolithic redbrick walls, fortified watchtowers kept guard, its windows were nothing more than sinister, elongated slits. Architecture as intimidation. It evoked the harsh, triumphalist style favored by the Soviets, or a medieval version of something Albert Speer might have conjured up for his demanding boss. But the most astonishing thing about this deeply disturbing edifice was that it wasn't a fortress or a prison, it was the Cathédrale de Sainte-Cécile in Albi.

Now why would the church want to go and build something like that? "Well, you have to remember that construction began in 1282, only forty years after the Cathars were finally defeated at Montségur," Peter paused to order a plate of *saucissons*, cornichons, and two glasses of wine, "and the bishop of Albi clearly felt that the cathedral had to assert the church's absolute victory over the heretics."

Looking back at this grim monument to orthodoxy I could see that the bishop had won the architectural war, but I also knew that seven hundred years later the heresy and the people who died for it had not been forgotten.

"Absolutely. We are still fascinated by them, how else to explain the fact that this book was a huge best seller? Here's what Laduric says: 'Today Catharism is no more than a dead star whose cold but fascinating light reaches us now after an eclipse of more than half a millennium.' "

I turned to face the sun and closed my eyes as Peter read me choice extracts about the local priest, Pierre Clergue, a secret Cathar, who appeared to have had a distinctly modern view of sex and sin: "One woman's just like another. The sin is the same, whether she is married or not. Which is as much as to say that there is no sin about it at all."

"A lady who sleeps with a true love is purified of all sins. With Pierre Clergue, I liked it. And so it could not displease God. It was not a sin," was how Grazide Rives justified her affair. The châtelaine of Montaillou, Beatrice de Planissoles, took a more practical view: "What if I do become pregnant by you? I shall be ashamed and lost." *Pas de problème*, Pierre assured her. "I have a certain herb. If a man wears it when he mingles his body with that of a woman, he cannot engender, nor she conceive."

It sounded remarkably similar to my own home life. I took another sip of wine and went on listening, still mesmerized after all these years by the same voice that had seduced Maureen, the receptionist at Weidenfeld's.

WHEN WE GOT BACK TO La Migoua, Peter returned to New York, but I stayed on, with the children, for a few more days. It was getting harder, and more painful for my mother to walk, but she loved seeing her old friends, so Nick and I organized a small dinner at the house. Madame la Princesse, Sylvia, came minus Prince Azamat, who had disappeared long ago to Nassau with an aging blond heiress, Francette and the pungent Éloi, of course, and Bill Deakin, minus bossy Pussy, who had died earlier in the year. Unable to drive—maybe like Freddie, he never could—Bill was brought over from Le Castellet by Alain, who deposited him on our terrace *sans culottes*, or at least with his trousers down around his knees. Bill couldn't have cared less, but Alain, embarrassed on his client's behalf, yanked them up as best he could before helping Bill over to the table.

After a couple of whiskeys Bill was chattering away about his adventures with Tito in Yugoslavia during the war ("He spoke remarkably good English and he loved girls, so we didn't have a bad time at all"); Francette described her first meeting with Freddie in Paris around about the same time, causing my mother to shut them both up. "Jesus, while you guys were cavorting with fun-loving partisans and that old fart Duff Cooper at the British Embassy, I was freezing my ass off on a parade ground in Canada. Nobody ever said life was fair!"

I caught Nick's eye across the table; we both smiled—this was just how we had hoped the evening would turn out.

Alain came back at ten to get Bill, who managed to make it to the taxi without losing his pants, but about half an hour later I got a frantic call. "I've just left Monsieur Deakin at his house, and he says he has lost his teeth, he wonders if perhaps you have them?" Not about my person, but they could be lurking somewhere on the shipwrecked table. Please tell Monsieur Deakin I will do my best to find them. After I'd hung up the telephone, I went outside where my mother was sitting in the dark. "Bill's lost his teeth." "Yeah, and I've lost my leg." I froze. Had she really said that? "It was hurting, so I took it off and now I can't find it." I got down on my hands and knees. "Well, it can't have gone far," and retrieved it from its hiding place beneath her chair.

"I really think she was trying to kill us." I had heard the story before and knew the attempted murderer's name. Sand dunes, an endless wide beach, sun sparkling on giant waves rolling in from the Atlantic, the woman in the black bathing suit waded into the water and beckoned for her two small children to follow. A powerful swimmer, she plowed through the waves, never once looking back as the children, struggling to keep up, were knocked over and dragged down into the churning ocean. My mother was three, her older brother, Jackie, almost five. She didn't tell the story often, in fact she usually avoided talking about her mother at all, but that night, more than seventy years later, sitting in the dark with her missing leg, the memory haunted her. "When I was about ten, she said she despised me." There was no way I could contradict or even soften these memories when all I had ever heard about my grandmother just confirmed the damage she had inflicted upon her daughter.

Alain arrived the next morning to take us to the airport—he always had a little packet of Kleenex on hand for my tears—and this time what I feared most came true. That was our last summer together in the house.

EACH MORNING Alexander would walk the two blocks to school with his dad, identifying the make of every single parked car along the way.

After he had been dropped off at 8:45, Peter would buy *The Times,* cross
Sixth Avenue, and head for the diner on the corner of Eleventh Street.
By the time he heard the first plane roar down the avenue and saw it hit
its target, nobody was reading the newspaper anymore. I turned on the
television the minute he called, and at 9:03 the word "crash" was replaced
by "attack" and I was running toward the school. "Give blood *now!* We
need blood. *Now!*" Doctors and nurses stood on the steps of St. Vincent's
Hospital, screaming, but how could I stop? I needed to get Alexander
safely—as if anywhere was safe—home.

The children had been told about the "accident," and as soon as we got
back Alexander sat down at the dining room table with a glass of milk,
cookies, a piece of paper, and some crayons, and drew me a picture of a
jaunty toy plane heading straight for the two Dunhill lighters. "That's
lovely, darling, thank you," I said, attaching it to the fridge with a magnet shaped like a strawberry. The only way Peter could reach Rebecca,
whose school was way up in the nineties on the East Side, was on foot. He
gallantly set out as soon as the second plane hit, stopping along the way
for necessary news updates and refreshments, and seven or eight hours
later, stunned and exhausted, they finally arrived home.

Laura Bush, that sensible mother and librarian, advised us to keep our
children from watching the death images repeated on an endless loop,
but did she seriously expect we would be able to turn our televisions off?
In any case, beyond producing his drawing, Alexander didn't seem to be
particularly interested in the "accident," and soon disappeared upstairs
to play in his room, while I went on watching. Loath to admit that such
a boring woman could be right about anything, I didn't bother to think
what effect the horror might have on an *adult,* never mind our sensitive
children. It wasn't good, it was driving me to madness, I needed to go out
and do something normal and comforting and primal—like buying food.

She sat alone beside me, shrunken, gray-haired, silent—no, after
shopping, I hadn't been able to keep away from the TV suspended above
the bar, or from the bottles lined up behind it—and I offered to buy her
a drink.

"Ach, you are too kind, and it's my birthday, you know!" she replied a
little too cheerfully, in a heavy German accent. Drowning in unfocused
compassion, consumed with a desire to help all mankind in our terrible
hour of shared tragedy, I bought her another, and listened while she talked

about herself, telling me the story of her difficult life, in perhaps greater detail than was strictly necessary—or becoming, on this of all days. By the time I got up to leave I had invited her to a birthday dinner—"I'll bake a cake!"—the next night. "*Please* say you will come. My husband is half German; he will be so happy to meet you."

Peter was not happy at all.

"Christ, what have you done now? What on earth makes you think I would want to have dinner with some drunken old German bag you picked up in a bar?"

"Shut up. It was her birthday yesterday. And anyway, there's the doorbell."

"Ach, I see you have cats. So much better than children." She appeared not to have noticed Rebecca and Alexander sitting on the sofa. "I tell you I have had so many abortions I can't even remember the number now."

Well, never mind about that, I'll be in the kitchen, while you two have a nice chat in German, I said with a bright smile. Peter glared at me.

When I set down the osso buco and risotto at the center of the table, they were babbling away happily in her native tongue: "I was just asking your husband when I would get my television reception back. Ever since those towers fell down, my set is *kaput*. I can watch nothing, absolutely *nothing*."

She must have been starving and was busy sucking the marrow out of the veal bones before I had even sat down. And yes, she *would* like some more, *danke schön*. Alexander and Rebecca fled upstairs, not even the promise of cake and ice cream could keep them sitting with us for another minute. Her eyes darted around in search of more food, and grabbing a piece of bread, she buttered it and with her mouth half full, said she had one more question for Peter: "You and I are both Germans"—he nodded warily—"you know what the British did to Dresden, you know how many civilians burned in *that* holocaust, you know how many Germans died in the war, so please tell me this—why are Americans making all this Sturm und Drang about two towers?"

Hard to say. Strange country. Not accustomed to being attacked. Maybe it's time I helped you fall down the stairs, you Kraut Witch.

"Promise me you will *never* have that cunt in this house *ever* again."

I promised.

~

MONTHS BEFORE, my father had invited me to lunch on September 13 at his club on the Upper East Side. He and Melissa would be arriving on the *QEII* that morning, and they were planning to spend a few days in New York before proceeding to Washington. What a civilized itinerary, how nice to travel that way, it sounded positively Whartonesque in its stately Old World decorum.

"Just calling to confirm our lunch! We've had a helluva time, the ship couldn't dock in New York." No, I didn't imagine it could. "So we're in Boston and are catching the train. See you there at one!"

Walking along Sixty-sixth Street you would never have known that anything had happened. No trace of trauma, no smell, no ash, nothing but stolid robber-baron mansions, emaciated ladies with tightly drawn faces and champagne-colored hair walking midget dogs, and there, standing in the doorway of the Lotos Club, a tall, handsome man holding out his arms to me. We went downstairs to the Grill Room, sat at our table, and as the waiter handed me a menu, my father said, "So how was your summer in the south of France?"

I looked at him in disbelief. My *what?*

"Never mind the summer. There's only one thing we are talking about in New York right now."

My dear, sweet, kind father hadn't wanted to upset his daughter. If you steered clear of unpleasant subjects, refused to acknowledge horror, maybe it would just go away. It worked for him, but I fear it is one of his many talents I have failed to inherit.

"I'm sorry, I didn't think you would want to discuss it."

Immediately regretting my rudeness, I told him about Montaillou, lied and said my mother had never been better, and when Melissa joined us we moved on to the only subject the world was talking about.

"WHY THE HELL did those people jump?"

The telephones were finally working again and this was the first time I had been able to get through to London.

"Mum, you can't say that. How about we play our favorite game,

'Which Would You Rather?' and *you* choose between being burned alive or jumping?' "

Maybe you had to have been in New York on that day to understand. Or maybe both my parents were totally insane in their very different ways.

Over the next couple of years my mother spent more and more time shuttling between her house and Saint Mary's Hospital in Paddington. In June 2003 she was back there with fluid in her lungs, nothing serious; the doctors said she would be able to leave just as soon as they had put in a stent to prop up yet another one of her collapsing arteries. Nick visited every day, Rebecca came from Oxford, Claus brought her a huge bag of cherries and watched as she bombarded the fire-breathing head nurse with their stones—surely an excellent sign. She told me not to be ridiculous when I suggested flying over from New York. But what if she was just trying to calm me down? I checked with my aunt and Nick, who backed her up—the doctors said she was in no danger—why didn't I wait until she was out of the hospital?

She died—under general anesthetic, she felt no pain, she knew nothing, or so the doctors told me, and Christ do I need to believe them—on the operating table the next day.

Although there was no escaping the Golders Green funeral pyre, none of us wanted anything more to do with Stalinist meeting halls, and her memorial service took place in the journalists' church, Saint Bride's, on Fleet Street. George Melly did his best Bessie Smith impersonation, we sang the "Battle Hymn of the Republic," Susan Crosland remembered the days when they were young, pretty American journalists who ended up marrying two of the most interesting men in London (Tony Crosland had been the foreign secretary in Harold Wilson's government), and I talked about having a mother who was more fun than anybody else on earth. How could I resist telling the story about our double date at that hotel in Oxford with Hylan and Martin? Here's what Paul Johnson wrote the next week in *The Spectator*.

Atheists' funerals always pose a problem. Where are we speeding them off to? Oblivion? Annihilation? It's all very well calling them a "celebration." But death, whatever else it is, is not an event to be celebrated. I was thinking about this when I attended the service for Dee Wells in

St Bride's. I suppose she was an atheist: anyone who married Freddie Ayer not once but twice must have been.

Dee was the wittiest woman I ever met . . . the service had magnificent music, but I could not hear one word of any of the encomiums, save a brief tribute from the ravishing Susan Crosland, and a superb Dee joke told by her delicious daughter, Gully, whom I used to know as Little Miss Naughty when she was a teenager. . . ."

The two lovers, Martin and Hylan, were there; my old nanny, Cele, was there; Robert, the man with the convoluted eyebrows whom she was going to marry before she fell for that "menace," Freddie, was there; my godmother from Burma, Sue, was there, and my father, without whom I could not have survived that day, was there. Peter, Rebecca, Nick, and Alexander formed a protective cocoon around me, and I was really doing quite well, or at least I thought I was, until somebody—who I can't even recall—said, quite innocently, "I expect you will be going to the house in France this summer." Do you not *understand?* That house *is* my mother, I have never been there without her, not once, and now that she is dead, how could you possibly imagine I would ever want to go back?

La Rentrée

I T T O O K M E S I X Y E A R S to change my mind. Sometimes the house
inhabited my dreams, and I would wander through its rooms, opening
the "Drawer of Death," examining the desiccated lizards, grasshoppers,
and scorpions inside, Freddie would look up from his work as I passed
by and smile at me, my mother would be clattering around in the kitchen,
and I would always wake up crying—why didn't they know that they
were dead?

As we rounded the last corner on our way up the hill, past the yellow schoolhouse and the wasp-infested mailboxes on the left, and the
temperamental septic tank, overgrown with bushes, on the right, Peter
honked the horn, just as Alain used to, to alert the welcoming committee. Not looking the least bit alerted, Nick was swinging in the hammock
under the lime tree, and I heard his girlfriend, Stephanie, calling to him
through the window, "How would you like a nice glass of cold rosé and
some of the tapenade I made from the olives we got this morning at the
market?" (Not for the first time I marveled at Nick's enviable talent—
inherited from his dad?—for acquiring adoring and adorable girls, who,
happy to cosset him like a pasha, managed to make the rest of us resemble
the truculent shrews we doubtless over time had become.)

Stephanie, wearing one of Vanessa's naughty French maid's aprons—
the sole survivor of my mother's wrath and scissors—emerged through
the clackety wooden beads, and, after a miniorgy of hugging and kissing, we all sat down at Freddie's table to drink our rosé and devour the
still-warm garlic toast spread with tapenade. I reached across to the basil
bush, picked off a few leaves and scattered the torn-up pieces on top of the

crushed olives. I was home. And at that moment, gazing at the overgrown lavender bushes our mother had planted when Nick was a baby, inhaling the scent of basil on my hands, I no longer remembered why it had taken me so long to come back to where I belonged.

Over dinner that night — *pâté de campagne* studded with pistachios, Brousse, tomato salad—Nick and I started to talk about the house and all the things that needed to be done. Rightly suspicious of my demonic mania for throwing things away, he did go so far as to allow that a little cleaning up and clearing out might be in order. A *little?* While he had been upstairs I had already had a go at the kitchen cupboards, and had put a bulging black garbage bag in our car, with instructions that Peter should take it down to the trash under cover of dark. But what about all our mother's clothes? Not to mention Freddie's. The voluminous linen shorts he had worn that day when Martin's snakeskin boots had provoked his mouth-frothing tirade, the faded espadrilles, the neatly folded piles of handkerchiefs were all in a chest of drawers on the top floor. And what about the closets, full of abandoned bathing suits, Nick's old toys, dead typewriters, broken lampshades, stacks of *New Yorker*s, dating back to the sixties, tied up with string, and the dusty box of twenty-year-old tampons I had found in my bathroom? And talking of bathrooms, how come there was no light in one of them? Nick sighed. "The bloody wiring is all fucked up, we'll have to get the electrician in." I said I'd call him first thing tomorrow morning, and tactfully avoided all mention of the closets.

Monsieur l'Électricien, bowlegged but not without a certain weaselish charm, shook his head ruefully. The wiring was *très vieux* and *complètement foutu*, it didn't conform to EU safety regulations, our insurance company would undoubtedly refuse to pay up if there was a fire, and if anybody should be injured that would, of course, be even more *grave*. Our only hope was to rewire the entire house, a job that he graciously offered to take on, but not anytime soon. *Il faut comprendre* that he was a very busy man, much in demand, and *pour l'instant* he had *trop de travail;* however, he should be able to squeeze us in *après l'été*. Oh dear. But since he was already here, couldn't he *peut-être* do something about the *triste* lack of *lumière* in the bathroom? Stephanie led him upstairs, where, she later reported, giggling, he had allowed himself a quick, good-natured grope of her irresistable bum while examining the lamentable state of our electrics. Nick and I were delighted. "Darling, you *know* we don't have any money . . . he'll probably give us a break on the price . . . you did *say* you wanted to help with the house. Oh, all right, *be* like that. I guess we'll just have to go on peeing in the dark."

THE DAY AFTER our visitation from the lascivious electrician I decided to make a pilgrimage to the market in Toulon where my mother and I used to do our shopping. In the old days she would be up at dawn, waiting impatiently for me in the kitchen because God knows there was absolutely no point in going there unless you got to the Cours Lafayette well before nine in the morning. Any later and you could never hope to park the car, it would be hotter than Hades by the time you reached the Cours, and all the best food would be gone. Like all her pronouncements, this was an incontrovertible fact. There was never any point in disagreeing.

But now that I could do anything I wanted, I took perverse delight in lingering in bed until after ten. Then I lounged about some more on the terrace, prolonging the evil pleasure, drinking coffee, painting my toenails Barcelona Red, and when the polish was dry, I had another cup of coffee, and after that, with the sun already high in the sky, I set off for Toulon. Around noon I parked the car—*pas de problème*—on a side street, and wandered slowly down the Cours Lafayette, filling my basket with whatever nonsense caught my eye. Miniature mauve mussels, squash blossoms with baby courgettes still attached, long red shallots, *haricots verts*, two boxes of *fraises des bois*, a log of *fromage de chèvre* rolled in ash, and a bag of inky, wrinkled Niçoise olives, no bigger than raisins. What would I cook with all this? Who knew, who cared? I had willfully, voluptuously, wickedly shopped without a list because she always had one.

A mild breeze blew up from the waterfront, cooling the back of my neck, and I reckoned it might just be time for a restorative *vin blanc cassis*. From a sidewalk café I gazed back through the dappled sunlight, at the piles of apricots, enormous, goiterlike tomatoes, thick braids of fresh garlic, and the baskets of figs laid out on their own soft fuzzy green leaves. On one stand square blocks of *savon de Marseille* had been built up into a huge Mayan pyramid of green and honey-colored soap, each one stamped with the guarantee *Pur Végétal* and its weight in grams as well as the precise percentage of olive oil it contained. Once, long ago, Francette had taken me to a ramshackle factory outside Marseille, and I remember watching an old man slowly stirring an enormous copper cauldron full of green sludge with a broomstick. He told us proudly that he had been making soap this way since he was a boy, and that the method—*fabriqué à l'ancienne*—dated back to *avant la Révolution*. (Actually the statute that laid down the law on what constitutes real *savon de Marseille* was passed in 1688. But this method of making soap has probably been around for almost a thousand years.) The Oliver Twist–like cauldron of porridge was stirred over a fire for ten days, poured into a mold, then left in the sun to dry, before being cut into cubes the size of a Parisian paving stone. Just like the one, ripped up from the rue Gay-Lussac during the revolutionary *événements* of '68, which my mother kept on her desk as a paperweight. Everything about the market, even the soap, led me back to her, and all the times, so many lost years ago, when we used to come here together, early in the morning, the scribbled list firmly in hand, and barrel through all twenty blocks of the Cours, and still be back home—exhausted—in time to make lunch.

But if I had been vindicated—you *can* get up late, find a parking space, wallow in the heat, buy whatever you damn well please—why were my cheeks wet with tears? Why had I gone to such pointless lengths to prove that my lazy self-indulgence had defeated her ingrained New England belief in doing things the hard way because life is tough and that's the only way to beat it? How could I have imagined that winning this perverse childish game would make me feel good, when all I longed for was to have her sitting beside me at the café table saying we couldn't possibly hang about here another instant or we would get heatstroke *and* a parking ticket *and* never be back in time to make lunch. I could not stop crying and would have done *anything*—given Monsieur Maurice a blow job, gobbled up a toad *en croûte*, worked on the Bandol dump for the rest of my life—just to see her walking toward me now.

I LEFT MY mother's room until last. It was bad enough dealing with the 2001 calendar still stuck to the front of the fridge with a cow magnet—missing one leg, like its owner—covered in her scribbled notes. July 30 "Gully arrives"; August 4 "Doctor in Toulon"; August 15 "Bill to dinner"—the night he had lost both his teeth and his trousers. Withered wishbones from chickens she had basted with mashed-up butter, garlic, and tarragon, still waiting to be snapped and make all our wishes come true, hung from hooks above the stove; a handwritten sign on how to operate the washing machine was stuck to the wall with yellowing Scotch tape; the salad plates shaped like cabbage leaves that we had bought together on an expedition to L'Isle sur la Sorgue when Rebecca was three, were stacked on the shelf, along with the blue-and-white jug she used to make lemonade in. In the cupboard I found tins of dog food for the awful, and long-dead, Éloi's cocktail-hour visits; a cardboard box of Frank Sinatra cassettes and a nylon mesh bag filled with decades of different-colored slivers of soap, waiting to be boiled up into a money-saving glob (a Depression-era trick she had learned from my grandmother, but thank Christ never actually got around to doing). All this I could just about handle, but still I refused to go into her room.

Everything was just as she had left it at the end of the summer in 2001, the last time we had been in the house together. Her little gold traveling clock sat on the bedside table, her address book was in the desk drawer with a shopping list—olive oil, eggs, capers, lightbulbs, parsley, stamps—and a stack of cards with "Lady Ayer: 10, Regent's Park Terrace. London N.W.1." engraved across the top. I opened the closet: Her clothes still smelled of Guerlain's L'Heure Bleue, the same perfume she had worn since I was a child, and there in the back, leaning against each other were her legs, the toes of the "swimming" one painted bright red—as if nail polish could make a joke out of something so unbearable.

At the bottom of the big mahogany bed stood an old trunk, plastered with the tattered remnants of stickers from the ships, the *France,* the *Constitution,* the *Queen Mary,* that she had sailed on, back and forth across the Atlantic—sitting in deck chairs, wrapped in a blanket, sipping hot bouillon in the winter, swimming in turquoise pools in the summer—never quite able to make up her mind which side she belonged on. Heavy linen sheets from the market in Le Beausset (carefully wrapped in plastic, far too precious for the saggy beds in our ramshackle house) were stacked up inside along with pillowcases, napkins, and a pair of strange, split-crotch Victorian bloomers that she had once tried, unsuccessfully, to palm off on me, "Hey, you'd look great in these. Will you get a load of the embroidery!" Just as she used Deyrolle in Paris as her decorators, my mother had always regarded the women who sold antique clothing in the market as her personal couturières. Huge billowing Edwardian men's shirts—tiny pleats running down the front with a tab at the bottom to anchor it inside your trousers—served as both dresses and nighties; petticoats became skirts and a curiously modern-looking linen shift was the perfect beach cover-up. I picked up the bloomers—maybe it was time to reconsider them? Then again maybe not. Instead I put them back in the chest and walked over to the closet, where I took one of the gentlemen's evening shirts off the shelf, undressed, and slipped it on over my head.

ON OUR LAST NIGHT Stephanie and I cooked ratatouille in the one-armed pot; we served grilled sardines and fennel on the crooked red platter that Sylvia had made with some mad potter in Ollioulles; and drank our wine from the glasses Francette had found at her favorite *antiquaire* in Toulon. At the center of the table sat the thirsty wasps' old drinking bowl, now filled with fresh figs. I reached up and unhooked a basket hanging from one of the beams, filled it with bread, and passed it around with the Reblochon that was already escaping over the edges of the marble slab we used as a cheese plate. More candles were lit—the bloody electrics—and after dinner, with Sinatra crooning away on the rackety cassette player, Nick produced a bottle of Madame Tricon's *vin d'orange,* while Alexander played chess with his sister on the same board that Freddie and Martin had fought to the death on almost forty years before. Outside the wind was starting up—maybe it was that ill-tempered Monsieur Mistral up to his odd-numbered tricks—and Nick and Peter had launched themselves onto the always choppy waters of the French Resistance. After a while I slipped off to bed and fell asleep listening to their voices drifting up the stairs—just as I had as a child. "Aaron Bank was the real hero . . . parachuted into the Var with the Jedburghs . . . the maquis rose up . . . the beaches between Le Lavandou and Saint-Raphaël . . . did you know that Le Beausset was liberated by Moors from Algeria?" *La vie continue.*

But the house will always be hers.

Acknowledgments

First I must thank the two infinitely understanding people—my husband, Peter, and my son, Alexander —who had to live with me while I was writing this book. Their wife/mother went AWOL for almost three years, but they never complained and now she's back. My daughter, Rebecca, was lucky enough to be living in England at the time. I am also deeply and forever indebted to my dear friend and agent, Irene Skolnick, who had faith in my idea from the day I first described it to her. Irene led me to Knopf where I was fortunate enough to find myself in the company of Sonny Mehta and Shelley Wanger. Need I say more? Well, just a bit. Shelley snipped and trimmed and restrained me from including some of the more exuberant and embarrassing moments in my life, and Sonny liked it enough to publish it. Peter, Rebecca, my brother, Nick, and his girlfriend, Stephanie, my aunt Beegoonie, and my old friend Hylan Booker all read the manuscript and put me right where I'd gone wrong. My godmother, Sue Boothby, Hylan, and Claus von Bülow were all kind enough to lend me letters from my mother and allowed me to quote from them for which I am truly grateful. I would also like to thank my publisher in London, Alexandra Pringle, and my agent, Clare Alexander, for their many helpful suggestions. I promise that I have made nothing up, but I have changed one or two names for reasons you are free to imagine.

A NOTE ABOUT THE AUTHOR

Gully Wells was born in Paris, brought up in London, educated at Oxford, and moved to New York in 1979. She is the Features Editor of Condé Nast *Traveler* magazine for which she writes regularly from all over the world. She is married, has two children and lives in Brooklyn. This is her first book.

A NOTE ON THE TYPE

The type used in this book was designed by Pierre Simon Fournier *le jeune*. In 1764 and 1766 he published his *Manuel typographique*, a treatise on the history of French types and printing, and on what many consider his most important contribution to typography—the measurement of type by the point system.

Composed by North Market Street Graphics,
Lancaster, Pennsylvania

Designed by M. Kristen Bearse